Game

The Segmentation, Implementation and
Protection of Land Rights in China

Series on Chinese Economics Research[*]

(ISSN: 2251-1644)

Series Editors: Yang Mu *(Lee Kuan Yew School of Public Policies, NUS)*
Fan Gang *(Peking University, China)*

Published:

*For the complete list of volumes in this series, please visit
www.worldscientific.com/series/scer

Series on Chinese Economics Research – Vol. 12

Game

The Segmentation, Implementation and Protection of Land Rights in China

ZHANG Shuguang

Chinese Academy of Social Sciences, China
Unirule Institute of Economics, China

W World Scientific

NEW JERSEY · LONDON · SINGAPORE · BEIJING · SHANGHAI · HONG KONG · TAIPEI · CHENNAI · TOKYO

Published by

World Scientific Publishing Co. Pte. Ltd.

5 Toh Tuck Link, Singapore 596224

USA office: 27 Warren Street, Suite 401-402, Hackensack, NJ 07601

UK office: 57 Shelton Street, Covent Garden, London WC2H 9HE

Library of Congress Cataloging-in-Publication Data
Bo yi. English.
    Game : the segmentation, implementation and protection of land rights in China / [compiled] by
Shuguang Zhang (Chinese Academy of Social Sciences, China).
        pages cm. -- (Series on Chinese economics research, ISSN 2251-1644 ; v. 12)
    "Originally published in Chinese by Social Sciences Academic Press (China). © 2011"
    ISBN 978-9814623377
    1. Land use, Rural--Government policy--China. 2. Land tenure--Government policy--China.
3. Land titles--Registration and transfer--China. 4. Land reform--China. I. Zhang, Shuguang,
1939– II. Title.
    HD928.B6313 2015
    333.3'151--dc23

                                                        2014050115

British Library Cataloguing-in-Publication Data
A catalogue record for this book is available from the British Library.

《博弈：地权的细分、实施和保护》
Originally published in Chinese by Social Sciences Academic Press (China).
Copyright © 2011 Social Sciences Academic Press (China).

In-house Editors: Dong Lixi/Dipasri Sardar

Typeset by Stallion Press
Email: enquiries@stallionpress.com

Printed in Singapore

Preface

From 2006 to 2010, three research reports on the topics of land in China were completed under a project organized by Unirule Institute of Economics, with ZHANG Shuguang as the lead researcher and author. We now compile them into a book for the convenience of readers.

I

The research is conducted in response to the increasingly acute land problems in China.

China used to be a large agricultural country, in which farmers formed a large majority of its population. However, China is now in a stage of a transition from an agricultural country to an industrial one and from a traditional society to a modern one.

Considering the fundamental realities of the country, the Chinese Communist Party had achieved great success in democratic revolution[1] by focusing on land problems and relying on farmers. After that, in the 30 years from 1949 to 1978, the Party accumulated adequate capital for industrialization using the scissors difference between the prices of industrial goods and agricultural produces, but owing to overseas blockades and

---

[1]The period from 1840 to 1949 in China is regarded as the democratic revolution period in the country. It consists of two parts: the old democratic revolution led by bourgeois, which lasted from 1840 to 1919, and the new democratic revolution led by proletariat, which lasted from the May Fourth Movement in 1919 to 1949.

the implementation of the division system between urban and rural areas, China was on a path of endogenous industrialization, which deviated from the characteristics of economics of scale and the principles of international division of labor for industrialization, and was unsuccessful. Although an independent and integrated industrial system was built, it was shattered to pieces in the tide of the market economy after the reform and opening-up.

After the reform and opening-up, China changed its strategy and started to pursue an exogenous industrialization path by vigorously utilizing external resources and markets to form the economics of scale and participating in the system of international division of labor. The country has obtained great success in industrialization over the past 30 years since then, proving once again that the exogenous industrialization is a successful path for industrialization. At the same time, China has also witnessed a rapid urbanization process, with an urbanization rate exceeding 46% at present. But urbanization is highly distorted due to the division system between urban and rural areas. Consequently, the current urbanization is incomplete, as the 210 million rural migrant workers in urban areas have not become the real urban residents. It is also deformed, as the expansion of urban areas is faster than the increase of urban populations, which is faster than the change and improvement of city life, leading to a tedious, vulgar, limited and uncreative city life in modern urban facilities.

In the processes of industrialization and urbanization, land has not only retained its status in agriculture as a main resource and an essential production base, but also gained new vigor and vitality. The land no longer produces only grain, farm and sideline products. It also bears a large number of factories and industrial products, as well as large areas of urban buildings and communities. Meanwhile, it goes beyond the guarantee for the subsistence of farmers and becomes a production factor with the fastest growing value and a wide range of uses, as well as a reliable guarantee and security for non-agricultural industries and urban investment and financing. Thus, the land commercialization and capitalization have become not only an engine for high growth and a secret for the economic miracle of the whole country, all regions, all cities and even villages, but also the focus of contention among the central government, local governments, land users, rural collective economic organizations and farmers. The game and contention have caused a chain of serious social and economic problems on one hand, and have promoted the transition of land systems on the other.

The central government aims at food security and social stability, and to this end, it mainly relies on the current laws and systems to strengthen the control and law enforcement on land. However, on one hand, the central government receives not cooperation and support but alienation and resistance from local governments, farmers and land users as the food security and social stability are not their aims. On the other hand, the central government itself has limited means to achieve its goal. It not only has to rely on local governments to carry out land control system and the law enforcement on land, but also needs to restrict and meet to some extent the local governments' demands for land expansion. Meanwhile, the central government cannot completely protect farmers' rights and interests as it can only increase the compensation for land expropriation but not give the complete land property right to farmers and it also wants to rely on farmers to counterbalance the behaviors of local governments. Therefore, the government has run into a dilemma with land problems and finds it difficult to break through the *status quo* and launch new reforms.

Local governments aim for local economic development and income growth. On one hand, due to the limitation of the current fiscal system, local governments lack funding resources for carrying out more work and therefore they seek to achieve their goals mainly through expanding land expropriation and urban construction. As a result, they grab the land benefit from farmers by using the current laws. On the other hand, while local governments are required to implement the land policies issued by the central government, they do not fully follow such policies and partly change them for their own purposes. Furthermore, in order to get around the control of the planning made by the central government, local governments usually support and protect the creative behavior of farmers. As for their relations with farmers, local governments need to grab the benefit from land appreciation but without driving farmers to the wall. Thus, in the game of land development, local governments are not only land law breakers, but also a strong power to promote system innovation. Meanwhile, they are not only strong grabbers of farmers' benefit, but also new policy makers to compromise on farmers' interests.

Farmers aim at maintaining and increasing the value of their land rights as much as possible. On one hand, as the vulnerable group in the system, farmers cannot protect their own interests in an official and legal way in the game, and their land rights are usually harmed. On the other hand, as the direct land owners and users, farmers directly exercise land property rights and directly contact other players on all land-related activities, including administrative arbitrariness, legal acquisition, or deception. Once their interests are harmed, farmers will be likely to negatively react both at the individual and collective level.

The land users have simple and clear aims, which are how to obtain the land development and use rights at the minimum cost and maximize their own profits to the greatest extent. They can either cooperate with officials or with farmers, and can either accommodate under current policy or find a way around the government's controls.

On the whole, the transition of the land system is completed in the interaction of the players above, where equilibrium is reached in the game.

It can be seen from the analysis and discussions above that in the processes of land policy implementation and land system transition, the central government is in a position to stick to and maintain the current land law systems. It not only does nothing in system innovation, but also inhibits the institutional innovation of local governments and farmers by relying on the current legal framework. In comparison, local governments play dual roles. They are not only the executors of land policy and the grabbers of farmers' interests, but also the main land law breakers. Meanwhile, in order to get out of this awkward situation, they are dynamic and energetic to conduct land system innovation, and so usually play a role of reformer in the current land system. Furthermore, in order to avoid the planning regulation of the central government by the way of land system innovation, local governments usually support and protect the creative behavior of farmers at lower levels. As for farmers, with the appreciation of land value and the increasing scarcity of land, they rapidly become more aware of their property rights, making it more and more expensive and difficult for the central government to implement the current land policies. Thus, in the past 30 years, local governments and farmers have struggled in all possible ways to find a way out in the face of a land system strewed with glaring defects, promoting the transition of land system towards property subdivision and limited property rights. The three reports give a clear description and in-depth analysis on this process from different perspectives.

II

Over the research of institutional transition concerning land property rights, people advocate land privatization, while many others plump for full nationalization. For that, we have no ideological preference and will not judge these ideas on the criteria of whether they are politically correct, or virtuously good or bad. Here, suffice it to say that these arguments either proceed from a certain principle lacking fact-based evidence, or from utopian designs based on a certain ideal. Hence, there is not much of a practical use.

Normally, such research focuses on both organizational and systematic design. In recent years, however, people have started to give more attention to the institutional evolution, which is not without its reasons. The idea not only provides a basis for us to set foot on, but also presents the process in which players involved interact with one another. Sadly, both are woefully neglected by those dim-witted revolutionaries.

The truth of the matter is that we do not start from scratch with a clean sheet, where we could possibly proceed with whatever blueprint we prefer. In reality, we are living with the existing system or inherited regime, not only the evolutionary consequence of our long history, but also the result of the development over the past 60 years. Whether such a state of nature is good or bad is rather irrelevant in this regard. What is real is that we have to move on with our historical baggage that is here to stay. Bearing that in mind, it seems that the folks with the idea of total privatization or nationalization are living in the middle of dream land where they could conjure up any fancy item at will.

What is more, given the *status quo*, not only is it nigh impossible to come to pass, but also preciously undesirable. The costly outcome aside, it will be fairly hard to tell whether those radical ideas are an equilibrium solution in the play-out of the game. Besides, it is not clear of how to do it: is it going to be based on the current land system or the one before the cooperative movement and previous land reform,[2] or be done for all lands by a decree issued by the state? Nor is it clear whether the state of existence then will be improved or worsened, especially for the rural folks. The answer to all these questions is inherently uncertain. The author did advocate land privatization before, but the realty has made us think otherwise.

That said, the crucial issue that strains the system then is hardly whether the property is owned by the state or the collectives and whether the rights are public or private in nature. What is important perhaps is the ability to exercise the rights and to gain benefits resulting from such an action. If the farmers can do it, then it does not matter who owns what. Would it not be true, for instance, that the government has the power and the will in land control? And would not it be true, again, that the collective property rights are expressly stipulated? And yet, the powers that be have repeatedly and pathetically come to nothing in that thankless battle over the so-called "sub-right housing". That is exactly because farmers have taken the rights in their own hands. All local governments are now busying themselves running their own pet projects of "urban village", but none of those going against grain, namely, the rights of original villagers, is progressing smoothly. Conversely, those that tag along face no obstacles.

Having said that, there are many factors that can affect this ability, including traditional custom, legal system, the degree of ease with which to conduct direct control and the scale of implementation, but the most

---

[2]Land reform (1950–1952): Following the liberation of China in 1949, the central government of the People's Republic of China published a Land Reform Law on June 30, 1950. The law abrogated ownership of land by landlords and introduced peasant landownership. During the winter of 1950–1951, land was confiscated from former landlords and redistributed to landless peasants and owners of small plots, as well as to the landlords themselves, who now had to till the land to earn a living. By the spring of 1953, with the exception of Taiwan and the ethnic minority regions of Xinjiang and Tibet, the land reform was basically completed.

Land cooperative movement (1953–1956): With the consolidation of the regime and the recovery of the national economy, the Communist Party of China decided in 1953 to carry out the agricultural cooperative movement in rural areas, which aimed to turn the farmer's private ownership of land to collective ownership, so as to meet the need for commodity grain in the large-scale industrial development of the country and improve agricultural productivity. By the winter of 1956, agricultural production cooperatives became the form of organization in rural areas.

important may be the state of subdivision of the property rights. Both the subdivision and exercise of property rights are the focus of the three reports compiled into this collection.

The property rights have a complex structure composed of multiple functions rather than a single entity. For the land property rights, it possesses both natural and social idiosyncrasies. In the natural context, there can be rights for farming, passage, underground and air, while in the social context, they can take shape of the rights to own, manage, use, benefit, and so on. These functions can be interacting and overlapping. Nonetheless, commonly practiced land rights have been the rights to own, manage and benefit. If the integration of the three is the classical structure of property rights, the subdivision can be looked at as the evolved form in the process of their practices in real time. Hence, it can be said that the transition of land property rights is by and large the process of subdivision of their functions, which can be demonstrated by numerous cases over the past 60 years.

Over the past 60 years, the land property right transition in China has gone through three stages, including cooperative stage, household-contract responsibility system stage and current scale transfer stage.

In the cooperative stage, all lands change from privately-owned to publicly-owned, and the rights to own, management and benefit are integrated and owned by the collective to a considerable extent, and the farmers are only laborers who are paid according the amount of work. Due to the prevalence of opportunism resulting in a wide-spread negative externality and moral hazard, the project had well and truly become a poverty trap, leading to the failure of the communization.

The household-contract responsibility system made a subdivision of property rights, in which the rights to own and that to contracted management were separated from each other. The rights to own were still with the collective economic organization, but the rights to contracted management were delivered to farmers, who got incomes from labor and operating. Accordingly, a clear and relatively stable connection between land use and output was established, and thus farmers become the tenants of collective land and the takers of agricultural surplus. As a result, a balance between the state, collectives and farmers was formed, which resolved the incentive problem occurred during the stage of the communization and promoted the development of agriculture. However, the limitations in the pattern of collective land property rights plus the equally distributed land use rights not only made the collective economy hollowed husk, but also were adverse to the modern development of agriculture and formed a "subsistence trap".

After that, as the scale land transaction occurred with the large scale population mobility and the change of employment structure, another subdivision of property right occurred, in which the rights to own, contracting and management were separated from each other. The right to own was still held by the village collective, the contracting right was owned by the contracted farmer, while the management right was transferred to large growers, land stock cooperative organizations and external agriculture-related enterprises. Therefore, as Adam Smith (1983) and Young (1928) said, "The division of labor depends on the expansion of market scale, while the expansion of market scale also depends on the division of labor", in a sense the scale land transaction not only creates the conditions for agriculture industrialization and modernization and promotes the specialization of agriculture before, during and after the production, but also promotes the agriculture marketization. Meanwhile, it not only helps set up the labor market within the agriculture, land market and land price, but also expands the product market beyond regional level to national or even international level. Thus, farmers can get both labor and property incomes, meanwhile, the land rent becomes the price for contracted land transaction, and farmers who join the cooperative may obtain the dividend income. Accordingly, the farmers' income can be increased and their property right can be ensured, and the collective economic organizations also get rid of the dilemma of being hollowed out.

Consequently, although the property right subdivision has not yet completely changed the fact that the land is collectively owned, it still largely expands and improves the capacity of exercising property right for farmers, and enables different right owners to have their own limited property right and perform their own powers and functions in their respective ways, thus promoting the development of production collectively. Although this is not a classic privatization, it can be considered a special privatization in the sense of the exercise of property rights.

The reason why the property right subdivision can strengthen the capacity of exercising property rights is that the process of property rights subdivision is also a process of property rights reallocation by the transfer of rights, by which the property rights will be allocated or transferred to those who can effectively use them. Therefore, the property rights subdivision is both a market process of property rights transaction and a process of optimal allocation of property rights. The change above largely avoids the artificial coercion and administrative intervention and returns to the normal path of property right transition and economic development. In fact, the property right subdivision occurred very early in the history of economic development of China, but it was distorted as a result of political struggle.

In the *Case Study on Chinese System Transition* (Land Volume) edited by the author, the paper *Land Property Right Differentiation and Institutional Arrangement of Villages in the South Region of the Yangtze River* by Wang Jingxin *et al.* in 2010 described in detail the arrangement of land property rights in rural areas in middle and late Qing Dynasty and early Republic of China. At that time, the rural land was divided into three types according to the property rights structure, the first type was called the Qing field, which has both the rights to own and use; the second one was called the civil field or large Pi field, which has no right to use but the right to own; and the third one was called guest field or small Pi field, which has no right to own but the right to use. The property rights of all three types of land could be freely traded and transferred, but their prices were different. The price for Qing fields was the highest, while that for the guest fields was the lowest. Civil lands could have been traded under the premise that the trade would not deprive the permanent tenants of guest fields of their cultivation right. Besides, the right of lease for guest fields also could be traded in a very flexible but solemn way. That is, the transaction could be carried out as long as both sides of the transaction agreed with each other, but a contract should be signed and the trade should be conducted on the spot through an intermediary. In this way defaults seldom happened. Now that there were so advanced property rights differentiation and transaction in the history, some people may start to ask why the current land system cannot develop toward that direction, or could it be said that the modernization is not the further differentiation of property right and the further development of property right transaction, but returns to the classic form of property rights that integrate multiple rights. As a matter of fact, historical development has shown that the function of private land property right must and can be differentiated, and the function of public land property right needs to and can be differentiated, which is favorable for the implementation and protection of property rights. In addition to the reasons above, the reason why the claim of land privatization and nationalization is unrealistic is that those advocates focus on the ownership of property rights rather than the exercise of property rights. However, the property rights that cannot be exercised or effectively exercised are meaningless. Thus, there is no way out for any idealized social research.

If the property right differentiation is assumed to be meaningful and the exercise is assumed to be important, our policy conclusions will be clear. After all, the current land law systems focus on the protection of ownership, which is only suitable for the classic property right form in which the property right is not differentiated other than the modern property rights form in which the property rights are subdivided. After the land contract right is confirmed in the *Property Law as a* real right for usufruct, all land laws should be adjusted and revised in this direction. That is, the focus of current land laws should shift from the protection of ownership to the protection of the real right for usufruct.

III

All discussions above clearly demonstrate that China's land problem is certainly not a pure economic problem but a complex social problem or social science problem involving politics, law and economy, which is also closely related to the current system structure, development model and interests relationship. Therefore, any simple idea or behavior cannot solve the problem and will even make things worse.

How to solve China's land problem certainly becomes a widely concerned question, and accordingly various designs and viewpoints have been proposed and all kinds of explorations and experiments have emerged. Many people advocate that the reform should rely on the central government and should be carried out from the top down and nationwide.

As a result, various reform schemes emerge everywhere and numerous seminars are held, and it seems that everyone is talking about the land problem. However, the general pattern of China's reform and the basic experience of land system transition demonstrate that the reform cannot be purely designed and there was never a catch-all reform scheme. Just think, over 30 years after the reform and opening-up, whether any reform was designed in advance, whether there was a reform scheme that was really carried out, or whether there was a successful reform that is carried out according to the designed scheme. Obviously, the answer to all questions is no. It would be like this even in the early stages of reform when there was a common social consensus (of course, there is a limitation in the degree of understanding), therefore, the reform that is designed in advance and is carried out from top down is only a kind of Utopian idea now when the society is divided into different interest groups and the consensus on reform basically cannot be reached. It cannot be denied that this is another reason in addition to the consideration of the vested interests why the central government can only be put in a dilemma and take no action. Hence, some are outraged and think that the reform results have been stolen by vested interest groups, and that China has completely moved toward crony capitalism and a great revolution is inevitable. Some feel confused and think that the reform remains half dead and there is neither new reform impetus nor activists to promote the reform. Some also feel satisfied and think that China's reform has been successfully completed, a successful so-called China Model has been created, and China's reform is enough to become something worth flaunt and the model to be learnt by other countries.

But in fact, the reform is still carried out constantly. However, it is not conducted from the top level but from the bottom level, not from top down but from bottom up; it does not have the uniform model but different explorations and experiments; and it does not have any breakthrough affecting the overall situation but small advances and accumulations. Thus, at the national or top level, it seems that the reform is stalled and backward, but at the basic levels or bottom level, there are some new stories. Although the reform at the bottom cannot solve the reform problem in the whole country or at the top, it will have serious effect on them. In view of these living creations at the bottom, the answer to the land problem only can be found by "Down-to-earth study".[3] In fact, the three land investigation reports presided over and completed by the author are an attempt of down-to-earth study. All the three reports systematically review and briefly comment the current related systems and policies, but we are not complacent about that. Such a review is mainly to provide some backgrounds for our research, and our main aim is to obtain various cases from the actual survey and get the theoretical understanding by refining and summarizing the cases.

In the first report, we introduce and discuss four cases as follows:

— Land-centered rural industrialization model in Nanhai County of Guangdong Province;
— Real estate compensation and property replacement model in the economic development zone in Dezhou City, Shandong Province;
— Three types of farmer's cooperatives in Kunshan City of Jiangsu Province;
— Community-type enterprise in Dongsandao Street, Haicheng City, Liaoning Province.

In the second report, we analyze the following six cases from three aspects, including "Methods and Effects of the Government's Control and Law Enforcement on Collective Construction Land", "Worrying Comprehensive Reform Experiment of Overall Urban–Rural Development: Is Homestead Exchange for House a Breakthrough?", and "Innovations and experiments by farmers, collectives and basic levels":

— Forcibly removing illegal cottages in Qinglongtou, Beijing;
— Emergence of painter village and property disputes in Songzhuang, Beijing;
— Blocking of government-led overall urban–rural development in Jiulongpo District of Chongqing City;
— Government-led and financial-supported comprehensive supplementary reform in Huaming Model Town of Tianjing City;

---

[3] "Down-to-earth study" is brought up by Huang Xiaohu (Vice Chairman of China Land Science Society) for comments on Liu Shouying's research style.

— Farmer-subjected land capitalization in Zhenggezhuang Village, Beijing;
— Land property rights game between villagers and government in urban villages of Shenzhen City.

In the third report, we tell six interesting cases as follows:

— Land transaction and scale management in Qianfu Village, Jiawu Town, Tongzhou District, Beijing;
— Land cooperative in Aoxiaoying Village, Yongledian Town, Tongzhou District, Beijing;
— Organic vegetable specialized cooperative in Zhenglong Village, Jiangji Town, Ningyang County, Shandong Province;
— Case of western flower world in Lingyun Village, Xinminchang Town, Pixian County, Chengdu City;
— Case of the industrial park for new and high-technology modern agriculture in Qiquan Town, Chongzhou City, Chengdu City;
— Case of scale plantation of Chongzhou Grain and Oil Reserve Ltd. in Sichuan Province.

We reached all the places above and saw and heard all cases or stories by ourselves. Thus, all our empirical findings and theoretical ideas are refined and summarized from these cases.

Facing with such a fickle economics society in China without foundation, accumulation, experience or deep thinking, we pose and discuss the problem for a large percentage of domestic economists in academic research who are superficial and only focus on the top level. Indeed, there are only a few people who conduct down-to-earth study, but a large number of people work behind closed doors and in ascetic meditation, all of them have neither thought of new information but only instruments and techniques, so all of their so-called research is at best only one school work or exercise. It is not that there are no good papers, just that there are only a few, which do not correspond to abundant practices of China's reform and the large team in the economics community. In most cases, theoretical papers have no theoretical hypothesis and analytical framework but a mess of formulas, while empirical papers only firstly copy or just slightly revise others' models, and then conduct some processing such as regression analysis based on a lot of data from the statistical yearbook, which is finally so-called highly successful. Obviously, only a few observe and understand practically, propose the hypothesis from experience, and think about how the existing models are constructed and their agreements and disagreements with China's reality. Only God knows how such research can interpret the realistic economic process and propose useful policy recommendations. However, this would never matter, these papers not only can be published but also can be awarded, and even become an asset for promotion, but who will refuse such things that save trouble, effort and worry? But, on the other side, the adverse effect on China's economic research level is obvious. Therefore, we sincerely hope that in addition to a good theoretical basis and professional skills, China's economists can complete their theory creation by going to the basic levels and repeatedly observing and systematically thinking in practices.

The research is funded by Germany Foundation, Boyuan Foundation and the "Research on Current Rural Land Transaction System and the Protection of Farmers' Rights in China", an important subject of philosophy and the social sciences hosted by the Ministry of Education. During the compilation of this book, we have received wonderful comments from many experts and professors and have got guidance and help in multiple aspects from ZHOU Qiren, WU Xiaoling, HE Di, JIANG Xingsan *et al.*, and we thank all of them here.

August 16, 2010
Beijing

Foreword

This book combs through the transition of China's land institutions over the last 60 years. By investigating 26 cases, it illustrates the mechanisms and implications of this transition, and provides theoretical explanations. The publication of the English edition will help English readers get a comprehensive understanding of China's land institutions, policies, and the policy effects on China's reform and opening up.

I would like to thank Social Science Academic Press (China) for the support; the dedication and hard work of Mr. Eric Fish, the translator of this book; and the World Scientific Publishing Group. Mr. MA Junjie from Unirule Institute of Economics has also contributed to this venture, and for that I am grateful.

ZHANG Shuguang
June 1st, 2015, Beijing

Contents

Implementation and Protection of Land Property Rights in the Context of Urbanization

This report carries out detailed examination of the regime and the policies governing rural land and its conversion, revealing the fact that the government as the sole regulator monopolizes the primary market, leading to a separation of rights from the property intrinsic in trade. Also, the report conducts an analysis of the implementation mechanism of the current policies and an evaluation of their resulting consequences. By introducing and reviewing cases relating to ongoing innovations in both areas at the local level, the report puts forward possible methods of rural land reform. Namely, under the present state of public-cum-collective ownership, the government should loosen its regulation and monopoly over land conversion and encourage trade, especially pertaining to transfers of collectively-owned land for construction purposes. With it, there should be suggestions regarding improvements feasible in policy-making and amendments of the law.

1. Introduction

The land issue was the central factor during the Communist Revolution. It also plays a key role in China's modern day development. The economic reform began land policies in rural areas and the economic growth in the last 20 or 30 years has to a high degree relied upon land conversion in rural areas to construction sites for urban expansion. However, there are fundamental shortcomings in current land laws and policies which impede economic growth and give birth to social instability. Therefore, land laws and policies must be reformed, and only then will China's long-term stability and smooth development have a solid foundation.

The reform of China's land policies should head towards relaxation of government regulation and development of the land market. More specifically, under the current state of collective and public ownership, the state monopoly over land conversion in rural areas for non-agricultural purposes should be terminated. The government's regulation of the conversion of collectively-owned land should be relaxed and the trade of those for productive uses should be encouraged. This should be the only way out of the present quagmire. For this argument, some may disagree. All the same, before getting into details, perhaps some theoretical findings as well as empirical evidence may be helpful here to clarify the issue somewhat.

First, opponents argue that development of the land market will lead to over-concentration of land in the hands of a few. This has not happened in the past and is almost impossible in reality. The history of land laws and policies can be found in the book *History of China's Land Laws and Policies* (2006) by Zhao Gang and Chen Zhongyi. Today, we seek to have collective ownership over land and our purpose is to encourage land transfers and trading to convert farmland for commercial and industrial uses. Then the collectives and farmers will be in a good position to share the gains from incremental values accrued to their land and have long-term protection against infringement by governments. The decisions should be land owners' alone while the government exercises proper regulation. Both history and reality have proven that so long as there is no patronage of a government, the price mechanism and market negotiation between property owners can effectively stave off any encroachment by abusive market powers, provided there is a proper regulatory environment.

The second objection is that land transfers and trading will lead to land waste. But actually, the root of over-expansion of China's cities and land waste lies in land requisition rather than market transaction. With the requisition, the shortage of land is not reflected in the prices that are too low and underpaid by the governments. What is more, besides its function of forming a price system and, with it, resource allocation, the market performs another important role. Namely, it forges economies of scale. In other words, the more traders there are in a market, the more efficient the market will be and the lower the average trading cost. Economies of scale are also apparent in network externalities. Namely, the more traders there are in a market and the higher the transactional utility of every trader and the higher the transactional utility of the whole market. Therefore, the convergence of people to cities has a positive feedback. Given that there are many people in a city, many more people will come. But two factors will play a counteractive role, slowing down the whole process, one is the rise of land prices and the other is over-crowding. The law of diminishing urban land return is the proof and example of application of the law of diminishing marginal return. The price mechanism will hence restrain the over expansion of cities and prevent the in-efficient use of land.

The third objection holds that land transfers and trading will harm food security. In theory, foot security should not be a problem. But in reality, attention should be paid. This is not because China has too large a population and limited cultivated land, which leads to a shortage of grain supply, but because China does not have a good mechanism to prevent famines. Nobel Prize winner Amartya Sen (1999) once conducted a study of famines and other historical crises and contended that 'incurable misunderstanding will be produced if famines are understood as a shortage of per capita grain supply.' Famines and crises appear because 'part of the population suddenly loses their economic rights and benefits.' He put forward an economic theory against famines. This theory advocates making use of reasonable price incentives, which help raise production (including grain production) and income; expansion of employment, which will turn the possible victims of famine into the possible preventers of it; and also a democratic system serving as 'protective insurance' and 'transparent guarantee' which provides political incentives against the onset of famine. The development of land markets and the encouragement of land transfers and trading are in line with the principles of this economic theory. Furthermore, the development of the land market and encouragement of land transfers and trading will protect cultivated land by restraining over-expansion of cities and reducing land waste, and help implement basic farmland protection policies by eliminating the incentives of local governments for land requisition. China has a large population but limited cultivated land and it is therefore inevitable for China to encourage international trade and import grain. The attempts are neither correct nor practical in an attempt to attain an autarky concerning grain production. It should be an important national policy to import grain and ply efficient use of farmland.

Having said that, we move on to the second part of report which elaborates and evaluates the current land policies and their implementation, with emphasis on the huge disparity and acute conflict between policy goals and actual results. The third part introduces and discusses several examples of innovation, showing the possibility for the modification of laws and reform of policies. The fourth part makes specific suggestions on those changes.

2.   Current Land Policies and Their Implementation: Results and Evaluation

2.1.   Evolution of land policies

The land policies in China form a complex system composed of a series of state laws, government statutes, rules and regulations of various departments concerned. But the most apparent feature of the system is that the state monopolizes and regulates land conversion and there exists separated systems of land management for rural areas and urban construction, referred to as a 'dual system'. The two kinds of land use are with different systems of rights, and in turn governed by different institutions and rules. The government, as the sole arbitrator in land conversion and the monopolist in the transfer markets, is the real 'owner of land'. After land in rural areas is converted for non-agricultural purposes, the government enjoys the exclusive right to acquire the land and transfer it to urban customers. The results and problems arising from the implementation of land policies all originate from this monopoly. A detailed discussion is needed on these policies before a comprehensive evaluation can proceed.

2.1.1.   Policies concerning land in rural areas

The notion of "land" in rural areas is the collective one for the land of agricultural use and other rural purposes. According to the *Law of People's Republic of China on Land Contract in Rural Areas*, land in rural areas 'includes the arable land, forestlands and grasslands owned collectively by the farmers and by the State and used collectively by the farmers according to law, as well as other lands used for agricultural purposes according to law'. Because most of the land in rural areas is collectively-owned, all the policies concerned are towards collective land, so is the following discussion hence.

There are two basic points in the current policies. The first basic point is the adherence to collective ownership of land and household contracting. The other basic point is that land in rural areas should be mainly used for agricultural purposes and certain procedures must be undertaken before land can be converted for non-agricultural purposes.

The current policies of land in rural areas have undergone an evolutionary process. The collective ownership was established in the 1950's and has not changed significantly up to now. Previously collectives managed the land and after the implementation of the reform, the household unit began to manage the land. In the last 20 years, with the transformation in the overall economy, including that in grain supply and demand coupled with land regulation, significant changes have occurred to the policies governing land regulation and household contracting. The changes are summarized as follows:

— The nature of contracting rights has changed. The land contracting right was considered as a creditor's rights in *Land Administration Law*. Beginning with the *Land Contracting Law*, the land contracting right has been gradually transformed into a real right, or property right. With the promulgation and implementation of the *Real Right Law*, the contracting right is transformed in essence into a real right.
— The land contract term has been repeatedly lengthened. At the beginning, the term was several years. Then it was lengthened to 15 years and then 30 years. The 20th Article of the *Law of the People's Republic of China on Land Contract in Rural Areas* stipulates that 'the term of contract for arable land is 30 years; the term of contract for grassland ranges from 30 to 50 years; the term of contract for forestland ranges from 30 to 70 years; the term of contract for forestland with special trees may, upon approval by the administrative department concerned for forestry under the State Council, be longer'. This article helps boost farmers' incentives for long-term investment in land.

— The rights and obligations of the party awarding the contract and the contractor are clearly defined. The intention is to restrict the rights of the party awarding the contract and protect the rights of the contractor. It is especially stipulated that in the terms of the contract, the party awarding the contract shall not take back or adjust the contracted land. This stipulation terminates the usual practice of the party awarding the contract from terminating the contract arbitrarily or repeatedly intervening in the contracted land. Furthermore, the *Supreme Court's Interpretation on the Application of Law in the Trial of Land Contracting Disputes in Rural Areas* promulgated in 2005 makes it possible for farmers to claim their rights by resorting to laws to substantiate their claims.

— The procedures for implementing contracts are established and the registration and certification procedures of the rights to contractual management are initiated in preparation for the establishment of land ownership infrastructure.

— It is clarified that the contractor shall enjoy the discretion to transfer the rights, i.e., land contractual management right. Document No. 1 in 1984 allowed for the first time transfers of the rights. The *Stipulations on Transfers of Rights to Land Contractual Management* promulgated in 2001 makes it clear that farmers are the main players in the transfer markets. Article 32 of the *Law of the People's Republic of China on Land Contract in Rural Areas* stipulates that 'the rights to land contractual management obtained through household contracts may, according to law, be transferred through subcontracting, leasing, exchanging, demising or other means.' The Law also stipulates that 'the rights to land contractual management' shall be transferred in adherence to the following principles:

That transfers shall be based on consultation of an equal footing, voluntary and compensatory in nature. No organization or individual shall coerce the contractor to transfer his/her rights or prevent him/her from doing so;

that no change shall be made in the nature of the land ownership or the utilization of the land designated for agriculture purpose.

From the above analysis and summary it can be seen that the policies are heading in the correct direction. The rights are becoming genuine, the owners of the rights are increasingly individuals and the rights are becoming more and more exclusive. Those changes assist the implementation, help protect farmers and gradually transform the rights into claimable legal ones. Farmers can get legal remedies and compensation if the collectives in rural areas or state employees infringe upon their rights to land contractual management and cause damage. But there are still restrictions on the conversion of land in rural areas, especially concerning the conversion for non-agricultural purposes, which reinforces to a certain degree the dual systems of land rights.

2.1.2. *Policies of conversion of land in rural areas*

The policies of conversion of land in rural areas are another dimension to the regime. In the *Regulations Concerning Land Requisition for State Construction* promulgated in 1982, the *Land Administration Law* and the *Implementation Regulations* promulgated in 1999, the *Decision of the State Council on Deepening Reform and Strengthening Land Administration* (hereinafter referred to as Document No. 28) issued on October 21st, 2004 and the *Circular of the State Council on Intensifying Land Control* (hereinafter referred to as Document No. 31) issued on August 31st, 2006, there are many differences in specific articles but the principles remain the same. The first principle is that governments at various levels are the decision-makers and regulators of the conversion of land in rural areas for non-agricultural purposes rather than the players in the transfer markets. The second principle is that the conversion of land in rural areas for non-agricultural purposes is strictly restricted. In recent years, faced with the uncontrolled conversion of land in rural areas for non-agricultural purposes, the central government has given repeated orders and even implemented strict administrative control. The key points of the policies are as follows:

— The conversion of land in rural areas is controlled by mandatory plans. Chapter 3 of the *Land Administration Law* stipulates:

- that overall planning of land utilization shall be conducted and the total amount of the conversion shall be controlled;
- that the land owned by collectives and villages shall be governed by plans;

- that the *Regulations on the Protection of Basic Farmland* shall be implemented, protection zones of basic farmland shall be established and the conversion of cultivated land for non-agricultural purposes shall be restricted.

Document No. 28 decided to put the annual plans for conversion of agricultural land under mandatory management and Document No. 31 stipulates that leading officials shall be responsible for land management and protection of cultivated land.

— Applications for land conversion shall be examined strictly before approval is given. Paragraph one of Article 44 of the *Land Administration Law* stipulates that 'for occupation and use of land for construction involving converting agricultural land into land for construction, procedure of examination and approval for converting agricultural land into other uses should be conducted'. Document No. 28 stipulates that 'the rights for approving conversion and requisition of agricultural land reside in the State Council and the governments of autonomous regions, provinces and municipalities under direct central direction'. Occupation and use of land involving the conversion of agricultural land into land for construction projects of roads, pipelines, cables and large infrastructure approved by people's governments of the provinces, autonomous regions and municipalities directly under the Central Government and construction projects approved by the State Council shall be subject to the approval of the State Council. Converting agricultural land into land for construction for the implementation of the said planning within the scale of land for construction of municipalities and villages and townships determined by the overall planning for land utilization shall be subject to the approval of the organ that originally approved the overall planning for land utilization in batches in accordance with the annual land utilization plan. Within the scope of agricultural land converted into other uses already approved, land for specific construction projects can be approved by people's governments, such as municipalities or counties. Requisition of basic farmland exceeding 35 hectares and cultivated land other than basic farmland exceeding 70 hectares shall be subject to the approval of the State Council. Besides, *Measures for Administration and Preliminary Examination of the Land Used for Construction Projects* stipulates that no conversion of agricultural land or requisition of land shall be approved if it is not examined preliminarily or it does not pass the preliminary examination. In 2003, examination and approval of land conversion was even frozen temporarily.

— Next, we would like to say something about the policies governing the conversion of agricultural land for non-agricultural purposes. Article 43 of the *Land Administration Law* stipulates that 'any unit or individual that needs to use land for construction must apply for the use of state-owned land in accordance with the law. The state-owned land referred to in the preceding sentence includes state-owned land and the land that originally belonged to collectives of farmers but has been requisitioned by the state.' In other words, before land in rural areas is converted for non-agricultural purposes, the land must be requisitioned by the state first. Only when the collectively-owned land is transformed into state-owned land can the land be converted for non-agricultural purposes. The essence of Article 43 is to reduce the extent of collective ownership through land conversion and expand state-ownership of the land.

In this article there is an escape clause, which stipulates that the 'use of land collectively owned by farmers by the respective collective economic organizations approved in accordance with the law for the establishment of rural and township enterprises and residential construction for villagers, or use of land collectively owned by farmers approved in accordance with the law for village (township) public facilities and non-profit undertakings is not bound by this article.' This escape clause is very important in that it opens an alternative possibility for the conversion of land in rural areas by collectives of farmers. But this escape clause is not in line with the spirit of the *Land Administration Law* and is even against many articles of the law. What is more important is that the escape clause is against the nomology of laws. The land belongs to collectives of farmers and why should the collectives of farmers need approval according to laws for the conversion of the land? Who approves the conversion according to what laws? Strictly speaking, the *Land Administration Law* is a tortuous law as far as this clause is concerned.

In recent years, because of over requisition of land in rural areas, the central government has strengthened its administrative control and paid attention to the transfers of collective land for construction purpose. Document No. 28 stipulates that 'the rights to the use of such a land owned collectively by the farmers in villages and towns can be transferred according to laws under the prerequisite of compliance with planning'. But Document No. 31 strictly legally forbids 'leasing in place of requisition.'[1] The contradictions between policies are manifested in this example.

— Next, we would like to say something about the policies of compensation for requisition. Article 47 of the *Land Administration Law* stipulates that 'for requisition of land, compensation shall be given in accordance with the original use of the requisitioned land.' In other words, the increment in the values of converted land resides with the party requisitioning the land and is not shared by the owner of the land. This is one of the fundamental shortcomings of the current land policies. Compensation for requisitioned cultivated land includes land compensation fees, subsidies for resettlement as well as compensation fees for ground appendixes and seedlings. Compensation fees for requisitioned cultivated land shall be 6 to 10 times the average annual output value in the three years prior to requisition. Subsidies for resettlement shall be calculated on the basis of the agricultural population that needs resettling. The agricultural population that needs resettling

---

[1]According to a report given by the Xinhua News Agency on March 20th, 2007, the director of the Law Enforcement and Supervision Bureau of the Ministry of Land and Resources, Zhang Baoxin pointed out that most of the cases concerning land involved 'leasing in place of requisition' guided by local governments. 'More and more village collectives and farmer-group collectives illegally lease land or sell land under disguises. Some village collectives lease land on their own. Some enterprises go to village collectives to rent land. Some governments rent land from farmers and then lease the land to enterprises.' According to Zhao Baoxin, there were 7,316 cases involving illegal leasing of land by village collectives last year, representing a rise of 51.1% over the same period in the year before last. The involved land covered an area of 9,100 hectares, representing a rise of 119.8% over the same period in the year before last.

shall be calculated on the basis of the amount of cultivated land requisitioned divided by the per capita occupancy of cultivated land measured by the number of units requisitioned. The rate of subsidy for resettlement per head of the agricultural population that needs resettling shall be four to six times the average annual output value in the three years prior to requisition of the said cultivated land. However, the maximum per hectare subsidy for resettlement shall not exceed 15 times the average annual output value in the three years prior to the requisition. If those farmers cannot maintain their original living standards on the basis of land compensation fees and subsidies for resettlement, additional subsidies for resettlement may be provided if people's governments of provinces, autonomous regions and municipalities directly under the Central Government approve. But the total land compensation fees and subsidies for resettlement shall not exceed 30 times the average annual output value in the three years prior to requisition of the land. Document No. 28 stipulates that 'if the total land compensation fees and subsidies for resettlement have reached the upper limit but the farmers whose land has been requisitioned cannot maintain their original living standards, local governments can provide additional subsidies using the revenues from the compensation of using state-owned land.' The land compensation fees belong to collectives, compensation fees for ground appendixes and seedlings belong to the owners while resettlement subsidies belong to those resettled.

— Next, we would like to say something about the policies governing the provision of construction land. After conversion, land in rural areas is either allocated or transferred. The land is allocated to state organs, military facilities, urban infrastructure, public facilities, key national power, communications and irrigation projects and other purposes stipulated by laws and regulations. The land for other purposes is transferred at a price. Transfer and allocation are the two methods of land provision. But under current policies, they serve as the base for compensation. Theoretically, the compensation for land should be the discounted value of future gains from the land no matter how the land will be used. But currently the compensation for the land to be used for infrastructure is given according to the original use of the land. In essence, the farmers whose land is requisitioned shoulder part of the cost for building the infrastructure. The compensation for the land to be transferred at a price is also given according to the original use of the land. In essence, the farmers are deprived of the increment in the values of the land after conversion. That is one reason that exacerbates present land problems.

— Next, we would like to say something about the distribution and utilization of the revenue from the paid use of land (i.e., compensable use of land). The state implements the system of paid use of land according to the law. Construction parties shall pay land use fees such as fees for land use and other fees. Because the land use fees were low, which led to inefficient use, the state doubled land use fees in 2006 and tripled the land use tax in urban areas. At the same time, foreign-funded enterprises were asked to pay the urban land tax. Of the land use fees paid for new construction, 30% is going to state treasury and the other 70% is for related local governments to be used exclusively for the development of cultivated land. Of the cultivated land, 50% of the occupation tax (i.e., the tax for using cultivated land) is for state while the other 50% is left to local governments' disposal. This policy fuels the competition between central and local governments for land use fees and taxes and is one of the important causes for the distortion of government behavior concerning land.

From the above it can be seen that the policies of conversion of land in rural areas for non-agricultural purposes fall into the mode of command-economy characterized by a high degree of state monopoly and all-sided regulation by government. The collective construction land in rural areas is covered by state plans and approvals of related governmental departments are needed prior to land conversion. Land in rural areas to be converted for urban use is requisitioned by governments before governments transfer the land to other parties. When governments requisition land, compensation is given according to the use of the land before conversion. All gains from the transfers reside with, and are distributed among governments at various levels. From the above-mentioned, it can be known that the same piece of land contains different rights before and after conversion and its transfers follow different rules. Farmers are excluded from the conversion of land in rural areas for non-agricultural purposes. In other words, farmers and village collectives have little say on the conversion of rural land for non-agricultural purposes and there is no protective mechanism for their rights and benefits. This is the source of the problems concerning land in China.

2.2. Structure of the land regime

In line with the dual systems of land rights, there exist corresponding dual frameworks of laws and institutions in the implementation of land policies. 'The state practices control over land use.' 'The state conducts overall planning for land utilization, classifying it as farmland, construction land and unutilized land. Strict restriction shall be imposed on converting farmland into construction land. The amount of lands for construction uses shall be controlled and cultivated land shall be protected specially' (Article 4 of the *Land Administration Law*). From the above it can be known that the target of the regulation is not state-owned or construction land, but collectively-owned, agricultural land. Therefore, the essence of the law is state regulation and governments' control over collectively-owned and agricultural land.

In order to enforce the government's control over collectively-owned and agricultural land, two sets of laws and regulations are made. One set of the laws consists of the *Law of the People's Republic of China on Land Contract in Rural Areas*, as well as related documents issued by the State Council and Ministry of Agriculture, such as Document No. 1. Those laws and regulations are applicable to collectively-owned and agricultural land alone and have no binding for state-owned land or construction land. The second set consists of the *Land Administration Law* and its implementation regulations. As the land problems worsening, the State Council and the Ministry of Land and Resources issued many red-headed documents, such as the *State Council's Decision on Deepening the Reform and Strengthening Land Administration*, the *Circular of the State Council on Intensifying the Land Control*, the *Measures for the Administration and Preliminary Examination of the Land Used for Construction Projects* and the *Measures for the Administration and Annual Planning of the Utilization of Land* issued by the Ministry of Land and Resources. These laws and regulations do not relate to the administration or utilization of land in rural areas proper, nor do they relate to the existing state-owned land or construction land. They only relate to newly converted state-owned land and construction land alone. In other words, they are meant to regulate and constrain the activities of land conversion in rural areas for non-agricultural purposes.

On the surface, the current framework of laws governing the regulation of land utilization is rooted in the two public ownerships of land. 'The People's Republic of China practices socialist public ownerships of land, namely ownership by the whole people and collective ownership' (Article 2 of the *Land Administration Law*). In the nomology of laws, since the two ownerships are both socialist in nature, the subjects of both ownerships should enjoy the same rights concerning land. Since the land under state ownership can be converted for non-agricultural purposes, the land under collective ownership should be allowed to be converted, too. Since the land under state ownership can be transferred at some price, the land under collective ownership should be allowed to be transferred at some price, too. Since the utilization of the land under state ownership is determined by the owners of the land rights, namely, the State Council and governments at various levels, the utilization of the land under collective ownership should be determined by the owners of land rights, too, namely, the village collectives and their members. Thus the public ownership remains whereas the 'regulations over land utilization' will lose the foundation.

In order to strengthen and put into practice land rights in the dual systems, there are dual systems of land administration. The land in rural areas, its conversion for non-agricultural purposes and construction land are administered by different governmental departments. Land in rural areas is administered by the Ministry of Agriculture and departments, bureaus and sections of agriculture at various levels. The conversion of land in rural areas and construction land are administered by the Ministry of Land and Resources and departments, bureaus and sections of land at various levels which are at the same time responsible for the protection of cultivated land. The predecessor to the Ministry of Land and Resources was the Land Administration Bureau established in 1987. In 1998, in order to strengthen land administration, the Land Administration Bureau was upgraded to a ministry. The following is the current institutional structure of land administration.

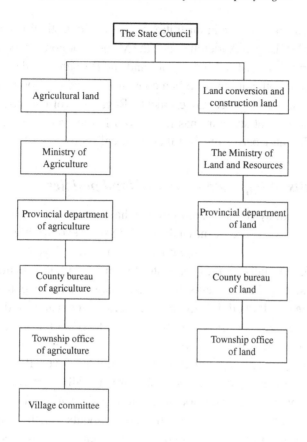

From the institutional structure it can be known that the administrative system of land in rural areas and the administrative system of conversion of land in rural areas and construction land are strictly separated. The administrative system of land in rural areas covers the contracting and utilization of land in rural areas while the administrative system of land and resources covers the conversion of land in rural areas and construction land. Though the administrative system of land and resources does not cover the contracting and utilization of land in rural areas, it is responsible for maintaining the total amount of land in rural areas for cultivation and housing. Therefore, it can be seen that land comes under the administration of different institutions according to the use of land, which serves as the institutional guarantee for the implementation of separate land policies.

Besides, as far as land administration is concerned, institutional functions overlap. The Ministry of Agriculture and the Ministry of Forestry both administer land in rural areas. The Ministry of Land and Resources and the Ministry of Construction both administer urban construction and rural housing. There are similar cases among local governments. Regardless of these overlapping functions, the current structure has provided a fertile ground for the rivalry amongst different departments over their political spoils.

2.3. Results of implementation of land policies

The current dual systems of land policies have their roots in history, and that indeed gives a sense of inevitability as to their evolution into the present form. Before the reform, the dual systems once played an important role in the industrialization of the state. During the rapid urbanization of recent years, the dual systems have also played an active role which should not be overlooked. But there are generally downsides in the current policies. For example, utmost attention is paid to general principles while inadequate care is given to specific rules; lower-level laws overrule higher-level ones; and the policies are ambiguous. Even if those shortcomings are ignored, the dual systems are actually self-contradictory, which gives birth to complex social relations and rivalling interests, such as the state versus the collectives, the governments versus farmers, the collectives versus farmers, the central versus local governments, governmental departments versus different local governments. Such policies not only distort the incentive mechanism but also social and market behavior, leading to competing interests, serious social conflicts, enormous waste of resources and possible economic or financial crisis.

2.3.1. Infringement upon and protection of farmers' land rights

The current land policies, in their implementation, extensively and severely infringe upon the land rights of farmers. First, the land contracting right is the sole property right for farmers, which is protected by the *Constitution* and *Land Contract Law*. Only when farmers exercise the right can they possibly make a living under the current system. Most of the requisition under the present policies is not aimed at public welfare but commercial purposes. Such a policy not only lacks legitimacy but represents abuse of power by the authorities. Some estimates show that up till now there have been 40 to 50 million farmers who have lost their land. A large proportion of them lost their jobs too. This is because requisition under current land policies does not involve negotiation with farmers and is not appealable. The requisitioning party has the *Land Administration Law* in their hand and the support of the authorities whereas farmers have no power or any law on hand. In the sense that the owners of rights have no way to express themselves or claim their rights, there is no difference between requisition and deprivation. The *Land Administration Law* is in essence a land deprivation law. It is not only more powerful than the *Land Contract Law* and the *Constitution*, but also contradictory to them.

Second, the *Land Administration Law* stipulates that land compensation and resettlement subsidies shall be provided for farmers. The law stipulates that compensation for land shall be given according to the original use of requisitioned land. The standards of compensation and resettlement subsidies as well as the ceiling are also in the law. Because of that, some people say requisition is not deprivation. This statement may be reasonable. But we would like to point out that the compensation principle, standards and ceiling are stipulated by the government and are not the results of equal negotiation between owners of rights. Therefore, they are not the expression of the free will, but a coercive mandate. Furthermore, compensation is something in consideration of damages, yet the livelihood and development of the farmers whose land is requisitioned are not taken into consideration. The most important point here is that the compensation according to the original use is seriously inadequate. When land is converted for non-agricultural purposes, there will be a big increment in the value of the land, and according to the current land policies, the increment will be taken by the requisitioning party and the user of the converted land instead of the original owner. The increment is tremendous. The ceiling of compensation and resettlement subsidies, 30 times the average annual output value in the three years prior to requisition, is usually 20,000 to 30,000 Yuan per *mu* (one *mu* is approximately equal to 667 sq. m). According to the data provided by the Shanghai Academy of Social Sciences, the expenses of requisition in the Long River Delta are RMB 375,000 to 450,000 Yuan per hectare while the transferring price is

RMB 2,100,000 to 5,250,000 Yuan per hectare (in the primary market) and the market price is RMB 11,250,000 to 22,500,000 Yuan per hectare (in the secondary and third markets). What the farmers receive for the requisition of land is only one-tenth of the price of land transfers, which is about one-fifth of the market price. Namely, the compensation and resettlement subsidies are only one-fiftieth of the incremental values. According to the calculation of experts from the Land Association, the incremental values of requisitioned land reach RMB 3 billion Yuan[2] each year and not a penny goes to farmers.

Third, according to current laws, the compensation for requisitioned land is given to collective economic organizations, resettlement subsidies are given to those to be resettled and only the compensation for ground appendices and seedlings is given to individual farmers. Under the current arrangement, the heads of collective economic organizations are the personified representatives of collective land rights and agents of state power in rural areas. They enjoy great power and often conspire with the requisitioning party rather than standing up for farmers. Because of graft, money-seizing, appropriation, inefficient investment and other waste by the heads of collective economic organizations, the compensation and resettlement subsidies which finally go into the hands of farmers are much smaller. Though farmers can claim their rights according to the *Land Contract Law* through legal means, the interpretation of the Supreme Court stipulates that 'the people's court shall not accept and hear the case when members of collective economic organizations bring a civil action on the amount of compensation distributed.' Because of this, the State Council issued a document stipulating that all the land compensation shall be given to farmers. But there is a huge difference between practice and the stipulation of the document.

Because farmers' property rights, personal rights and economic interests are seriously infringed upon, farmers take actions to claim, fight for and protect their land rights, especially since their awareness of rights was awoken by the implementation of the reform policy. Because legal remedies are not available, farmers hold together and appeal to higher authorities for help. Among all the appeals, those concerning land compensation

---

[2]Economic Report in 21st Century, June 22nd, 2006.

rank first. But appealing to higher authority for help is not an efficient arrangement. Bureaucrats shield each other and try their best to create obstacles; therefore most appeals are usually rejected unless the State Council or the Premier pays attention. A good example is the administrative reconsideration of land requisition in Longquan City Zhejiang Province, which became a success for farmers only after the media and lawyers participated.[3] Because the chances for success are low in appealing to higher authority for help, farmers choose to safeguard their rights collectively and a lot of group incidents happen. According to a survey, there were around 80,000 group incidents two years ago and 30% of them involved farmers safeguarding their rights. About 70% of those group incidents involving farmers safeguarding their rights were caused by unfair compensation for requisitioned land, which impeded the building of a harmonious society and endangered social stability.

2.3.2. *Conflicts over policy goals and competing interests of central and local governments*

Surrounding the issue of conversion and compensation, there have been conflicts over policy goals and competing interests between central and local governments, which is the inevitable result of current land policies.

The central government has a hierarchy of goals. On the top level is the goal to protect cultivated land and ensure food security. On the second level is the goal to protect the interests of farmers and maintain social stability. On the third level is the goal to properly expand construction land and maintain economic growth. Apart from the things in common, there are conflicts among them. For example, food security is a goal of the central government, but not that of local governments or farmers. In a certain sense, the central government has to keep farmers engaged in agriculture in order to protect cultivated land, which is against the interests of farmers that lie in participating in urbanization and industrialization. For another example, there is a conflict between the protection of cultivated land and the expansion of construction land. In order to keep economic growth at a

---

[3] 'Farmers in Zhejiang Province beat provincial government in court', *China Net*, July 11th, 2007.

certain speed, the central government is usually not strict with applications for expansion of land conversion and sometimes even compromises other goals. Local governments have double goals. The first goal is to maintain economic growth and meet certain targets. Expansion of construction land can help industrial development and economic growth. The second goal is about local finance and interests, namely, to increase local revenues and attain more financing. The two goals are highly consistent with each other. Quick conversion of land in rural areas and expansion of construction land will both boost economic growth and increase financial revenues. Therefore, as far as these goals are concerned, the central government and local governments are at loggerheads. Furthermore, if the legitimacy and rationality of the goals are taken out of consideration, goals of local governments are more valid and realizable than goals of the central government.

In terms of the means employed to realize policy goals, the central government is less powerful than local governments. The means of the central government mainly consist of administrative control, such as defining basic farmland, making an overall plan and an annual plan for land usage, examining land-law-enforcement, etc. But those means are heavily dependent on the cooperation of local governments. Therefore, the rationality of land policies stays with the central government while the effectiveness is more dependent on local governments. To be specific, the effectiveness is dependent on the conformity of goals between central and local governments, the controlling capacity of the central government and the loyalty of local governments. In the command economy, the three above-mentioned conditions were basically met. But against today's back-drop of de-centralization and marketization, none of the three above-mentioned conditions are met and the effectiveness of central control is not ensured. In China, there is an old saying which goes 'the far-away central government is often less powerful than local governments.' Local governments directly administer the land and farmers in their jurisdiction and are responsible for the specific handling of land conversion. Local governments and their officials may employ many means to evade admin-istrative control of the central government and seek favorable results of policy implementation. For example, they can adjust basic farmland, con-vert agricultural land before the approval is given, or give inaccurate or even false information on land conversion to the central government. The central government has to deal with 30 provinces (or autonomous regions), 70 large- and medium-sized municipalities, 600 cities, over 2000 counties and tens of thousands of townships in this game. Therefore, the central government often loses, leaving its goals unfulfilled. On the other hand, the goals of local governments concerning land conversion are often fulfilled unless they are extremely unlucky, thus catching the attention of the central government. Actually, the supervision and regulation employed by the central government work only accidentally.

In the current game of land policy implementation, due to local governments' superiority in both information and operation at local levels, the threats from the central government are not real, a serious consequence is that the scale of conversion of agricultural land is far bigger than the planned scale and the needed scale. According to some surveys, some provinces exhausted their 10-year quota for land conversion in just 5 years' time and some provinces used up their quota of land conversion up to 2010 by the year 2000. The central government gave an eastern province a one-million-*mu* quota for conversion of agricultural land into construction land from 1997 to 2010. But from 2000 to 2004, the province converted an average of 0.5 million *mu* of agricultural land into construction land each year, with the peak reaching 0.7 million *mu*. The quota for the capital city of a western province was 135,000 *mu* for conversion of agricultural land into construction land but by 2003, 171,300 *mu* of agricultural land had been converted.

At the same time, development zones mushroomed. By 2005, there had been 6,866 development zones of various kinds around the country, with a planned coverage of 38,600 sq. kms, which accounts for 1.1% of the total land area of the country and exceeds the total area of existing construction land of 31,500 sq. kms. Streamlining of development zones reduces the total number to 1,568 with a planned coverage of 10,200 sq. kms.

In the implementation of current land policies, local governments leave no stone unturned when gaming with the central government. In doing so, local governments can increase the supply of construction land, boost economic growth, heighten local officials' achievements and increase local financial revenues. There are three specific ways for governments to requisition and distribute land. The first is administrative allocation. From 1998 to 2003, 35% of the construction land in Zhejiang Province and 50% in Shanxi Province were allocated. The second is contracted transfer and 45% of construction land in the two provinces was distributed in this way. The third is auction through a market or semi-market mechanism. During that period, 20% of the construction land in Zhejiang Province and 5% in Shanxi Province were auctioned. The interests and revenues of local governments are boosted by three aspects, too. First, industrial land can be expanded. Low land prices or even free land helps a lot in attracting investment, which helps boost the growth of local GDP and tax revenues. According to a survey conducted by the Statistics Bureau of Zhejiang Province covering all the province's industrial development zones, the land development cost is RMB 98,800 Yuan per *mu* and in some places reaches RMB 200,000 Yuan per *mu*. But the average transfer price for industrial land is RMB 88,300 Yuan per *mu* and the average transfer price for one fourth of the land in industrial development zones is lower than half of the development cost. Second, low land prices can serve as subsidies for the development of infrastructure, and thus, improvement of the investment environment. Third, local governments can monopolize primary land markets, control secondary land markets and increase extra-budgetary revenues from the incremental values of land obtained through bidding and auctioning. Though only a small proportion of the land is transferred through bidding or auctioning, the revenues are enormous. From 2000 to 2003, the revenues from bidding or auctioning reached RMB 910 billion Yuan and in the year 2005 alone the revenues reached RMB 550 billion Yuan. In many places those revenues account for more than 60% of the extra-budgetary revenues. Besides, through conversion of land in rural areas and expansion of cities, the sales and income taxes of the construction industry and real-estate industry are increased and in some developed counties and cities, revenues from the two taxes account for 37% of the total local tax revenues. If the data in 1999 serves as the reference, the tax revenues from the construction industry and real-estate industry of the Chang'an district of Xi'an city increased by 5-fold and 19-fold respectively in 2003. Actually the increment in revenues comes from the deprivation of farmers because no incremental land values go to them. It is estimated that from 1987 to 2002, financial departments at various levels got a net income of RMB 1,420 billion Yuan from the land of farmers. As a result, another serious consequence arises, namely the chances of rent-seeking dramatically increase, which leads to serious corruption.

Furthermore, because land is closely related to financial departments of governments and the financial market, it becomes an important tool for getting bank loans. In some counties and cities on the south–eastern coast, the investment in infrastructure often reaches several million Yuan each year. Government investment accounts for only 10% of the total and land transfer funds around 30%. The remaining 60% has to be borrowed from banks with the land mortgaged. Bank loans account for even a higher proportion in western provinces. Since 2000, the city of Xianyang in Shanxi Province has been engaged in 15 projects, some of which have been finished, with an actual investment of RMB 0.953 billion Yuan, 76.7% of which is bank loans. The loans were obtained by land reserves centers of governments, policy-oriented companies or administrative committees of development zones with the land mortgaged or the financial credit of governments as the guarantee. If the loans on the mortgage of real-estate agents and citizens as well as the loans to universities for building new schoolhouses are taken into consideration, the total amount of loans is too large. Serious financial risks and crises are hidden in the approach to economic development that depends on the conversion of land in rural areas. But people are not adequately alert to those hidden risks and crises.

2.3.3. *Conflicts between the protection of cultivated land and urbanization*

China has a huge population but relatively limited land and it is a basic national policy to protect cultivated land. China is amidst quick urbanization. Therefore, urban expansion as well as expansion of urban land will be inevitable. But the implementation of the current land policies not only makes worse the contradiction between the protection of cultivated land and urbanization but also causes inefficient use of land, resulting in enormous waste.

From the preceding discussion it can be known that the current land policies have three pillars. The first is that the central government strengthens its administrative regulation and control over the conversion of land in rural areas. The second is that local governments try everything in their power to accelerate the rate of requisition in the process of urbanization. The third is that rural collectives and farmers have no say in the conversion of land in rural areas. From the cost-benefit perspective, rural collectives and farmers are net losers, local governments are net beneficiaries and the central government is somewhere in-between. The central government may lose more than it gains. Because rural collectives and farmers are disadvantaged and have no power and their interests are infringed upon, the central government cannot rely on them to restrain local governments. Collectives and farmers are powerless in the face of the infringement. Therefore, in the game between the central government and local governments, the goal of cultivated land protection is often unfulfilled and the process of urbanization distorted, which is the inevitable result of the current policies.

On the one hand, cultivated land is invaded and becomes smaller and smaller at an increasing speed. From 1996 to 2002, 10,275,000 *mu* of cultivated land disappeared each year. In recent years, despite the central government adopting strict measures, cultivated lands have been disappearing at a higher and higher speed. Cultivated land was reduced from 1.951 billion *mu* in 1996 to 1.829 billion *mu* in 2006. At the same time, per capita cultivated land was reduced from 1.59 *mu* to 1.39 *mu*, representing 40% of the world average.

On the other hand, cities are over-expanding. Because it is very cheap to obtain construction land, its users are encouraged to take up too much land. Because of the low cost and high return in the transferring of land in rural areas, urban areas are over expanding. From 1998 to 2005, urban areas increased from 21,400 sq. kms to 32,500, representing an annual increase rate of 6.18% and a total increase rate of more than a half. Local governments expand urban areas by transferring entire counties into cities or city districts, or simply building them anew. Worse, some county-converted cities expand their constructed areas by a rate of 5 or 6 sq. kms per year. According to the statistics of 664 cities, per capita land area of urban residents reached 133 sq. m in 2005, surpassing the highest quota for urban construction land stipulated by the state by 33 sq. m. Per capita land area of the United States is 10 times that of China, but the per capita land area in American cities is 112 sq. m. The urban per capita land area in some European countries is only 82.4 sq. m while their level of urbanization is much higher. The increasing urban land areas and over-expansion of cities lead to low efficiency in land use and high waste of land. The floor area ratio of Chinese cities is only 0.33 while some cities in other countries have reached or surpassed the floor area ratio of 2.0. According to a survey covering 400 cities, idle land in urban constructed areas exceeds one fourth of the total. Here in cities, it is common to see extraordinarily big public squares, expanses of green land and amazingly broad roads everywhere and even the roads in some counties have four or six lanes. And the office buildings of governments are usually the biggest and most beautiful in cities. For example, the government of Huizhou district of Zhengzhou city spent tens of millions of Yuan in building a White-House-style office building covering an area of 250 *mu*. And the office areas of many county governments are built against the backdrop of incredibly wonderful scenery.

2.3.4. *Two ways of conversion of land in rural areas and development trends*

There are two ways of converting rural land and increasing the level of construction areas. The two approaches will be discussed separately because they differ in nature and lead to different results.

The first approach is that governments requisition land in rural areas and then convert the land for non-agricultural purposes. The legal basis of this approach can be found in paragraph 1 of Article 43 in the *Land Administration Law*. In the requisition and conversion, governments play a dominant role. Governments become the real 'owner of land' through requisition backed by administrative power. Through monopoly of the primary land market, governments engross the incremental values from the conversion of land in rural areas. That is the major way in which local governments implement land policies, which leads to many problems, dilemmas and even conflicts. The industrialization done in that way is more of state-led one, and the resulting urbanization is more of that for governments and its officials, rather than farmers and rural areas. They represent a distorted form of industrialization and urbanization.

Different from requisition and conversion dominated by local govern-ments, the second way represents the conversion of land in rural areas initiated by farmers and rural collective economic organizations on their own through innovations on the basis of current land policies, or direct participation in industrialization and urbanization. The legal basis for it is in the escape clause in Article 43 of the *Land Administration Law* and there are two reasons behind such a practice. The first is the business opportunities involved in land conversion and incentives for farmers and collective economic organizations to interpret the current policies in some innovative manner and apply the escape clause according to their own understanding. The second reason is the tolerance, permission, or even encouragement of local governments. Despite the fact that the practice is like toeing along the borderline that separates legal from illegal, it repre-sents the development trend of rural land policies. The second part of this report will describe some related examples.

That said, there is another ominous trend developing here. Given that the land requisition of local governments causes serious consequences, the central government simply strengthens administrative control over land conversion. As a result, the game between the central and local governments becomes intensified. In that, local governments use legal means on the one hand and administer against the law on the other. Therefore, the strict control of the central government on land conversion leads to more and more concealed transgressions. From 1999 to 2004, since the implementation of the *Land Administration Law*, there had been one million incidents of transgressions involving a land area of five million *mu*, which was one million *mu* more on the 4.02 million *mu* newly converted in the whole country in 2004. In the last two years, there have been many similar incidents of transgressions. In the first half of 2006, there were 25,000 of them involving a land area of 0.25 million *mu* and in the first half of this year, there were 24,245 cases involving a land area of 220,000 *mu*. In paid transfers of land, local governments, land developers and banks conspire to arbitrate and easily manage to get away scot-free. Therefore, the strengthening of government control over land conversion not only fails to solve China's land problems but further exacerbates the situation.

It is a blessing that the serious contradictions and even conflicts con-cerning land have made decision-makers reflect upon the current land policies, and as a result, some new features have appeared. Document No. 28 of the State Council puts forward the issue of land conversion and Guangdong Province took the lead in issuing local regulations encouraging transfers of collective construction land. Those new things plus policy innovations around the country make it possible for us to blaze a new path in the market-base development for rural land.

3. Local Experiences and Policy Innovation: Cases and Analysis

3.1. *Brief introduction*

Since the implementation of the reform, urbanization, industrialization and market-bases, development has hastened in China. From 1978 to 2005, the rate of urbanization had increased from 18% to 43%, the rural population was reduced from 82% to 43%, the proportion of primary industry was lowered from 27.9% to 12.6% and GDP growth was maintained at an annual rate of 9%. As a result, China is transforming itself from an agricultural society to a modern industrial society.

Land and labor are the two initial resources for the rural population. In the transformation of the society and the rural areas, the 700-million strong rural population and grassroots organizations made full use of existing resources and made many innovations. Those innovations helped the rural population and grassroots organizations overcome policy obstacles and technical difficulties on the one hand, and on the other helped them participate in industrialization and share in the fruits of economic growth. More importantly, those innovations showed the correct direction for the future development in the rural areas. In general, there are four ways for rural populations and grassroots organizations to participate. The first approach is that rural laborers go to cities and join industrial workers. We call that migrant labor participation. The second way is that the rural areas build village and township enterprises and develop such non-agricultural industries as tourism or manufacturing. We call that industrial development participation. The third way is that expansion of townships and industrial zones assimilates neighboring rural population. We call that township radiation participation. The fourth way is that the traditional agriculture undertakers who are far away from townships cooperate with each other for the industrialization of agriculture and participate in domestic and international labor division (markets). We call that rural participation 'on its own'. If the first half of the 1990s serves as a dividing line, rural population and grassroots organizations participated in the first two ways prior to that and continue to participate in those two ways up to now. The final two approaches are the innovations that came later on and work in many places.

Farmers encounter new problems in every path they choose, which places new requirements on public governance. In 'migrant labor participation', farmers, as laborers, are scattered. Up to now, more than 100 million farmers have gone to cities as laborers or businessmen. And another 200 million are expected to go to cities in the next 20 years. The maintenance of the rights of farmers as migrant workers is a serious social challenge. There are other problems too, such as problems relating to large-scale migration, small-scale migration, social security, unpaid salary, unpaid premiums, employment, medical service and schooling of migrant children and children who stay at home. In 'industry development participation', there are usually no obstacles for land conversion, and the success of farmers depends on chosen industries and technologies at hand. If there are such resources as natural or cultural landscapes, or agricultural produce generated with modern environment-friendly technology, farmers' endeavors will be fruitful and incomes will rise. Otherwise, farmers will be in difficulty too. In recent years, because of pollution, many village and township enterprises have been closed down. Since the purpose of this report is the implementation and protection of land property rights, we will not further elaborate on 'migrant labor participation' or 'industry development participation'.

The following cases involve policies concerning land rights in 'township radiation participation' and 'rural participation on its own'. In 'township radiation participation', farmers cleverly exercise their legal rights and take advantage of the inconsistency and loopholes in current land policies and laws when converting cultivated land into that for non-agricultural purposes. By doing so, they turn land rights into their eternal possession and participate in the transactions of land markets. In this way, their land becomes part of townships and they turn themselves from farmers into urban residents or quasi-urban-residents. Then they can say goodbye to their traditional way of life and create new ways of life.

In 'rural participation on its own', those farmers who are far away from industrialized metropolises need not go away from home or give up agricultural activities while participating in industrialization. Generally speaking, urbanization does not mean that all rural residents go into cities. Instead, metropolitan industries and the farming industry can well co-exist. As long as the traditional peasant economy is reformed, market and natural risks can be effectively reduced and the problems associated with provision of public goods in rural areas can be addressed. But people need to make corresponding changes in their agricultural institutions where implementation and protection of farmers' land rights are always central to it.

3.2. The model of land-centered rural industrialization in Nanhai of Guangdong Province

Nanhai, located in the center of Zhujiang Delta to the east of Guangzhou, is a county-level city surrounding Fuoshan. Beginning from the 1990s, Nanhai gradually implemented a joint-stock cooperative system where land is always the central issue. Statistics show that the GDP of the city in 2000 reached RMB 33.87 billion Yuan, 3.4 times higher than that in 1992 when collective economic organizations were first established, with an annual growth rate of 23%. At least, 163 administrative villages had an revenue higher than RMB 100 million Yuan and 82 had a net income (i.e., after interests paid) higher than RMB 10 million Yuan, accounting for 66% and 32.8% of the total respectively. Per capita income of farmers reached RMB 6,764 Yuan, 1.7 times higher than that in 1992 and repre-senting an annual increase of 13%. In the table of total-factor economic strength of all counties (cities) in China, Nanhai sits at the top.

The so-called model of land-centered rural industrialization is that while the governments of villages and townships in the processes of indus-trialization requisition some parts of land on behalf of the state, they accept the practice of collective economic organizations in planning their own overall use of the remaining part without changing land ownership, which is then rented out to investors and manufacturers. This way, collective economic organizations and farmers can share the incremental gains accrued to the converted land. In 2004, industrial land in the city covered an area of 150,000 *mu* whereas the collective ownership of 73,000 *mu* was retained, almost half of all industrial land. Moreover, when Nanhai was upgraded from a county to a city in 1992, many village collectives turned their residential sites, fringes of villages and some parts of orchards into non-agricultural uses. Most of the conversion was not reported because no cultivated land was involved and farmers and village collectives chose to remain silent. Take Pingzhou, a district, according to the statistics of the Land Bureau of the city, the collectively-owned non-agricultural construction land in the district should cover an area of 2,000 *mu* while the actual coverage is 8,000 *mu*. The cases in another 19 districts and townships are similar. At the same time, when local governments requisition land on behalf of the state, they will leave to farmers 10% to 15% of the land for each *mu* requisitioned. What is more, the threshold of industrialization was lowered. In Nanhai, the cost to convert one *mu* of cultivated land into state-owned industrial land was RMB 130,000 Yuan. The cost was RMB 220,000 Yuan to convert one *mu* of comprehensive-purpose land and RMB 250,000 Yuan to convert one *mu* of housing sites. If an enterprise needed 200 *mu*, it would have to pay RMB 9 million Yuan for land alone. But it would be much cheaper to rent it at the price of RMB 0.8 Yuan per month for one *mu* of hillside land, RMB 1.5 Yuan per month for one *mu* of cultivated land and RMB 2.5 Yuan per month for one *mu* of road-side land. It is the flexible land use approaches that attract many enterprises to Nanhai and have transformed the city into a famous industrial zone in the Zhujiang Delta.

For the model to be practicable, the land regime should undergo some institutional changes. At the beginning of the 1990s, a few villages in Nanhai attempted to set up a joint-stock land system. In 1993, the Party Committee and government of the city reviewed the practice of those villages and advocated the system in all the rural areas within its jurisdiction. There are two basic approaches to the system. The first is the 'three zones' planning, namely, land is classified according to its function into three zones: protection zone for cultivated land, economic development zone and commercial residential zone. The classification helps protect basic cultivated land, makes it easier for overall planning in urban construction and utilizes land resources in an efficient way. The second approach is capitalization of collective assets such as land, contracting rights, residential sites, etc. by converting them into stocks. Meanwhile, rules are made for the issuance of stock rights, dividends distribution and rights administration, which is called 'village constitution' by farmers and followed strictly. Under such a system, collectives own land instead of enterprises. Thus, it is ensured that not only collectives share the incremental gains accrued to the land, but ambiguity of property rights and drainage of collective assets are avoided. Also, due to the stock conversion of their rights, the resulting dividends will be there to stay. In this way, the right to use and the right to own are separated, quickening the process of transferring farmers from agriculture to the secondary and tertiary industries. In 2002, 92% of the farmers were transferred to the secondary or tertiary industries.

In short, the policy innovation of Nanhai involves reform in the former household contract system, replaced by the collective land stock system. To be specific, collective assets and land are converted into stocks according to their monetary values, and an administrative district (now administrative village) or the economic commune (now village group) plans, manages and runs the land. Stock are issued on the basis of residential registration and classified as basic stock, contracting stock, contributing stock and so on, in line with the specific circumstances of the members in the village (or group). Hence, different grades of the stocks can be worked out and dividends distributed accordingly. This way, household contracting certificates are replaced by stock certificates, making the stock cooperative operation of land at long last come to pass.

The key to the success of the land stock system in Nanhai lies in the fact that when the contracting rights are replaced by the stock rights, farmers are protected. Compared to the former system, two things stand out. One is that under the current system, not only do farmers benefit from utilization of land like before (i.e., through land rent), but also enjoy incremental gains accrued to the land. Second is that stocks once issued are enjoyed by farmers over a lifelong period, perpetuating their rights, whereas the former contracting system has, at least on paper, a time limit.

The land policy innovation of Nanhai does not violate the regime of the collective ownership while it maintains the rights of members of collective economic organizations to the dividends resulting from the incremental gains of land converted for non-agricultural purposes. Yet, the innovation is not without its flaws. First is its exclusiveness: Only members of the community have the rights to land stock. Second is that the innovation is heavily colored with welfare. When the land stock system is implemented, farmers will usually get shares for free. Moreover, like that in the corporate world, the notion of shareholders' value in the system more often than not encourages shortsightedness in the operation. The farmers only care for the size of dividends alone, reluctant to shoulder their obligations and risks.

3.3. *Real-estate compensation and property rights exchanges in the development zone of Dezhou, Shandong Province*[4]

The development zone of Dezhou was established in 1992 and became prosperous in 1998 when many enterprises came to the area. The locale of the development zone was enlarged from 1 sq. km at the beginning to 23 sq. kms. By 2006, 19,000 *mu* of land had been requisitioned accounting for 67% of the rural land in Dezhou. Per capita cultivated land was reduced to 0.56 *mu*. An estimated 8,644 farmers had less than 0.3 *mu* of cultivated land on average and 5,616 farmers had 0.3 to 1 *mu* of cultivated land, accounting for 84% of all farmers in Dezhou.

In the development of the zone, the local government gave two kinds of compensation: monetary compensation and retained-land compensation. The monetary compensation was RMB 30,000 Yuan per *mu*, equal to 30 times the average annual gains from one *mu* of land and reaching the highest compensation standard stipulated by the *Land Administration Law*. Different from other local governments, the local government of Dezhou development zone gave all land compensation fees and resettlement subsidies to village collective economic organizations instead of farmers for them to develop the collective economy. At the same time, the

[4]The data of the Dezhou case was provided by Professor Liu Xianfa with the Comprehensive Development Research Institute and the comments were given by the author of the report after field visits.

local government gave retained-land compensation and combined in a clever way the monetary compensation with that of retained-land. That combination represents a new model for property compensation. In the development zone 2,440 *mu* of land were retained for 20 villages and townships. Monetary compensation fees were worked out according to the principle of '1 for 10', namely, for every 10 *mu* required, compensation fees for 9 *mu* would be given leaving one *mu* retained by each collective. Those compensation fees could only be used in the development of the retained construction land for non-agricultural purposes, for example, building industrial workshops, stores or other commercial uses. The ownership of the retained land was not changed in the short run to lower the costs of development by village collectives. When the land begins yielding returns, ownership will be transformed into state ownership accompanied by payment of overdue taxes and fees to the state. But the rights to use will still be in the hands of village collectives. In this way the land will turn into "active capital". In other words, when the ownership of land is transformed, it will become possible for the land to be used as collateral for bank loans. At the same time, land with transformed ownership can be easily transferred, which is helpful in stabilizing the expectations of village farmers.

Contrary to Guangdong and Zhejiang, Dezhou did not allow village collectives to develop the land on their own. Rather, Dezhou took it as part of the overall planning for the development zone. To be specific, the local government established an inward investment agency which is responsible for inviting investors and makes sure that village collectives build facilities on retained land according to renters' design and requirements. Up to now, eight enterprises have been invited by the inward investment agency that has rented out the industrial facilities with the same standards as the state-built facilities.

Dezhou authorities also combined compensation with the project of rebuilding old villages. In the process, the compensation for requisitioned collectively-owned residential sites took the form of commercial housing, which was built by the state-owned construction companies responsible for the rebuilding of old villages. Because of the coordination of the local government, some proportion of the commercial housing high in market value, the so-called "the gilded", was given back to village collectives as compensation. Up to now, the village collectives inside the development zone have invested RMB 0.353 billion Yuan and built property covering 614,400 sq. m. For example, the roadside commercial buildings built by Shierli Village and Songuantun Village are rented at a high price of RMB 12 Yuan/m² per month. In another example, Diaoligui Village and Liuji Village contracted with Himin Solar Energy Group and Jinguang Group respectively and built workshops according to the planning and standards of the latter for an annual rent of RMB 60 Yuan/m². Thus, with compensation taking the form of commercial real estate, villagers whose land was requisitioned had their basic livelihood ensured and could gain benefits for a long time in the future.

Moreover, Dezhou development zone built new housing first and resettled farmers before it demolished the old. That practice was in line with state policies of land requisition, land conversion and land-transferring in public bidding, and incremental gains were shared by farmers through newly-built commercial housing sold back to villagers at a discounted price. In the 1980s, some villages in the development zone tried a 'new village' initiative, giving each household a standard housing space of 360 sq. m and a building area of 100 sq. m. In the rebuilding of old villages, each household could get a compensation fee enough to buy only 30 sq. m in the commercial market according to the standards of compensation for requisitioned residential sites. In order to transfer more benefits to the farmers, the development zone made and implemented a 'space compensation' policy and gave each household a compensation fee of RMB 150,000 Yuan, which was RMB 85,000 Yuan higher than the monetary compensation.

During the rebuilding process, old housing sites were traded for new ones. To be specific, while the building area of new housing to be sold at a low price to the villagers was in accordance with the number of households and the number of family members in each household, the villagers paid RMB 680 Yuan for each square meter of new housing, which is at cost, from the compensation fee of RMB 150,000 Yuan for the old. That compensation fee could well cover the expenses of the villagers (150,000 − 680 ∗ 200). Thus, every household could get two new apartments worth RMB 400,000 Yuan (2,000 ∗ 200). They usually lived in one of the two apartments and leased out the other with monthly returns of

RMB 600 Yuan. The costs of the rebuilding were balanced, on the other hand, by the land saved due to re-planning in the process (i.e., 4/5 of the total), and newly built commercial housing. In this way, smooth project development is sustained.

At present, the Dezhou innovation is in an evolutionary phase. The major problem is that the property rights of the village collective economic organization are not defined clearly in that the village collective economic organization as an enterprise is mixed with the administrative body of the village. With the growth of assets, development of the collective economy and beginning of dividends distribution, such a problem and others related to it will emerge. The way out is to introduce rural stock cooperative organizations, clarify the rights and run the organizations like corporations.

The lessons learned from Dezhou model.

First, the model makes dynamic and sufficient compensation possible. The Dezhou development zone is newly-established. Being a late comer, it is inevitable for it to opt for high-speed or leap-frog development. The key question the zone faces is how to focus on development. At the beginning of it, the incremental values of land did not show up and land compensation fees according to the original use of the land were not sufficient. The land-retaining mechanism atones for the shortfalls, allowing for a sustainable livelihood. When the rebuilding of old villages has done, the incremental gains of land emerges, leading to an actual compensation higher than the monetary one, fairness of the development is achieved.

Second, through trade in property rights, farmers participate in the process of urbanization and industrialization directly. The key to Dezhou's combination of monetary compensation with retained-land one lies in the use of the funds from former for the development of the retained land. On the surface, the monetary compensation is to make up for requisitioned land, but in essence it is a trade in property rights when land is exchanged for commercial assets, which allow them to participate in the process of industrialization and urbanization. Though they are still farmers, they share the benefits from the process.

Third, the land requisition, resettlement, compensation and property right exchanges are planned by the local government and implemented by the villages and townships with the participation of farmers. The major responsibility of the government is to make plans, put forward related policies and attract investors. The governmental plans do cover the development of the returned land by taking it as part of overall planning. As a result, random development and unauthorized land occupation are prevented and possible mistakes of the village collectives, stemming from lack of knowledge, information, accesses or capabilities, are avoided. The specific arrangements of land requisition, resettlement and compensation are decided by villagers' assemblies after repeated discussion. In that process, not only self-governance of the villagers is strengthened, but also the resources of traditional communities are given a full play, which leads to cooperation and a win–win result.

Fourth, the practice of the Dezhou development zone brings new angles to the notion of property rights. Like in rental markets, the rights to own and the rights to manage are separated in the process. Even though the land is owned by collectives, the decision on its development cannot be made by village collectives alone but by the administrative committee of the development zone and township governments (or economy administration office) jointly. Moreover, the government of the development zone assumes dual roles in the process, both as the administrator and as a market player, not only making plans but also peddling the project to investors. Such a practice might be useful in under-developed regions with incomplete market mechanisms. First, heads of village collectives are effectively prevented from putting compensation fees into their own pockets or abusing compensation fees. Second, mistakes of village collectives in building factories on their own are largely avoided. Third, funding for collective property development is ensured. Fourth, successful operation of collective property is enhanced.

3.4. Three kinds of farmer cooperatives in Kunshan, Jiangsu Province

In 2006, per capita net income of farmers in Kunshan city was RMB 10,508 Yuan, 1.5 times higher than that of the province and 2.4 times higher than that of the country. Around 40% of the net income came from wealth, 45% from wages and salaries and 15% from fiscal transfers. Here, farmers' cooperative economic organizations played an important role in that per capita dividends from land cooperation reached RMB 3,407.6 Yuan. There are three kinds of cooperative economic organizations: Fumin cooperatives, rural land stock cooperatives and community stock cooperatives. 1/3 of the farmers joined cooperatives and nearly 1/4 of the farmers had reached the goal put forward by the local government that 'every household shall have stocks in cooperatives.'

3.4.1. *Fumin cooperatives*

Kunshan is near Shanghai and in the 1990s with the arrival of many foreign investors including Taiwanese and also domestic investors, migrant laborers swarmed in. Investors needed factory buildings and migrant laborers needed accommodation, which provided a great business opportunity: leasing of factory buildings and boarding of houses.

Seeing the business opportunity, Shen Weiliang, the party secretary of Chetang village of Lujia township, Kunshan city was determined to seize and make use of the opportunity together with other villagers. After repeated discussion with other villagers, Shen Weiliang and some of the villagers established first 'farmer investment association' in 2000. The association was mainly engaged in standard construction for factories, boarding houses, shops and marts, which were then leased out with dividends distributed at the end of the year. At the beginning, no license was required nor taxes levied. Because the risk was low and returns high, many farmers requested to join. Then the 'investment association' was transformed into 'Fumin cooperative', which is called in Jiangsu Province by the uniform name of 'rural specialized economic cooperative'.

In the development of cooperatives, the attitude of city heads played an important role. At that time, an assistant party secretary was inspecting Chetang when he found the existence of the association and reported it to the city government. On February 25th, 2002, the city government of Kunshan held a meeting in Lujia township to popularize the practice of Chetang, maintaining that farmers should 'invest and join cooperatives on a voluntary basis', cooperatives should 'be established by farmers and managed by farmers and beneficial to farmers', no fund should be raised forcibly, no promise should be given on dividends distribution, no government should be involved in dividend distribution, there should be rules in cooperatives while members should be registered, the major activity of cooperatives should be that of standard construction for factories and boarding houses, there should be an overall plan. And also, construction, leasing and management should be taken into overall consideration with the plan made by the city government and the actual construction should not proceed before investors are found.

After the meeting, Fumin cooperatives quickly became prosperous in the city and increased in number from 48 in 2002 to 178 in 2006 with an investment of RMB 500 million Yuan. The land managed by Fumin cooperatives covered an area of 2,465 *mu*, including 1,973 *mu* of construction land rented from collectives and 492 *mu* of requisitioned land. The cooperatives have built 310,000 sq. m of boarding housing, 410,000 sq. m of standard factory buildings, 135,000 sq. m of stores buildings and 5 marts covering an area of 380,000 sq. m.

3.4.2. *Community stock cooperatives*

In community stock cooperatives, collectively-owned assets that still have market value are quantified and distributed to bearers of land contracting rights. That kind of cooperative is governed like a share-holding company and distributes dividends at the end of the year. The purpose of establishing that kind of cooperative is to protect collectively-owned property, safe-guard resettlement compensation of farmers and make sure that farmers can participate in the decision-making processes of village collectives. The prerequisite to the establishment of cooperatives is that village collectives have net assets that are capable of generating returns.

There should be association rules in community stock cooperatives which should be followed strictly. Before the establishment of those cooperatives, two standards must be established. One is for evaluation of collective assets and the other is serving as cut-off date in household registration for every villager. Therefore, the following three 'confirmations' are needed in order to work out the shares of each villager.

First, the net value of the collective assets which are to be converted into shares should be confirmed. An auditing team consisting of members from the village and township administrative bodies and democratically selected financial groups should inspect and verify the net worth of village economic cooperatives and clarify ownership according to the law. Village economic cooperatives should convene members' assembly or representatives' assembly to check and approve the verification results and report the results to the rural working office of the city government for examination and approval. If most of the members require asset evaluation be done by an intermediary agency, legally qualified evaluation agencies could be contracted to do the work.

Second, village and cooperative membership and shareholders should be confirmed. Village members refer to those who are registered with the village before the base line date for household registration. Cooperative members refer to those villagers who have the rights to enjoy one basic share. These include all villagers aged over 18, as well as those who live in the village but are not registered members of the village and those who do not live in the village because of land requisition but are registered members of the village. Shareholders refer to those who are ineligible for basic shares and yet enjoy preferential treatment. Different statuses in the system have different kinds of shares, ranging from 0.09 shares to 0.5 shares.

Third, rights of shareholders should be confirmed. Two kinds of shares are issued: collective shares, which account for 30% of the total shares, and individual shares, which account for 70%. Individual shares are further classified into basic shares and enjoyment shares. Members of cooperatives get basic shares and other holders get enjoyment shares. Holders such as members of cooperatives, in-service village cadres only receive basic shares.

Community stock cooperatives were increased from three in 2002 as a pilot project to 24 in mid-2006, involving 11,957 rural households. The total assets of those cooperatives reached RMB 0.336 billion Yuan with 42,332 members holding shares and net worth reaching RMB 0.228 billion Yuan. There were altogether 65,800 shares including 57,000 individual shares and 11,800 collective shares and net worth per share reached RMB 3,500 Yuan.

3.4.3. Land stock cooperatives

In order to realize large-scale industrialization of agriculture, local governments guide farmers into establishing land stock cooperatives which are mainly engaged in crop and animal farming. Township and village land transfer service stations play a key role in that they combine the construction of agricultural products bases, building of agricultural parks and agricultural investment with the establishment of cooperatives. Farmers, if they volunteer, can exchange their land contracting rights for shares in cooperatives to get dividends within the framework of the law. That kind of cooperative is popularized in southern and northern Kunshan where there are large expanses of agricultural land. As long as the overall planning of land use is not violated, the original use and ownership of the land are not changed, holders of land contracting rights are clarified and stock values are reasonable, a land stock cooperative can be established and registered.

The first land stock cooperative in Kunshan city is called Shibei land stock cooperative. Each *mu* of land contracted to farmers is converted into one share. At the same time, shares that can be bought over counter are issued at the price of RMB 1,000 Yuan per share. In the contracting period of 30 years, shares can be inherited, sold or transferred after the cooperative and village committee gives their approval. The guaranteed annual minimum dividend of land stock is RMB 300 Yuan per *mu*.

Meanwhile, the city government sets up rules to regulate land stock cooperatives. First, farmers exchanging their land contracting rights for shares shall act in line with the aim of developing large-scale industrialization of agriculture. Second, consistent with the reform in agricultural land use and on the basis of crop and animal farming, land stock cooperatives should make effort to move into secondary and tertiary sectors aiming at broadening product bases and increasing productivity of land. At present 1,668 rural households (5,225 people) have joined land stock cooperatives with the land stock covering an area of 4,832 *mu*. These cooperatives are mainly engaged in the production and marketing of agricultural products and by-products, including flowers and saplings.

Local governments issued a series of favorable policies mainly in the form of subsidies, tax reduction, preferential treatment in land use, bonuses, etc. By the end of 2005, the annual income of the household in three kinds of cooperatives mentioned above had been increased by RMB 1,700 Yuan on average and per capita income by RMB 570 Yuan. The incomes of the 80 Fumin cooperatives of the city reached RMB 97.55 million Yuan with taxes paid reaching RMB 9.86 million Yuan. The subsidies received by Fumin cooperatives reached RMB 7.10 million Yuan and distributed dividends of RMB 25 million Yuan, plus bonuses of RMB 4.60 million Yuan. The dividends distributed from the 24 community stock cooperatives reached RMB 5.62 million Yuan, representing a dividend of RMB 104 Yuan per share. The actual dividends distributed from the 10 land stock cooperatives reached RMB 2.07 million Yuan, representing a dividend of RMB 428 Yuan per *mu*.

Concerning three kinds of cooperatives in Kunshan, there are three points needed to be discussed.

First, land contracting rights can stand independently as tradable assets for farmers. In the township-radiation model, rural laborers are to become industrial workers and farmers are to become city residents. Part of cultivated land is to be converted into urban land and the remaining part is to be cultivated on a large scale. This process is in essence that of allocation of resources to their most optimal uses through free flow of labor and capital. Moreover, the land contracting rights originally given to farmers by law become a tradable asset, which not only helps farmers share in the incremental gains of land, but also provides farmers with social security when they go into cities and other industries. This way, the free flow of labor is ensured since farmers are no longer bound by their collective membership. Around 65% of the rural laborers of Kunshan have left for the cities.

Policy choices of local governments are determined by two factors — fiscal expenditure and costs of public projects. In the process of urbanization, whatever model is applied, the impact on farmers' livelihood is huge. Yet, the decisions to make are not is with farmers. In the case of Kunshan then, what governments should do to maintain welfare of farmers is to make rules that would regulate and safeguard their rights rather than spending their way out. That would be cost-effective. But with the model of simple requisition, where farmers' contracting rights are not tradable, the cost of projects in terms of compensation and resettlement would shoot up, placing a heavy burden on local governments' budgets.

As with economic costs, the city of Kunshan provided 'five securities[5]' for farmers, two of which are directly related to land requisition and resettlement. Among other securities, old age insurance is related to land requisition, resettlement and guarantee of re-employment. The details of the five securities are as follows. First, the minimum rural living standard is RMB 2,200 Yuan per person/year. Second, rural old age insurance is RMB 100 to 130 Yuan per person/month. Third, from the rural medical insurance premium of RMB 200 Yuan, 130 Yuan is paid by the city and township governments, 20 Yuan is paid by village collectives and the remaining 50 Yuan is paid by individuals. Fourth, a policy of 'trading land for social security' is implemented with the purpose of integrating rural and urban social security systems into one. Around 7,000 elderly farmers begin drawing the urban old-age pension, which is higher than RMB 500 Yuan. Fifth, in land requisition and resettlement, compensation fees are given to farmers and new housing sold at the cost price. On average, each household receives a compensation fee of RMB 250,000 Yuan, sufficient to buy new housing covering an area equal to that of the old. From the above, it can be known that the burden on governments will become much heavier in township-radiation industrialization (like in Kunshan) if the social security of farmers whose land is requisitioned becomes the same as those of urban residents. In short, direct compensation for requisitioned land and ensuing re-employment and social security of farmers will greatly increase the burden on local governments, and indeed this will be beyond the capability of most local governments.

Third, for a land market to exist, its price system has to be established, which means farmers have to be able to decide the price of their lands. Under the present regime in which private ownership is not possible, collective cooperation thus becomes a necessary systematic guarantee. There are two key factors in all three kinds of rural cooperatives in Kunshan. First is farmers' legal right to land. Second is their membership in collectives. In the practice of Fumin cooperatives, if individual farmers had converted their land for non-agricultural purposes or leased

---

[5] The five securities are the insurance on minimum rural standard of living, rural old age insurance, medical insurance, land requisition compensation and resettlement subside.

out their land instead of collectives, the local government would have neither accepted nor supported their practice. Under a framework where private ownership of land is strictly forbidden and land contracting rights of farmers do not tolerate any infringement, farmers will be faced with the problem of legitimacy if they convert or lease out their land individually. Cooperatives are the best choice for farmers under that framework. Collective cooperation is in line with the *Constitution* and laws and makes it possible for the free flow of labor and land. Furthermore, the law governing rural cooperative organizations, *the Law of PRC on Farmers' Professional Cooperatives*, was passed on October 31st, 2006 and implemented on July 1st, 2007.

3.5. Communal enterprises of Dongsandao in Haicheng, Liaoning Province

Dongsandao village is located in the mountainous areas in the eastern part of Bali township of Haicheng city, Liaoning Province. On the river side of Haicheng River, it is 15 km away from Haicheng city and surrounded by mountains (Qianshan mountain range) on three sides. At present there are 880 households divided into 17 groups with a population of 3100. The village covers an area of 24 sq. kms with 3,100 *mu* of cultivated land, 10,000 *mu* of woodland and 12,000 *mu* of orchards. Now there are 12 village-owned enterprises with fixed assets worth RMB 130 million Yuan. In 1994, Dongsandao established and registered the Haicheng Dongxin Industrial Company and in 1996, it established the Liaoning Haicheng Dongsandao Demonstration Zone for the Industrialization of Agriculture with the approval of the government of Haicheng city. In the eyes of local villagers and cadres, there are not many differences between Dongsandao village, the demonstration zone and the Dongxin company. In 2005, the village had net worth of RMB 7.52 million Yuan and paid RMB 1.5 million Yuan in taxes and the per capita cash income of farmers reached RMB 8,000 Yuan.

There were two innovations in areas of policy-making and operations, namely, conversion of land contracting rights into shares and setup of a large-scale commodity basis for vegetables.

The first is the establishment of the 5,000 *mu* commodity basis for vegetables.

In July 2001, a company in Hong Kong dealing in vegetables, after hearing the good reputation of the village, came with a contract to buy broccoli and *brassica campestris*. The village collective rented 96 *mu* of cultivated land from villagers to plant those vegetables to see whether they were adapted to the local soil and weather and whether the result was satisfactory. At the end of 2001, the two sides signed a contract worth 150 million HK dollars.

In order to meet demand, large expanse of cultivated land was needed. The secretary of the village party committee and the chairman of the board of the Dongxin Industrial Company, Ma Yuying went from house to house and convened assemblies of party members, assemblies of representatives of villagers and meetings of village committees and party committees to try to persuade the villagers. Finally the Dongxin company signed a 3-year cooperative contract with the villagers. According to the contract, farmers' households exchanged their land contracting rights for shares and the guaranteed minimum dividend per *mu* was RMB 260 Yuan which was paid to the farmers before seeding (after 2004 the guaranteed minimum dividend was gradually increased to the present level, from 350 to 400 Yuan per *mu*. Before joining it, the net income from each *mu* was only RMB 180 to 200 Yuan). The farmers could also work for the company for wages and salaries (the average annual pay is higher than RMB 3,000 Yuan). To scale up, they pieced up scattered lands together, totaling 3,000 *mu*. Meanwhile, they also merged with two other adjacent villages with cultivated land of 2,000 *mu*.

When the vegetable base was established, the village collective decided on the kinds of vegetables to be planted, what kind of land for what kinds of vegetables, and the method of land rotation. The village collective also hired 28 technicians from Shenzhen city and put aside 500 *mu* as a trial plot. The village invested RMB 6 million Yuan to build such infrastructure as roads, bridges and wells. In order to make vegetables free from pollution, all of the fertilizers, pesticides and seedlings were purchased by the village collective.

Through public bidding, 12 farmers got the sub-contracts from the planting administration. For them to join the project, they must pay expenses for electricity, pesticides, fertilizers, seedlings and salaries for workers as their investment instead of deposits or other fees. When vegetables were harvested, the company purchased them from those sub-contractors according to the quality, quantity and price of the time of the vegetables. The difference between the purchasing price and the selling price (the vegetables were sold to the HK company) was used to cover the guaranteed minimum dividends, salaries of the technicians, expenses of storage, packaging, processing and transportation of the vegetables, etc.

The subcontractors hired workers from the village and paid them on a daily basis. They worked together with their workers and knew perfectly well who worked hard or not. In the rural society of acquaintances, one incompetent worker might be punished by long-term unemployment, financial ruin and social exclusion.

When there are orders, the major risks in vegetables planting come from the climate. For example, because of persistent high temperature, the broccoli, which should have been solid according to the requirements of the Hong Kong company, became puffy and failed the quality standard test, which inflicted a sizable financial loss. At that time, the subcontractors felt that they were at high risk, claiming that some expenses in the early stage should be covered by the village collective. In the settlement at the end of 2002, they received a net profit of RMB 10,000 to 20,000 Yuan each while the households having shares got their dividends and salaries. But the Dongxin company suffered a loss of nearly RMB 400,000 Yuan. In the following years the company managed to get by through vegetables processing and exporting. Because of the 5,000 *mu* vegetables base, 10,000 *mu* of cultivated land nearby was used to plant vegetables with 1,200 households involved and 600 farmers finding employment in this process.

The second is the establishment of a 3,000 *mu* commodity basis for vegetable production through merging. In 2004, a Korean company signed a contract with Dongxin company to purchase 1,000 tons of peppers each year. According to the contract, the Korean company would provide seeds, fertilizers in the seedling period, pesticide and planting technologies and training. Dongxin Company invested RMB 2 million Yuan in building a quick-freezing production line to freeze the peppers before they were transported to Korea. In 2005, the total value of the contract reached 3.2 million dollars.

In order to deliver the contract, a lot of cultivated land was needed and the land around Dongsandao village was insufficient. Dongxin Company went to Yingkou and Benxi and offered guaranteed minimum dividends of RMB 280 Yuan and RMB 300 Yuan per *mu* respectively to the farmers there to persuade them to exchange land contracting rights for shares and successfully got 2,000 *mu*. Dongxin Company provided seeds, fertilizers and planting technologies and sent technicians after harvesting to help farmers store and transport peppers. At the same time, Dongxin Company sent agents to Korea to increase market shares. Dongxin Company also invested RMB 1 million Yuan in building water pipes onto a mountain in the hope of converting the land there into pepper fields. The experiences of Dongsandao provide for the following lessons:

3.5.1. *Market expansion is the basic inducement to land policy innovations*

Dongsandao, located in mountainous areas, is far from cities. If Hong Kong and Korea's need for vegetables had not reached the village, there would have been no requirement to establish large-scale production bases of vegetables or no inducement for innovations in the old household contracting system. Business opportunities arise with the expansion of markets. In order to take advantage of these opportunities, collective land operation is the only choice. Therefore, it becomes inevitable to establish 'communal enterprises' by converting the household contracting system into the stock cooperative system and converting land contracting rights into shares. The case of Dongsandao shows that when the rural opens itself to the processes of industrialization, the powerful functions of the market can help the industrialization of special agricultural produces. Maybe in China's rural areas special agricultural produces enjoy greater comparative advantages than cotton and grain. Nonetheless, what is important is that we should respect the choices and decisions of farmers as market players.

3.5.2. *Farmer cooperation is necessary if farmers are able to play a dominant role in the price system for land*

In China's agricultural sector, in order to avoid risks and conduct large-scale operations, farmers need to make a rational decision on whether to continue operations independently or to pool factors of production in collective operation. With the market development, the current household contracting system is not as stiff as before. At the village level, farmers may take various collective actions and try various systems to improve their own welfare. The different systems compete against each other and the most effective one will be selected as the winner and chosen by the farmers. The communal enterprises in Dongsandao represent one of the systems. In the competition, community culture, market demands and current laws are all taken into consideration by the farmers. Namely, as far as land policies are concerned, Chinese farmers have the wisdom to coordinate in a clever way the traditions, markets and current policies for their own benefits.

3.5.3. *In rural communities, an efficient communal enterprise is important for the success of rural industrialization on its own*

Dongsandao village plays three roles for three respective purposes. First, as an administrative body, the village has the function of governance, planning and mobilization. The rights it exercised includes the collective ownership of land stipulated by law and administrative authorities given by the state. Second, as a communal organization of individual farmers, it has the function of providing social security and public services. Third, as a market player, it performs the function of spotting market opportunities, avoiding risks and allocating resources. The third function is very important in that it is the basis for performing the first two functions, making them practicable and meaningful. The above-mentioned roles and functions show that the village collective is a 'community-based enterprise' rather than a branch of the higher-level government. It has clearly-defined property rights and its leaders act like entrepreneurs when exploring market opportunities and signing contracts. Inside the community there is division of labor such as administrative management, production management, and other functions of a market organization whose authority comes from the consent of the members and is mainly free of the interferences from higher-level governments. All of it exhibits the distinct feature of a typical market organization. But it is different from an enterprise in that the village collective spends the profits in performing the functions of a government in a traditional sense. As the bridge between farmers and the market, cadres of the village are both entrepreneurs and community-governors. Therefore, one of the key issues in the economic and social development of the rural areas is how to retain those visionary, yet clean cadres.

3.6. *Summary*

The above-mentioned cases lead to the following conclusions.

- **In developing their local economy, the above-mentioned villages stick to collective ownership of land in the development of land markets, conversion of rural land for non-agricultural purposes and transfers of land contracting rights.** They produced a result satisfactory to the farmers, local governments and central government. Therefore, it can be safely said that the development of land markets and transfers of land rights is not inconsistent to the two kinds of public ownership of land and represents a feasible way to maintain the two kinds of public ownership.
- **The conversion into and transfers of collective construction land necessitates the breaking of state monopolies on land conversion for non-agricultural purposes, relaxing of governments' regulation on the utilization of collectively-owned land and the direct participation of land-rights owners in market transactions and in determining the price of land.** This represents the general direction of land policy reforms and the only way to urbanization and industrialization.
- **Farmers' cooperation in the market is a systematic guarantee of farmers' participation in the processes of urbanization and industrialization.** There are different forms of farmers' cooperation with each form exhibiting unique advantages. The most efficient form of cooperation has the greatest vitality and will develop on its own. But governments' support and protection are also needed.

4. Suggestions on Policy Improvement and Law Amendment

4.1. *Uniform land laws should be formulated in order to terminate the dual systems of land policies*

4.1.1. *The principle of 'same land, same status, same value' under the prerequisite of public ownership should be implemented*

The *Constitution* stipulates that China practices socialist public ownership: urban land 'belongs to the state' and rural land 'belongs to the collective'. State and collective ownership should only reflect the difference in owners of property, not in the status and the value of it in a market. Namely, collective ownership should be equal to state ownership and enjoy equal market status. Since there are serious and wide-spread mistakes in understanding and practice, the Standing Committee of the People's Congress should give clear explanation and make and implement uniform land laws. Under the current mechanism, collectively-owned land can only be used for agricultural purposes and it must be requisitioned by the state and transformed into state-owned land before it is converted into construction land. That mechanism should be changed and land under the two kinds of public ownership should be given ensured equal status and opportunities to participate in the processes of urbanization and industrialization according to the principles of "same land, same status, same value". Otherwise, farmers and collectives will lose their rights to land due to urbanization and industrialization. Laws and regulations governing the conversion and transfers of collectively-owned construction land should be made as soon as possible to allow collectively-owned construction land to go into markets in various forms for transferring, leasing, mortgaging and other forms of transactions.

4.1.2. *Land laws shall be modified to establish a systematic basis for the protection of land rights for farmers*

The purpose of *the Land Contract Law* is to protect the land rights of farmers. But a parallel law, *the Land Administration Law,* confines this protection to rural land and deforms the land rights of farmers. The clauses of land law concerning collective ownership are not clearly defined, which leads to infringement upon the rights of farmers by collectives. Worse, not much effort has been made in this regard.

It is an urgent task to modify the conflicting laws for the protection of land rights and interests of farmers. Inside villages, it should be further clarified that collective ownership is equivalent to community members' rights in order to prevent collective economic organizations from exploiting the ambiguity in the definition of property rights. This would potentially infringe upon land rights and interests of farmers. The government should try its best to provide a systematic mechanism to protect the land rights and interests of farmers, including the issuance of long-term land use certificates, registration of farmers' land, registration of land transfers and the establishment of land courts for the protection of land rights and interests of farmers.

The specific suggestions are as follows.

— The 17th Article of the *Land Contract Law* should be modified by deleting 'keeping or using the land for agricultural purposes, and refraining from using it for non-agricultural development.'

— Paragraph 2 of Article 33 of the *Land Contract Law* should be modified by changing 'no change shall be made in the nature of the land ownership or the purpose of use of the land designed for agriculture' into **'no change shall be made in the nature of the land ownership'**.

— Article 4 of the *Land Administration Law* should be modified by deleting 'The state practices the system of land use control.'

— Article 12 of the *Land Administration Law* should be modified by changing 'Whoever changes land ownership and use in accordance with law should go through procedures of change in registration of land' into **'Whoever changes land ownership in accordance with law should go through procedures of change in registration of land; whoever changes the use of land should go through procedures to put the changes on record.'**

— Article 14 of the *Land Administration Law* should be modified by changing 'Farmers who contract and manage the land have the obligation to protect and utilize the land pursuant to the agreement in the contract' into **'people who contract and manage the land have the obligation to protect and utilize the land in a reasonable way.'**

— Paragraph 1 of Article 43 of the *Land Administration Law* should be changed to '**Any institution or individual that needs to use land for construction must apply for the use of state-owned land or collectively-owned land in accordance with law; rural collective economic organizations have the rights to use the land they own to construct commercial buildings or villagers' residential buildings, or construct village (township) public facilities and public welfare establishments according to law.**'

— Article 47 of the *Land Administration Law* should be modified by changing 'For requisition of land, compensation shall be given in accordance with the original use of the requisitioned land' into '**For requisition of land, compensation shall be given in accordance with the market value of the requisitioned land.**'

— Article 153 of the *Real Right Law* should be modified by changing 'In acquiring, exercising and transferring the right to use housing sites, the law on land management, other related laws and provisions of the state shall apply' into '**equity owners of rural housing sites and houses on the sites enjoy the rights of possessing, using, transferring the housing sites and houses according to law.**'

4.1.3. *Local and grassroots experiences should be reviewed and attempts made to upgrade local rules and regulations governing transfers of collective construction land into state laws*

Transfers of collective construction land could bring benefits to farmers but are forbidden by current laws. Though local governments start to game the system, the hidden worries remain. First, such transfers violate current laws; this is counterproductive to the protection of farmers' rights and interests, and is harmful to the expectations on the long-term development of enterprises. Second, perverse competition has led to too low a price in such transfers, which results in a drain of resources and distorts land markets. Third, because the property rights of collective land are not defined clearly, the collectives often grab the bigger share of the incremental gains and there is no systematic guarantee of farmers' dividends.

Transfers of collective construction land are forbidden by law and governed by no explicit policies from the central government. Under such a condition, local governments in Anhui, Jiangsu, Shandong, Fujian and the suburbs of some metropolises have made effort in searching viable ways to strengthen the administration of collective construction land, initiating some policies for the healthy and orderly transfers of collective construction land. The pilot projects launched by the Ministry of Land and Resources in Suzhou of Jiangsu, Wuhu of Anhui, Huzhou of Zhejiang and Anyang of Henan can be seen as a preparation for the modification of land laws and reform of land policies later on. What deserves attention is that the provincial government of Guangzhou issued the *Transferring Trial for Rural Collective Construction Land* which represents a big leap forward in protecting farmers' land rights and interests and making it easier for them to be tradable in the market. First, the trial puts forward clearly the principle of 'same land, same status, same value' and that 'rural collective construction land can be transferred, leased out or mortgaged' so as to 'establish a uniform, open and orderly land market.' Second, the trial puts forward principles of and conditions for the transfers of rural collective construction land. (1) The principles of "free will, openness, fairness, equal value in compensation" shall be followed. (2) Utilization or obtaining construction land shall be approved according to law. (3) The transfers shall be in line with the overall planning of land utilization and construction planning of related cities, townships and villages. (4) Land shall be registered and ownership certificates drawn according to law. (5) The rights shall be clearly defined to avoid disputes. (6) Rural collective economic organizations shall convene villagers' assemblies to discuss and sanction transfers, leasing or mortgaging of the construction land according to law before they apply to governments.' Third, in order to protect the market for state-owned urban land, the utilization of the rural collective construction land traded in such a market is restricted. 'The remised, transferred or leased-out rural construction land shall not be used in residential housing development.' 'The part of land used for construction purposes shall not be changed without the approval of the bodies authorized to act in such a manner.' Fourth, clear stipulations are given about the utilization of the proceeds from land transfers. 'Around 50% of the proceeds shall be distributed among farmers directly and part of the remaining 50% shall be left to the collectives to develop collective economy and the other part shall be used to provide farmers with social security.' It is suggested that laws governing transfers of collective construction land be promulgated as soon as possible to help orderly, healthy and lawful transfers of rural collective construction land in a unified urban and rural land mark.

4.2. Governments' monopoly in the primary land market should be broken to protect land rights and interests of farmers and collectives

4.2.1. The current land requisition policies should be reformed fundamentally to stave off the trend of nationalization of construction land

According to the current land policies, rural land must be requisitioned by the state before it is converted for non-agricultural purposes, which leads to governments' monopoly in the primary land market and a tendency for nationalization in rural land conversion for non-agricultural purposes. From 1987 to 2001, non-agriculture construction nationwide consumed 33.946 million *mu* of cultivated land, 70% of which was obtained through governments' requisition. This means that in the last 10 years, 24 million *mu* of collectively-owned land has been nationalized. According to a survey by the Ministry of Land and Resources, there are 250,000 sq. kms of construction land nationwide including 70,000 sq. kms of state-owned land and 180,000 sq. kms of collective construction land accounting for 72% of the total (land for transportation and water conservancy facilities is not included in this figure). The collective construction land is actually nationalized as well.

In recent years, cities have rapidly enlarged and encroached on rural land. A tendency of land nationalization is manifested in that villages inside cities are converted into residential areas, townships into urban neighborhoods and counties into districts. For example, Shenzhen city nationalized 260 sq. kms of rural land in Bao'an and Longgang districts not long ago for urbanization. The tendency of nationalization will definitely change the current situation for construction land, harm the land rights and interests of farmers and collectives, and reinforce governments' monopoly in the primary land market, which is harmful to healthy urbanization and sustainable economic development. Therefore, only when the current system of land requisition is reformed and governments' requisition is restricted and regulated will the governments' monopoly in the primary land market be broken and the tendency for nationalization in the process of urbanization be checked. Given that the current laws are yet to be modified, full use of the overall planning for land utilization and urban construction should be made. Such planning should be regarded as an equivalent of a law which governments cannot modify at will and everything should be consistent with the planning instead of breaking it. Large-scale occupation of rural land in so-called innovations such as the conversion of villages into residential areas, township into districts, etc. should be prevented.

4.2.2. *The current system of land supply by governments should be reformed and collective construction land should be allowed to directly enter the land market*

The current land supply system is an important part of the regime governing rural land conversion. Only governments have the right to requisition land and are the sole supplier of construction land. Governments' monopoly from land requisition to land supply impedes the direct entering into the land market of collective construction land and is harmful to future industrialization prospects. The large-scale allotment of land through administrative means often leads to serious land waste and infringement upon the interests of farmers and collectives. The purpose of transferring construction land through bidding, auctioning and listing is to prevent local governments from depressing land prices (they do so to attract investors) and to promote intensive utilization of land, to which things often go to the contrary. Since the lowest price of land is determined by the land classification of the Ministry of Land and Resources, the price of industrial land in developed regions is relatively low while that in central and western China, where industrialization is just beginning, is strangely high. China is in a key stage of industrialization, and labor and capital moving to central and western China are both dependent on the quick development of industrialization. Local experiences show that if farmers are able to lease out, transfer or remise their collective construction land directly to enterprises under the present state of overall land planning, the land cost of enterprises will be greatly reduced, farmers can also share the incremental gains of land for a long time to come, and local governments will get taxes revenues and land utilization fees from enterprises. If rural collective construction land is allowed to enter the market directly, many enterprises will be attracted to move to central and western China, especially manufacturing industries, which is helpful in maintaining manufacturing competitiveness in the world.

Along with the development of urbanization and industrialization, capitalization of increasing quantity of rural construction land has taken place. In developed regions in particular, spontaneous transfers of rural construction land happen in large quantities through remising, leasing, mortgaging and demising (including investment, acquisition, merger, joint operation and exchange of managing rights, etc.). Hidden markets for collective construction land are in existence where legal and illegal transfers happen simultaneously. It is a better choice to allow collective construction land to enter open markets than to see illegal transfers in hidden markets.

4.2.3. *Infringement upon farmers' rights in the construction of village residential sites should be prevented and commercialization of the sites should be promoted*

With the rapid expansion of cities accompanied by the promulgation of central government policies for strengthening the administration of land and developing a credit system in the real-estate sector, local governments and real-estate developers cast their selfish eyes on rural housing sites of farmers and begin infringing directly upon their rights. First, because housing sites are already classified as construction land, exploiting them in the name of rebuilding old villages or starting new ones not only increases the proportion of existing construction land used for development purpose but also conforms to administrative quotas requirement. Local governments in the developed regions in the east strive to be the first to undertake rebuilding of old villages and construction of new villages. Local governments in central and western China emulate this, which leads to deprivation or free transfers of farmers' housing sites. Second, local governments and real-estate developers join hands to develop commercial housing on the sites. With the incessant rise in prices of commercial housing and land in urban areas, farmers' housing sites on the boundaries between urban areas and suburbs represent a great opportunity for real-estate developers. Local governments establish policy-oriented companies that mortgage land for loans to invest in infrastructures in the suburbs with great development prospects. Real-estate developers demolish farmers' old houses before building new houses on the sites. Then they compensate for the demolished houses with new houses in the ratio of one to one and sell the remaining newly built houses in commercial markets. In that process, local governments receive proceeds from land transfers and achieve the construction of new villages, real-estate developers receive profits and farmers move into new houses but lose their land forever. Third, rural housing sites are nationalized in the name of 'urban–rural integration'. With the progression of urbanization, there appears to be a severe shortage of existing land in designated zones of some rich provinces or metropolises in the east. Those governments then convert village housing sites in designated zones into state-owned construction land, with an adjustment in administrative rules, by converting counties into cities, townships into districts with village committees turned into resident committees and villagers into urban residents.

Existing housing sites are heavily colored with welfare. Because the sites have not been recognized by law as either commodities or tradable assets, the arrangement of the property rights is clearly flawed. And that leaves loopholes for local governments and real-estate developers to exploit. Hence, proper property rights should be defined for the housing sites and uniform certificates with legal backing should be issued. Surveying mechanisms and the registration of farmers' housing sites should also be further improved. At the same time, pilot projects should be launched to look for effective methods of commercialization and transfer. Before effective methods are found, the State Council should stipulate that regions financially capable should rebuild or rearrange villages under the prerequisite of farmers' free will. But extra land saved from such an activity should be re-cultivated in principle instead of being used for construction purposes.

4.2.4. A 'requisition black list' should be made to ensure that land to be used for the purposes other than public benefits shall not be obtained through requisition

The land requisition system has its roots in the command era when land and other factors of production were all controlled by governments. During that era, land was usually used by state-owned enterprises, government departments or large state-run infrastructure projects (such as roads, railways and irrigation works). The *Land Administration Law* stipulates that 'the state can requisition according to law collectively-owned land for the sake of public benefits.' But large quantities of requisitioned rural land are in practice used by governments for purposes other than public benefits at various levels since 'public benefits' are not clearly defined. With the deepening of reform and economic development, the notion of land user is no longer confined to the authorities alone. Rather, it has been pluralized. As a result, land utilization has long been outside the range of 'public benefit'. In highly industrialized counties and cities in the east, industrial land accounts for 30% of all construction land and most of the industrial land is used by private enterprises. Around 20% of all the construction land is used by the real-estate industry, business and services industry. The remaining 50% is used for public facilities and infrastructure, which are meant to be for public benefit. But an ever-increasing part of those facilities and infrastructure is moving out of the domain of public benefit.

Land requisition must stick to the principle of 'public benefit' and the current practice that land used for economic construction is obtained through requisition should be changed. In order to prevent local governments from abusing their power in land requisition with the excuse that 'public benefits' are difficult to legally define, policies stipulating that land not for public benefit shall not be obtained through requisition should be issued. Also, a list of land uses that do not fall into the category of 'public benefits', a so-called 'black list', should be set up. This can serve as the basic reference in national land supervision. Whereas too much land is allocated for too many purposes, which leads to waste of land and corruption, it is suggested that strict restrictions should be introduced on the proportion of land allocated for public facilities, and land, while allocated in the name of public benefits, used for generating profits be reduced. It is also suggested that pilot projects be launched to compensate for land requisitioned for purposes with quasi-public-benefits according to market prices.

4.2.5. *Governments' land reserves should be confined to existing levels and it should be strictly forbidden to requisition collectively-owned land to add to land reserves*

Land reserves are obtained through purchasing or taking back existing construction land which should be strictly confined to existing construction land. Land reserves consist of land belonging to a user who no longer exists or has moved to another place, land which has not been utilized for two consecutive years, land whose use is changed by the user without authorization and is not corrected within given time, land whose terms of use expire while no application is forwarded by the user for another term or the application is turned down, land which has been idle for a long time, state-owned river beaches, land along roads, along railways, in airports and in mines which are discarded as useless after approval, land vacated for public benefit or in city planning, land in key areas vacated in the rebuilding of old cities, land vacated in re-structuring of enterprises, land of a user who has received the right to use according to the law but is not financially capable developing the land while the circumstances do not allow a transfer of the land, land where the user asks the government to take it back, land where the price of transfer is much lower than the market price, reserved land or idle land along passageways in planned areas of cities, and land which is to be requisitioned by governments according to planning. Whereas the system of land reserves has been in practice for 5 or 6 years in more than 1,000 cities, the central government should make as soon as possible laws and policies governing the purposes and goals as well as regulating range, institutional establishment, legal person status, mortgage patterns of and loans to land reserves in order to put an end to the present disorderly state and to prevent funding risks for centers of land reserves.

4.3. The fiscal structure should be changed and local property tax should be levied

4.3.1. The mechanism of revenue collection should be changed to eliminate incentives of local governments in land requisition and sale

At present, land transfers represent large amounts of money and the major source of extra-budget revenues for local governments. Collection of land-related fees is an important avenue for governments' departments to fatten their own welfare. Direct tax from land and indirect tax from urban expansion are two important sources of revenue in the budget. All in all, more than half of local government revenue comes from land, and in a sense, local governments' budgets are worthy of the name 'land budget'. This is the principal incentive behind local governments' passion for requisition and land sale. This fiscal arrangement is consistent with the monopoly of local governments over construction land. Only when the mechanism of revenue collection is changed so that it matches the administrative responsibilities of local governments will governments' monopoly over the primary land market be broken and governments be willing to give up their role as the 'landlord' or the land-dealer, putting an end to their current practice whereby land is requisitioned at a low price and supplied at a high one.

4.3.2. Incremental gains from land should be distributed in a reasonable way and the system of land property taxes should be improved

While changing the mechanism that has encouraged local governments in land sales, the central government should set about broadening land tax base and improving the existing system to stop the monopolistic bargaining power of local governments in the market. On the one hand, an institutional guarantee should be established to ensure that the owners of land rights and interests are treated fairly in the distribution of increment gains. It should be acknowledged that the owners of land have the rights to share these gains and research should be conducted on what are reasonable proportions of the total incremental gains that should go to farmers, land developers and governments at various levels, respectively. On the other, the system of land taxes should be reformed and a new land or property tax should be designed that the revenues of local governments can be sustained for years to come in the process of urbanization.

Practice of reform in land property taxes may take reference to the experiences of some developed countries with a complete market mechanism. The reform may begin with the easy part before moving on to the difficult and be implemented in steps. The present system where different taxes are levied by different offices should be changed into that where various taxes will be integrated into one collected by a single government body. It is suggested that taxes and fees related to land property be collected by the taxation office alone instead of many departments. It also argues that the current land taxes and fees should be unified into three taxes: land occupation tax, land tenure tax and land transaction tax. The land occupation tax is levied on the conversion of rural land for non-agricultural purposes, which is the combination of the current cultivated land occupation tax, cultivated land reclamation tax, and tax on paid utilization of new construction land. The land tenure tax is levied on the holder of construction land. Because land is not renewable and its values appreciate with economic development, taxation departments shall levy the land tenure tax on the holder of construction land which should represent a proportion of the price rise evaluated by independent land assessment agencies periodically. The land transaction tax is levied on the transfers of construction land; this serves as a stable tax source for local governments and encourages land to go to the most valuable use.

4.3.3. *Measures of including in the budget the revenue from land remise should be set up as soon as possible, which may serve as an interim mechanism for establishing the system of property taxes later on*

Document No. 31 stipulates clearly that 'all the revenue from remising management rights relating to state-owned land shall be included in the local budget, paid to the local treasury and managed separately.' The implementation measures should be made and put into effect as soon as possible, which is not only conducive to the efficient utilization and standardized operation of the funds, but also serve as a preparation for establishing later on the system of property taxes. However, in specific operations, attention should be paid to the two following points. First concerns of estimating the revenue from land remise. In other words, the budget is made at the beginning of the year and reviewed at the end of it. Governments can control the quantity of land to be transferred in the year, but the specific amounts of the revenue are to be determined by the market, even though it is monopolized by the authorities. Therefore, there needs to be detailed measures as to the ways of including land remise funds into local budgets. Second is how to use the tax properly, according to the experiences of other countries, the land property tax is usually a principal tax for local governments who are attracted to collect this tax. Because it is easy to spot any changes in land, the tax is usually fully collected. The rationale behind is to enhance efficiency in regulating and using the funds, rather than giving them another means to share land spoils after obtaining some detailed intelligence on land users.

4.3.4. *Fiscal regime should be upgraded so as to match financial power with administrative responsibilities*

In the current system, local governments have unlimited responsibilities but the financial power is in the hands of the higher-level governments. That is why local governments are unable to make ends meet and tend to derive incomes through selling land in the processes of urban expansion. In order to reduce local governments' incentives to try for extra-budget revenues, the fiscal regime should be upgraded in that the assumed role of governments as investors should be turned into that of governments as public services providers. While reducing heavy burdens for local governments, a pluralistic urban investment environment will come into being with governments being the principal provider of public goods.

4.4. Farmers whose land is requisitioned should be allowed to negotiate for compensation and proper measures should be set up

4.4.1. Actual compensation should be decided upon through negotiation with the comprehensive standard of a region (district) as the reference

Document No. 28 stipulates that 'the provinces, autonomous regions and cities under direct central administration shall set up public standards in annual output values of land in the cities and counties under their administration or comprehensive regional (district) land price as the reference in compensation for requisitioned land.' Compensation has already been based on the comprehensive regional (district) land price in many places in the provinces of Guangdong, Zhejiang and Jiangsu. This has led to a rise in compensation standards. The compensation standard in Jinhua city was RMB 8,000 to 10,000 Yuan per *mu* in 1999 and RMB 22,000 Yuan per *mu* between 1999 and 2003 while the standard was raised to RMB 30,000 Yuan per *mu* on the basis of the comprehensive regional (district) land price in 2003. Compensation on the basis of the comprehensive regional (district) land price was given in Yiwu city in 2003, leading to a standard of RMB 38,000 to 42,000 Yuan per *mu*. Actually, the current comprehensive regional (district) land price is not negotiated by owners of land and does not take into consideration increment gains. Therefore, the price can only serve as the minimal standard of compensation for requisitioned land. Farmers whose land is requisitioned should be allowed to negotiate directly regarding compensation and the actual compensation should be the result of bargaining between the two parties.

4.4.2. Land for development should be retainable and property compensation should be implemented

When monetary compensation is given, a proportion of the requisitioned land should be retained by the villages concerned. The collective economic organization of the villages can build standard factories or stores to rent out on the retained construction land with the rent distributed among the villagers as dividends. Besides the cases of Nanhai, Dezhou and

Kunshan, introduced in the second part, there is another case in Shaoxing County. In Shaoxing, when over 60% of the cultivated land of a village within the urban area of the county becomes requisitioned, part of this will be retained by the village for economic development. To be specific, when the land of over 1,000 *mu* is requisitioned, 25 *mu* will be retained. When the land between 670 and 1,000 *mu* is requisitioned, 20 *mu* will be retained. Exactly 15 *mu* will be retained when a part below 670 *mu* is requisitioned. When related taxes and fees are paid, the village with the retained land will receive a certificate for the right to use and can build standard factories, office buildings and stores to lease out or exchange the rights for shares. The land that is outside city planning shall be transferred through bidding, auctioning or listing with 80% of the net revenues distributed among the village collective. The profit-generating assets accumulated by the villages in Keqiaozhen range from RMB 12.7 million Yuan to RMB 56.939 million Yuan. When 'converting villages into residential areas,' those assets were converted into shares and per capita financial wealth ranged from RMB 5,000 Yuan to RMB 26,000 Yuan. Because the retained land helped to increase the revenues of the farmers' dividends, it was welcomed by the farmers and collectives. Practices show that retained land is helpful to the growth of the village economy and the rent plays an important role in providing public goods in rural areas where public finance is absent. Furthermore, land dividends represent an important channel for farmers in developed regions to share incremental gains. It is suggested that the central government issue documents governing the proportion and utilization of retained land and the distribution of proceeds.

4.4.3. *The practice of exchanging social security for land should be scrutinized to prevent any covert infringement on farmers' land*

Such provinces as Jiangsu, Zhejiang and Guangdong are promoting the practice of providing farmers whose land is requisitioned with social security and the Kunshan case in this report contains some relevant information. Actually, farmers, especially those in their prime of life, do not look favorably on exchanging land for social security. The practice is furthermore worrying in terms of its methods and funds needed. From the perspective of the whole country, governments tend to exchange social security for farmers' land in order to resolve the conflict of interest between farmers and governments. Though that practice represents clear progress, the social securities provided by governments, at least on paper, should be taken by farmers as worthwhile to trade their land rights while governments should be financially sound enough to fund such a project. In practice, city governments suffer from shortages of funds in providing old-age insurance and social security for urban employees and even in developed regions farmers whose land is requisitioned can only get RMB 200 Yuan each in social security. Guangdong estimates that expenditures on social security will increase the average cost of land requisition by RMB 60,000 Yuan per *mu*. Therefore, caution should be taken in 'exchanging social security for land' to prevent governments from falling into financial mire or infringing upon farmers' land rights in the name of 'providing social security'.

4.5. The effectiveness of quota management and institutional arrangement for protecting cultivated land

4.5.1. The current quota administration is basically of no effect because of easy evasion by local governments at various levels

As early as 1997, the central government, out of concern for food security, issued strict cultivated-land-protecting rules governing the compensation for requisitioned land, dynamic balance of total cultivated land, protection of basic farmland, etc. Before cultivated land becomes occupied, it must be approved by the central government, and the responsibility of local governments is to make up for cultivated land lost in order to maintain the dynamic balance of total cultivated land. But local governments try their best to evade the directives of the central government by reshuffling the quotas among areas of different level of the requirement for the purpose of occupying as much as possible of the cultivated land. Some provincial governments do it not only within the province but even beyond its borders with a certain amount of financial compensation. Some local governments include pools, riverside and hillside land into basic farmland in order to get approval

from the central government to convert more cultivated land for non-agricultural purposes since the total area of cultivated land 'is' maintained.
Some local governments convert land illegally and readily pay the fine
when land audits are conducted. And with the penalty paid, the land converted this way will become legalized. In order to obtain the approval from
the central government for land conversion, some local governments even
cook their books, leading to a farcical phenomenon that basic farm land
actually increases while growing part of it is converted for commercial and
industrial purposes. In some regions, though the total area of cultivated land
is maintained, the replenished land is of poor quality. For example, there are
irrigation facilities in two-thirds of the requisitioned land and only in one
third of the replenished land. To sum up, the balance of total cultivated land
is to be maintained by local governments. As long as local governments are
attracted by the current land system to requisition more land, local governments and the central government would have different goals and local
governments would try their best to evade, usually successfully, the quota
system of the central government. Strict rules cannot solve this problem
caused by the separation of land protection from economic development
and as a result cultivated land protection will exist only in name.

4.5.2. *The trade in quotas should be accepted and a mechanism for it should be established*

In the process of urbanization and industrialization, development levels
differ from region to region or from city (county) to city (county) in the
same region. Therefore, regions and cities (counties) vary in their need for
construction land. The current practice that construction land quotas are
traded within cities, counties and provinces or even beyond to resolve the
dilemma between basic farmland protection and the need for construction
land has not been accepted by the central government. When considering
economic development, the practice becomes more and more widespread.
It is suggested that policies be made accepting the trade in quotas and a
mechanism governing it be established. While quotas are allowed to be
traded from less-developed and agricultural regions, where there is not
such a strong need for construction land, to industrial and developed
regions, where there is a strong need for construction land, compensation
should be given by the latter to the former. Thus, the need for construction

land in those quickly-urbanized and industrialized regions will be satisfied while the poorer regions receive certain monetary compensations.

4.5.3. *Regional zoning for industrial development should be set up in a scientific way and a mechanism of food security be established*

Multi-discipline experts should be organized to study the regional lay-out of industries. On the basis of that study, national food security should be linked to the protection of cultivated land. The state should give compensation for cultivated land used to ensure food security and industrialized regions should give compensation to regions providing such security. Thus, local governments will have clear goals, responsibilities and fair compensation in cultivated land protection.

Bibliography

Amartya Sen, *Development as Freedom*, Oxford University Press, 1st edition, 1999.

Amartya Sen, *Development as Freedom*, Remin University of China Publishing House, 2002.

Circular of the State Council on Intensifying Land Control, also called *Document No. 31*, in effect on August 31st, 2006.

Constitution of the People's Republic of China, adopted by the 2nd meeting of the 10th People's Congress on March 14th, 2004.

Decision of the State Council on Deepening Reform and Strengthening Land Administration, also called *Document No. 28*, in effect on October 21st, 2004.

Land Administration Law of the People's Republic of China, amended by the 4th meeting of the standing committee of the 9th People's Congress on August 29th, 1998 and in effect on January 1st, 1999.

Land Contract Law of the People's Republic of China, adopted by the 29th meeting of the standing committee of the 9th People's Congress on August 29th, 2002.

Real Right Law of the People's Republic of China, adopted by the 5th meeting of the 10th People's Congress on March 16th, 2007 and in effect on October 1st, 2007.

Zhao Gang & Chen Zhongyi, *History of China's Land Laws and Policies*, Xinxing Publishing House, 2006.

Chapter 2

Implementation and Protection of Property Rights in Collective Construction Land — Involving the Issue of "Sub-Rights" Rural Housing*,†

The report, focusing on the rural housing system, describes and evaluates the process of transition in the current system concerning collective construction land. Based on six cases, it discusses the methods and effects of the government's control on the land, reveals the real purpose

*The report is organized by Beijing Unirule Institute of Economics, mainly written by ZHANG Shuguang, followed by LIU Shouying, LIU Xianfa, GAO Shengping, SHI Hongxiu, CAO Zhenghan, LUO Biliang and ZHANG Chi. ZHANG Shuguang has given a speech on the topic in the 379th biweekly forum of the Unirule Institute of Economics and in the seminars held in universities including SUN Yat-Sen University, South China Agricultural University and Fudan University, besides that other scholars such as ZHOU Qiren, WU Xiaoling, HUANG Xiaohu, ZHAO Shufeng, DANG Guoying, ZHENG Fengtian, PENG Bo, ZHAO Nong and SHENG Hong have given wonderful discussions. Meanwhile, the research is funded by the German Foundation and Boyuan Foundation, and we offer thanks for all above. The author takes sole responsibility for his views.
†Originally published in of the winter issue of 2009 *China Social Sciences Journal* (Volume 29).

of overall urban–rural planning and the nature of disguised land expropriation, and examines the emergence and the role of the spontaneous innovative activities by farmers, village collectives and the local governments. Moreover, the report demonstrates the significance of the ability to exercise land rights in the process of interaction among major players over their respective interests arising from the issue of so-called "sub-rights" rural houses. And with it, the report puts forward some specific policy recommendations about how to effectively protect farmland and achieve efficient land use as well as a market-based reform of collective construction land.

1. Introduction and Definition

The issues concerning farmers are not only the core in China's revolution but also a key to the country's modernization drive. The *Decision on Several Major Issues on the Promotion of Rural Reform and Development* points out that "the issues concerning agriculture, rural areas and farmers are relevant to the overall development of the Party and state" and "are a priority for the whole Party's work". The Decision also states that "agriculture is a strategic industry for peace, stability and modernization, the rural area's prosperity, stability and the farmer's well-being are the key in the entire process. However, the critical issue facing farmers is land problems."

According to current laws, China implements two types of public land systems, namely the state-owned land system for cities and the collective land system for rural areas. Under the current system, the two land systems constitute two different right systems and result in different prices and rights for the same land. The dual right system shows up either in the conversion process from agricultural land use to non-agricultural land use, or in the different status of property rights relating to rural and urban construction lands. The former one was studied by the Research Group of *Chinese Land Problem* of Beijing Unirule Institute of Economics in 2007, while the latter one is the topic of this report.

From the current situation of rural areas in China, collective land can be divided into agricultural land and construction land according to land use or four types of barren lands, including barren mountains, valleys, slopes and beaches. The agricultural land includes basic farmland and ordinary farmland, in which the former is the land that should be ensured for agriculture and constitutes the main part[1] of the so-called National Red Line of 1.8 billion *mu* (1,200,000,000,000 m²), while the latter is the farmland that can be converted to non-agricultural land. The collective construction land includes rural homestead, township enterprise land and the land for rural public utilities. Four types of barren lands can either be opened up as farmland or be converted as rural construction land. On one hand, with the rapid development of urban construction and the quick expansion of urban size, the demand for construction land becomes more and more acute, and on the other hand, the central government issues more strict protection measures for farmland out of consideration for food security. As a result, the rural collective construction land has become a focal point in the contention among local governments, property developers and farmers. Particularly, due to the size and the distinct characteristics, the rural homestead has become the target of local governments for expanding urban scale and increasing the total construction land after this round of strict land supply regulation. However, perceived from the general trend of China's economic development, the contest starts from villages on the outskirts of urban areas and rapidly expands and spreads outside, which not only represents the necessity in urbanization but also significant progress, but current land systems and policies make the process chaotic and characterized by cutthroat competition, which has not only threatened the maintenance of basic farmland but also violated the farmers' land rights, and thus has hindered and distorted the urbanization process of China to some extent. The report focuses on rural homestead surrounding urban areas, aims to reveal the inner contradictions and fundamental defects of the current collective construction land systems and policies, discusses how these systems and policies cause and provoke the opportunist behaviors of each player and result in current confusion, and further seeks the route and method for system reform and policy adjustment.

Therefore, the report consists of the following parts: In the first section, the problem is introduced and defined; in the second section, the historical transition of the legal system concerning rural collective construction land is analyzed based on rural homestead; in the third section,

---

[1]According to statistics, area of certain basic farmland in 2002 is 1,087,666,666,667 sq. m.

the methods and effects of the government's management and law enforcement on collective construction land are discussed; in the fourth section, the management of homestead by local governments in overall urban–rural reform experiments is discussed; in the fifth section, some creative cases involving the transfer of collective construction land at the local level by farmers, village collectives and local governments are analyzed; in the sixth section, the issues about the "sub-rights" housing is discussed; finally, some reform ideas and policy recommendations are provided.

2. Transition and Analysis of Collective Construction Land System: Based on Rural Homestead

2.1. *Process description on the transition of rural homestead*

With the collective construction land, the land area for rural public utilization is small in proportion, clearly defined by laws, and has clear land use regulations, so it generally has no problem; and even if there is any dispute on such land, it is easy to be settled. The land for township enterprise is also clearly regulated in the *Land Management Law, Property Law* and *Provisions on the Mortgage Registration of Rural Collective Land Use Right*, can be obtained by certain procedures, or can be self-used, transferred and mortgaged. Although, a gray area in the land use for profit-generating operations by township enterprises has appeared in recent years, but the land has become the major source for collective income and rural public goods, therefore local governments generally will not target it. The homestead, however, has a unique nature and presents an outstanding problem, and thus worth special attention. On one hand, it is the major part of rural collective construction land, composed of both housing land and the courtyard in front and at back of the house, and accounts for about one-quarter of total village land in the north but a smaller percentage in the south.[2] On the other hand, the legal systems and policies on this type

---

[2]According to statistics by the Ministry of Land and Resources, the total area of villages in the whole country has increased by 860,000,000 sq. m and reached 166,000,000,000 sq. m from 1996 to 1997, the per capita land area of rural population increased from 193 sq. m

of construction land are quite ambiguous, variable, contradictory and controversial, so this type of land has not only become the cause of disputes between farmers, but also become the main target of local governments and township organizations to gain land revenue from rural areas.

In the following paragraphs, we will review and comment on the transition of the legal system of collective construction land with rural homestead as an example.

Homestead, just as its name implies, is the land used for home construction for farmers, so the discussion on the transition of the homestead system should not only focus on the change of land ownership, but also on the housing system as a whole.

Since the end of the 1940s, the transition of the rural homestead system has basically undergone three stages, with both similarities and differences with the whole rural land system.[3]

The first stage was from 1949 to 1962, which was a stage of private rural homestead and farmers' housing.

At that time, the land reform was carried out based on private land ownership and aimed to achieve the goal of "land to the tiller" and "residents owning their homes". Poor peasants and farm laborers obtained the land and parts of houses simultaneously. According to the *Agrarian Reform Law of the People's Republic of China*, farmers had complete ownership of their lands and houses on the land and had the right to freely trade and rent homesteads, which indicates the market transaction of homestead rights. After the land reform, all local governments issued the

---

to 227 sq. m, and the area of homestead per household can reach 533 sq. m if the area of homestead is assumed to be 80% of total area of villages.

[3]Most of the data cited here is from the Perfect Rural Homestead System and Advance Land Registration and Certification-Research Report on the Policy for Beijing Homestead Registration written by the Research Group of Beijing Rural Research Center in 2008 and the Research on Initial Obtaining System of Use Right of Homestead — Comment Related Rules in Chapter 13 of Property Law written by GAO Shengping and LIU Shouying in 2007. The former divides the transition process of the homestead system into four stages, but there is no essential difference between the second and third stages, while the fourth stage cannot point out the essence of its variation and is improper to generalize and analyze its characteristics. The latter also divides it into four stages, including economic recovery, socialist transformation, socialist construction, reform and opening up, which also cannot reveal the essence of the problem.

land certificate (property ownership certificate), in which the area, location and boundaries of farmland, housing property and foundation were specified. Especially, the *Land and Property Ownership Certificate* of suburban districts of Beijing also specifies that it is a private property that can be freely cultivated, dwelled in, mortgaged, transferred and demised, etc. which shall not be violated by anyone.

In the initial stage of agricultural cooperation and communization, especially after the establishment of advanced agricultural producers' cooperatives, all farmlands, domestic animals and farm tools became collectively owned and belonged to the cooperative, but houses and homesteads were still privately owned. The *Regulations for Advanced Agricultural Producers' Cooperatives* approved at the 3rd meeting of the 1st National People's Congress in June 1956 regulates that the main means of production such as farmland, domestic animal and large farm tool owned by farmers who participate in the cooperative must be transferred to the cooperative, commune members' graveyard and homestead can be private, but homesteads for newly-constructed houses and graveyards for those members with no graveyard will be decided by the cooperative, and commune members have the freedom to withdraw and take land away. The Movement of People's Commune canceled the freedom of withdrawing, but the *Resolution on Several Problems of People's Commune* issued by the Central Committee of the Communist Party of China on December 10, 1958 confirmed that farmers' houses are means of livelihood and will be owned by members forever.

The second stage is from 1962 to 1998, which is a stage of public rural homestead for private use and private farmers' housing.

On the premise that the basic system remains unchanged, the stage can be further divided into the establishment and strengthening stages of rural homestead public ownership.

During the establishment of the system of public rural homestead for private use, the *Draft Amendment on the Practices for People's Commune in Rural Areas* (or the 60 Regulations) was issued in 1962 by the 10th Plenary Session of the 8th Central Committee, which advocated "Never forget class struggles" and opposed the trend of working individually and the system of setting farm output quotas for each household. The Draft provided in Article 21 that "all lands owned by the production team, including members' private plots, private mountains and homesteads, are not allowed to be rented or traded." The draft is the first document to change the private rural homestead to public and to specify corresponding right of use. After that, the ownership and management right of rural homestead are separated from each other. While the ownership right is with the production team, the right to use is owned by the communal member. Obviously, the change of rural homestead's ownership is not achieved by market transaction but by government's mandatory order. The transition of land property right system was confirmed by the *Constitution* in 1975, and meanwhile, the *Sixty Regulations* confirmed again that houses are still privately owned by the commune member and can be rented and traded. Since then, the basic system framework of separated house and land and two systems for one house has been established.

In the stage, the documents that purport to adjust the legal status of rural homestead include the *Questions on Commune Members' Homestead* prepared by the Agriculture and Forestry Office of the State Council forwarded in the *Notice on the Supplementary Regulations of Commune Member's Homestead by the Central Government* issued on March 20, 1963 and the *Opinions on Several Problems about the Implementation of Civil Policy by the Supreme People's Court*. The main contents of the former document are as follows:

(1) All members' **homesteads,** including those with building and those without building, are owned by the production team and cannot be rented and traded, but **will be used by members for a long time.** The production team should protect the use right of members and may not take back or adjust the right at will.

(2) **All attachments on the homestead,** such as house, tree, shed, sty and toilet, **are owned permanently and can be traded or rented by communal members. After the house is traded, the use right of its homestead will be transferred to the new owner, but the ownership is still with the production team.**

(3) If someone without homestead needs to construct a new house, he should apply for the homestead by himself, which will then be discussed by the Member Meeting for approval and be uniformly planned and decided by the production team. During the process, those idle and

scattered lands should be utilized as much as possible and farmlands generally should not be occupied, if farmlands must be occupied, it should be reported to the People's Council of the County for approval according to the regulations of 60 Regulations. **Whether or not newly constructed buildings occupy the farmland, the premium will not be levied.**

(4) The commune members cannot take house construction as an excuse to expand their own yards and homesteads by occupying collective farmlands, and those occupied farmlands should be returned.

During the process, the obtaining procedure and management of rural homestead have been improved and strengthened. In the 1980s, with the advance of rural reform, the development of agricultural production and the settlement of farmers' concerns over food and clothing, a tide of housing construction appeared in rural areas and the problems of unlawful appropriation of farmland and of home building on the contracted land occurred, and for that, the Central Committee of the Communist Party of China and the State Council issued related documents successively[4] to strengthen the management of rural homestead. In 1986, the first *Land Management Law* was issued and put into effect, determining the limit of homestead area and providing for more strict procedure for examination and approval of homestead. The Law stipulated in Article 38 that "When rural residents build their house, they should use original homesteads or idle lands in the village. The use of farmlands should be reviewed by the people's government at the town level and approved by the people's government at or above the county level. The uses of original homestead, idle lands in the village and other lands only need to be approved by the people's government at the town level. Besides, the lands used for home building for rural residents shall not exceed the standards specified by the

---

[4]For example, the Emergency Notice for the Prevention of Rural Housing's Occupation on Farmland (GF (1981) No. 57 document) and the Control Regulations for Village and Town Housing Land issued by the State Council in 1981 and 1982 respectively, the Report on the Practical Solution for Excessive Land Occupation for Housing issued by the Rural Policy Research Office of Secretariat and the Ministry of Urban–Rural Development and endorsed by the General Offices of the Central Committee of CPC and the State Council, etc.

province, autonomous region or municipality. The application for home-stead of anyone who sells or rents his house shall not be approved."

However, the transfer and transaction of rural homesteads were not prohibited in this stage, and non-agricultural populations in urban areas were still allowed to build houses using rural homestead. The *Regulations on the Management of Lands Used for Housing Construction in Villages or Towns* issued in 1982 states that "those retired and resigned workers and soldiers who go and settle in their ancestral villages, those overseas Chinese who come back and settle" and "those non-agricultural house-holds in market town areas can obtain the homestead for home construc-tion after the approval". The *Interim Measures for the Management of Lands Used for Housing Construction in Rural Areas of Beijing* issued in 1985 further expands the scope and regulates that those teaching and administrative staff, medical staff and scientific and technical personnel who work in outer suburbs for a long time and want to settle in rural areas and whose housing needs cannot be met by their units, and those overseas Chinese and the compatriots from Hong Kong, Macao and Taiwan who come back and settle, can apply for the homestead in the area where they live. Even the *Land Management Law* amended in 1988 still stipulated in Article 41 that the use of collective land by non-agricultural residents for home construction shall be approved by the people's government at the county level, shall not exceed the standards specified by the province, autonomous region or municipality, and shall be paid with the compensa-tion fee and resettlement fee according to the national compensation standard for land expropriation. Obviously, the only difference with the previous regulations is that it defines the principle that urban residents who use rural homestead to build houses should pay for it.

On January 3, 1990, the State Council endorsed the *Notice on the Instructions on the Strengthening of Rural Homestead Management by State Land Administration Bureau*, which gave more detailed provisions on the approval procedure of homestead application and established the pilot program for paid use of rural homestead. But in order to alleviate farmers' burden, the General Offices of the Central Committee and the State Council issued the *Notice on the Examination Opinions Involving Farmer's Load* in 1993, which formally repealed the use fees and over-occupation fees in rural homesteads.

The third stage is from 1998 to now, where farmers' private houses and right to use of rural homesteads can be traded but the transfer is limited.

Since the late 1990s and especially the start of this century, the urban construction land has been increasingly in short supply with the rapid development of urban construction and the sharp expansion of urban scale. Under the strict land policy, the battlefront of local governments and real estate developers on construction land has gradually moved to rural areas, and thus the homestead has become the target of real estate developers. Meanwhile, driven by the high housing price, many urban residents came to villages to purchase or build houses. Numerous resident communities with different scales suddenly appeared on the homesteads of villages around the city. They are the so-called "sub-rights houses." In response, the government has issued a series of policies and regulations to curb the trend. On August 29, 1998, the revised *Land Management Law* revoked the provisions in Article 41 as mentioned above. In May 1999, the General Office of the State Council issued the *Notice on the Strengthening of Management of Land Transaction and Prohibition of Speculation on Land Prices* (*Guo Ban Fa* [1999] No. 39), which announced that "farmers' houses shall not be sold to urban residents, urban residents shall not be approved to occupy farmers' collective lands for housing construction, and related departments shall not issue land certificates and property ownership certificates for the houses illegally built or purchased. In October 2004, the State Council issued the *Resolution on the Deepening of Reform and the Strengthening of Land Management*, which specified that urban residents are prohibited from purchasing rural homesteads. In November 2004, the Ministry of Land and Resources issued the *Opinions on the Strengthening of Rural Homestead Management*, which presented Two Prohibitions, namely the prohibition for urban residents to purchase rural homesteads and the prohibition for related departments to issue land use certificates for those houses in rural areas purchased or illegally built by urban residents. In December 2007, the General Office of the State Council issued the *Notice on the Strict Implementation of Relevant Rural Collective Construction Land Laws and Policies*, which reiterated that rural residential lands can only be distributed to villagers of the village concerned and that urban residents shall not come to villages to purchase homesteads, farmers' houses or sub-right houses. In particular, the verdict in Songzhuang's villager Ma Haitao versus painter Li Yulan, accepted by the Beijing Tongzhou Court and the Second Intermediate People's Court of Beijing, made the proprietary rights of farmers' houses more uncertain. After issuing *the Resolution on Major Problems about the Advance of Rural Reform by the Central Committee of the Communist Party* that states that some measures shall be taken to improve the rural homestead system, tighten management on homestead and ensure the real rights of farmers in rural homestead according to law, the Ministry of Land and Resources issued related documents, which states that it is strictly prohibited to build commodity houses on the homestead.[5]

2.2. Analysis on the rural homestead system and its advantages and disadvantages

Under the condition of separated urban and rural areas, China implements the homestead system of equal distribution by person and household, which can satisfy the natural demand of farmers to build houses for their livelihood, reflecting the nature or characteristics of equality at a low level and even playing an active role in stabilizing rural communities and protecting farmers' rights. However, since the reform and opening-up, this rural homestead system has obviously lagged behind and become retrogressive, as it not only fails to meet the needs for urban and rural construction and farmers' economic needs, but also provides loopholes keenly exploited by those seeking personal gains. In this way the system is unfavorable for protecting farmers' rights, their interests and cultivated lands, hinders the rural industrialization and the development of urbanization, and even directly threatens the stability of society.

The examination and evaluation of the nature of and changes in the rural homestead system cannot be too generalized and must be set in some context with a proper reference. Otherwise, we cannot grasp its essence and characteristics, or we may even have some unnecessary bias and misunderstandings. According to the actual situation in China, there are two

---

[5] See the *Land and Resources News* on October 29, 2008.

proper reference systems: urban residential land and rural agricultural land, which are closely related to the homestead system and have both similarities and differences to it. Therefore, the rural homestead issue will be discussed by the comparison with urban commodity housing land and agricultural land in the following paragraphs.

Some say China's rural homestead system is basically characterized by separated houses and homesteads, or two systems for one house.[6] Obviously, the summarization above is not accurate enough. In fact, regardless of where you are, urban or rural areas, China's real estates are characterized by publicly owned residential land plus privately owned houses. On the surface, the only difference is that the urban residential land is state-owned, while the rural homestead is collectively owned. However, the two types of land form two principally different systems with different functions, resulting in different rights and interests. Thus, it is improper to summarize the characteristics of rural homestead in that simple manner.

Firstly, there are different ways to obtain land. The urban housing construction land is obtained by transaction, and the primary market of construction land is monopolized by the government. The government will sell the use right of construction land for commodity housing to real estate developers by way of bidding, auction and listing. After obtaining the use right of state-owned land, developers can build commodity houses on the land. After that, they can sell the houses along with transfer of the use rights to recover costs for purchasing the use rights of land. Accordingly, a homebuyer can obtain a 70-year use right after purchasing the house. However, the rural homestead is collectively distributed or transferred to villagers for free. Although the experiment on the paid homestead distribution was once carried out in a short period, and the homestead used to be provided for urban residents on payment, both of these behaviors were formally prohibited by the government later. Thus, it can be seen that the major difference in obtaining housing land between rural and urban areas is about the difference between transaction and

---

[6] See the Perfect Rural Homestead System and Advance Land Registration and Certification-Research Report on the Policy for Beijing Homestead Registration written by the Research Group of Beijing Rural Research Center in 2008.

allocation, with compensation and without compensation. The difference causes two problems: First, the distribution for free homesteads encourages farmers' unlimited demand and can neither block the excessive occupation of homesteads nor retrieve the extra land taken by farmers on their spree and useless homesteads. Second, as size of urban construction land decreases, the supply dries up and land price increases, all governments, developers and urban citizens will focus on and battle for rural homesteads. During the process, some governments achieve it by exchanging newly built houses for land in the name of overall planning of urban and rural areas, the developers obtain the development rights of homestead by delivering benefits to village chiefs or township cadres, while urban citizens purchase the homestead through black market trade. Consequently, a trading network composed of seller, purchaser, intermediaries and protection parties is formed, and all of them play a fancy Tom & Jerry Kids Show.[7]

Second, in terms of commercialization, they are different in degrees. Urban houses have been commercialized. With complete commercial attributes and functions, they can be rented, sold and mortgaged, accordingly the use rights of their housing land will be transferred with the houses without any limitation and obstruction in terms of legal system and economic policy. These houses can be sold to both urban citizens and farmers, or to both Chinese and foreigners, and those purchasers will obtain the use rights of housing land. However, rural houses have not been commercialized, that is, although these houses are private property, they have no commercial attributes and functions under current policies and regulations. In other words, rural homesteads cannot be rented, sold or transferred, and it is prohibited to construct commodity houses on the rural homestead. Although these houses with the use rights of homesteads scan be traded and transferred between rural residents, they cannot be sold to urban citizens. Likewise, urban citizens cannot purchase rural houses and certainly cannot purchase or occupy rural homestead for home construction. Thus, rural houses are not commodities. They cannot be completely traded or mortgaged and are mainly for self-use, and so they have the characteristics of self-sufficiency in a natural economy. As in the

---

[7] See the *Southern Weekend* on November 13, 2008.

situation before the commercialization of urban houses, all above have blocked the process of rural market-based development and have caused the stagnation and backward situation of rural economy and social development.

Thirdly, they are different in quantities traded. Because urban commodity houses can be freely traded, one can purchase two or more commodity houses despite the fact that the central government has issued specific policies and regulations in an effort to restrict purchasing second commodity housing, and many people even specialize in trading and leasing houses, living off home rents. Some incidents, such as the existence of the Wenzhou house-purchasing team, do occur. Conversely, rural residents can only obtain one homestead under the policy of one homestead for one household. The farmer only can obtain one homestead with limited area and has no right to obtain a second one if the house on the homestead is rented out or sold. The government may think that the farmland protection problem can be solved by limiting farmers' rights on homestead with the policy of one homestead for one household, but in fact, some phenomena such as several houses owned by one household, excessive homestead and farmland occupation are overwhelming.

Fourthly, there is a difference where ownership is separated from decision-making. For urban residential land, the owner and decision maker are the same, the government is not only the owner of state-owned land but also the provider and approver of commodity housing land. However, the owner and decision-maker of rural homesteads are different, that is to say, according to current systems and procedures regulated by policies, the village collective as the homestead owner does not have the decision making rights to decide whether a farmer can obtain the homestead or not, but these rights are owned by local governments at all levels and related officials. As regulated by the *Land Management Law*, the quantity standards of homesteads are formulated by the governments of provinces, cities and autonomous regions. The obtaining of homesteads shall be reviewed by the people's government at the township level and approved by the people's government at the county level, and for those occupying farmland, the approval procedure for farmland conversion shall be required. Consequently, it is not the owner but the official that makes decisions, so the property right of the owner of land property right is directly violated. Undoubtedly, the *Land Management Law* is certainly a piece of legislation that encourages infringement of farmers' interests, but under the current system, the property arrangement is still a policy variable that can be changed anytime by the government. Since the reform, we have not established the basic system for the implementation and protection of property rights.

Finally, there is a difference between homestead and farmland. After the reform and opening-up, the management of farmland changed from a collective ownership and collective management system to household contract responsibility system; accordingly farmers have obtained the use right of farmland. Moreover, as the *Land Contract Law* and *Property Law* are issued and implemented, the use right of farmland has become closer to property rights and can be transferred without legal limitation. Especially, the Supreme Judicial Court issued the *Instructions on Applicable Legal Problems about the Trial of Rural Land Contract Dispute* in 2005, which makes the contracting and transfer of farmland become a right that can be applied for and carried out, which is then confirmed by the *Decision on Several Major Problems on the Promotion of Rural Reform and Development by the Central Committee of the Communist Party of China*. However, the policies for rural homestead and housing have changed in opposite directions. With the development of China's society and economy, the urbanization is accelerated, the urban size expands, and the urban construction land increases sharply, but simultaneously, numerous farmers leave their hometown and come to the city to make a living, which results in the large demand for rural housing land in the suburban areas. Besides that the rapid increase of urban housing price and the relatively favorable rural living environment also make some urban citizens purchase houses in rural areas. However, the current homestead system not only fails to adapt to the situation and make corresponding changes, but becomes even more backward than that in the command era of the planned economy. Driven by practical interests, all parties participate in the battle for rural homestead due to the absence of related legal systems. Urban governments want to obtain them to meet the demand of land for urban expansion, the developers to reduce the cost, expand the development scale of commodity houses and obtain high profits, and urban citizens obtain the houses at low prices and avoid the urban noise.

Meanwhile, considering the rapid increase of land prices and the worry of losing property, farmers are also unwilling to lose the land. Similarly, in order to protect basic farmland and ensure food security, the central government also does not want to see the chaotic situation of rural homestead battles, but it has been unable to take any specific measures to solve the problem fundamentally except blindly strengthening the government's regulation. The regulation will undoubtedly prevent the central government from achieving its policy objects, and even makes the existing problems more serious: The government not only has limited the decision making right of farmers and collectives on homesteads and violated the property rights of farmers on private houses, but also has encouraged behaviors of rent-seeking, collusion and opportunism, resulting in a vicious circle of "regulation begets regulation."

3. Methods and Effects of the Government's Management and Law Enforcement on Collective Construction Land

The government has established a series of laws, rules and regulations for managing rural collective construction land, especially for homesteads. On top of that, it has greatly enhanced its corresponding law enforcement mechanism. These actions can be divided into two types, the first one is the administrative regulations, which is organized and implemented by the departments of land and resources. For this reason, the Ministry of Land and Resources sets the Land Supervision Department and local governments set up the Land Supervision Office. Since the implementation of the *Land Management Law*, over one million cases of illegal land use have happened in the whole country from 1999 to 2004, involving over 5 million *mu* (3,333,333,333 m^2) of land, which is nearly 1 million *mu* (666,666,667 m^2) more than the total incremental construction land of 4.02 million *mu* (2,680,000,000) in 2004. Even in recent years, the behavior of illegal land use have shown a trend of continuous increase. From September 1, 2007, the Ministry of Land and Resources carried out a 100-day law enforcement inspection for some illegal land use activities, e.g., the rural collective farmland not requisitioned but rented for non-agricultural construction and the construction land size being enlarged without authorization; the over-all plan for land utilization is violated, the sanctioned four boundaries of the development zone are broken without authorization, and the land is occupied for industrial development in all kinds of names; construction is started without authorization and before legally obtaining the approval. During the inspection, relevant departments supervised and inspected 12 key areas and 37 typical cases, and dealt with three types of 31,000 illegal cases, involving 3.36 million *mu* (2,240,000,000 m²) of land, and by December 15, relevant departments had dealt with 26,700 cases, fined RMB 1.92 billion Yuan, confiscated 14.68 million m² and dismantled 7.72 million m² of surface buildings (structures).[8] The second type is through court hearing. Generally there are numerous legal precedents on the homestead dispute between farmers. Disputes over homestead and hous-ing between farmer and non-farmer are few, but they have drawn great interests.

3.1. *Forcibly removing illegal cottages in Qinglongtou, Beijing*

Qinglongtou Village, located in Qinglongtou Town, Fangshan District, Beijing, has 66 households that live sparsely in the northern slope of the village, is economically backward. The village has no cement road, and the villagers mainly depend on the planting industry with an annual per capita income of less than RMB 5,000 Yuan. It is a poor village in the suburbs of Beijing, and its best resource is the beautiful Qinglong Lake nearby.

In 2005, the village was listed as one of 150 experimental villages for new countryside construction by the government of Fangshan District. The village committee signed a contract with Beijing Jindiya Real Estate Development Company to conduct village reconstruction. According to the agreement, Qinglongtou Village will transfer 344 *mu* (229,333 m²) of land including 126 *mu* (84,000 m²) of farmland to the company for real estate development. Among these lands, 40 *mu* (26,667 m²) will be used for village reconstruction, of which 8,000 m²

---

[8] See the website of the Ministry of Land and Resources.

residential cottages and 8,000 m^2 commercial cottages will be constructed respectively for villagers, while 304 *mu* (202,667 m^2) of land will be used for real estate development to build 60,000 m^2 of commodity cottages. According to the planning of new countryside construction, farmers' cottages can be rented to tourists, so that the village will quit the traditional agriculture and pursue a path toward a tourist economy and ecological agriculture.

On October 28, 2005, the village committee published the planning scheme, according to which the developer will obtain RMB 15 million Yuan in profit through cooperative land development, while each villager will obtain 40 m^2 in the form of returned houses and 40 m^2 commercial house respectively, and the price of returned house is RMB 1,200 Yuan/m^2. Besides that, old houses can be mortgaged to get new houses. Meanwhile, local villagers reported that villagers can purchase fewer returned houses and are able to refuse any commercial house as required, all of which will be purchased by the village collective instead at a price of RMB 2,000 Yuan/m^2. For example, according to the agreement for compensation and resettlement signed by villager WEI Fengsheng and the village committee, WEI Fengsheng can purchase a cottage with an area of 160 m^2, and the payment of the cottage can be offset by his old house value and a RMB 50,000 Yuan moving fee. Besides that the commercial house with an area of 200 m^2 can be purchased at a price of RMB 400,000 Yuan. That is to say, after the whole family of WEI Fengsheng moves into the cottage, he can still obtain a net income of RMB 350,000 Yuan. Meanwhile, the village collective promises that those who move early will obtain a subsidy of RMB 3,000 Yuan, which can offset the property management fees.

According to the scheme, about 180 villagers will obtain RMB 800,000 Yuan of medical insurance and pensions, as well as some ecological agricultural greenhouses. The developer also promised to construct a road and some public facilities such as medical room, real estate management center and the village committee house for the village. Besides, the village collective will also hold a 10% stake in the commercial cottage project, and share 2% commission from the total sales revenue of commodity houses, which will be used for the maintenance of infrastructure in the new village.

In February 2006, the scheme of village reconstruction was approved by all villagers by vote. According to the plan, the cottage project will fully start in March and will be completed within 7 months, and villagers can dwell in the cottages in October. Consequently, villagers could not only live in the western-style building that they dared not even imagine in the past, but also can embark on the road to prosperity.

Soon after the construction was started, the developer began to sell the so-called Qianhutingyuan cottages at a price of RMB 3,500 Yuan/m². All purchasers signed a purchasing contract with the committee of Qinglongtou Village, in which it states clearly that the property is a two-storied house constructed by the village collective, with a service life of 70 years.

In May 2006, the Beijing Municipal Commission of Urban Planning found by remote sensing satellite that large-scale engineering construction was being carried out in Qinglongtou Village, Qinglonghu Town, Fangshan District, which was not reported to the planning department for review. The law enforcement officials from the Fangshan Branch of the Beijing Municipal Commission of Urban Planning immediately came to the village for field investigation and confirmed that the construction of cottages in Qinglongtou Village was illegal. On May 26, 2006, the Fangshan Branch issued the *Suspension Notice for Illegal Construction* to the construction unit and ordered to immediately stop their construction and accept relevant investigation. However, the construction unit did not stop but accelerated the construction, and not until September was the cottage project formally stopped. In April 2007, the law enforcement officials demolished 85 cottages aside the Qinglonghu Lake. Finally, the cottage dream of villagers of Qinglongtou Village was completely shattered.

In September 2007, the Ministry of Land and Resources issued a bulletin, which pointed out that in March 2006, in the name of new countryside construction, the committee of Qinglongtou Village in Qinglonghu Town of Fangshan District did not go through any approval procedure for project approval, planning and construction land, illegally occupied 326.12 *mu* (217,413 m²) of collective land (including 127.39 *mu* (84,927 m²) of farmland) to construct farmer housing, cottages, roads and other facilities, and altogether constructed 144 buildings, including 138 cottages. In April 2007, the Beijing Municipal Bureau of Land and Resources and related planning departments removed 85 cottages that were non-compliant with the overall planning for land utilization and confiscated the remaining cottages and buildings. The discipline inspection and supervision departments of Beijing gave a warning sanction to WANG Zhonghai, the Deputy Head of Fangshan District in charge of agriculture, a sanction of major demerit recording to YANG Dongsheng, the Director of Labor and Social Security Office of Fangshan District and former Secretary of the Qinglonghu Town Party Committee, a serious warning within the party to WU Baoxiang, the Party Secretary and original Chief of Qinglonghu Town, and a sanction of removal from the post to LIU Songhua, the Standing Deputy Chief of Qinglonghu Town.

In the case of cottage construction by illegal occupation in Qinglongtou Village, the government's law enforcement behaviors in a sense have maintained the dignity of the current *Land Management Law*, but are contrary to justice. For villagers, land is the only property for them and it's legally owned by all villagers, but villagers are still in poverty under the traditional way of land use for agriculture. Meanwhile, Qinglongtou Village is located in the well-known scenic spot of Beijing, therefore the land there has large potential value, which will only be visible through market transaction and inflow of capital from the city, and obviously villages have realized that the original land use must be changed to completely shake off poverty. According to relevant reports, Qinglongtou Village is to respond to the call of the CPC central committee to build a new socialist countryside, and all villagers agree to develop real estate using the lands owned by the village collective and approve the countryside reconstruction scheme by vote. In villagers' view, they are the main players in the new countryside construction and have the right to live the life that they want by using their only land resource and in the spirit of "democratic consultation and acting according to one's abilities." However, the real estate development in Qinglongtou Village also hits the limits of the current land management system, and obviously it not only occupies farmland but also applied for no approval. For this reason, the management departments of land and resources determined it an act of illegal land occupation and imposed punishment for it, which was unexpected and unacceptable for the villagers.

On the surface, the government's strict punishment for the behavior of cottage construction by illegal land occupation in Qinglongtou Village has maintained the seriousness of the current land system, but actually has revealed the inner contradiction and serious conflicts of the current land system, which will undoubtedly cause an internecine situation. It can be seen from the case that, firstly, due to the contradiction and conflict in the current law, the government's law enforcement in a sense has stopped the illegal land occupation in Qinglongtou Village, but also has canceled the rights of farmers to participate in the non-agricultural operation and gain benefits using their own lands, which certainly implies certain limitation and failure of the policy for a new socialist countryside. Secondarily, the road to prosperity for villagers is ruthlessly blocked, and since it will be costly to reclaim those farmlands under housing construction, the living conditions of the villagers are worse than before. Thirdly, the investment loss of the developer is self-inflicted, which will constitute part of the social cost in a society with effective law enforcement mechanisms. Nonetheless, it could become the actual loss if placed under an ineffective law enforcement environment.

However, why does illegal land use remain unabated in spite of the strong law enforcement of the Ministry of Land and Resources, and why cannot a situation of self-regulation be formed? The first reason is the irrationality of the law and the lack of the basis for self-regulation. The second is that the land occupation can obtain high benefits and so some people still commit the crime despite severe crackdown on it and take risks of losing their post and being imprisoned. And the third reason is that due to local protectionism, these illegal behaviors are unlikely to be discovered and will only receive a lighter punishment. Consequently, under the current system, illegal land occupation is here to stay, and a situation of no punishment for the majority has been formed. Accordingly, the government law enforcement has become an accidental event and has bad effects. The demolition of cottages in Qinglongtou Village only means that the village had bad luck.

3.2. *Rise of painters' village and property disputes in Songzhuang, Beijing*

Songzhuang Village, located in Tongzhou District of Beijing, is one of cultural pioneer parks of Beijing. It attracts over 240 domestic and overseas painters in various genres including some famous painters such as FANG Lijun, which is thus called Painters' Village.

In 1993, a painting teacher came to Songzhuang Village, purchased his student's house and became the first villager from outside. Over the next year, 6 painters came, and in 1996, 40 painters came from the Old Summer Palace and purchased 28 houses. Since then, numerous painters came to purchase or rent villagers' houses for dwelling and painting, and Songzhuang Village soon became a veritable Painters' Village.

With the arrival of numerous painters, an industry involving paint brushes and materials, painting mounting, paint auctions and transactions, art exhibitions, special painting training and other business services were promoted, and many local villagers gave up farming, entered into the tertiary industry and soon became rich. In 2005, the cultural center of Songzhuang was constructed and the 1st cultural festival of Songzhuang was held, with a total number of visitors of 100,000 and an annual trading volume of above RMB 0.3 billion Yuan. Many contemporary world-famous artists came here and many successful artists came from here.

On July 1, 2002, the painter Li Yulan signed a purchasing contract with the villager Ma Haitao to purchase eight houses and corresponding courtyards in Xindian Village of Songzhuang Town at a total price of RMB 45,000 Yuan. The purchasing contract was acknowledged by the village officer, and at that time, the household of Ma Haitao had moved to the urban area for a long time.

In 2006, the Beijing government planned to construct 10 cultural and artistic pioneer parks, including Songzhuang Park. Thus, the village decided to issue a new plan for the pioneer park and roads, and some farmer's courtyards will be removed, in which the house purchased by Li Yulan from Ma Haitao was included. Owing to the immigration of a number of painters and the establishment of Pioneer Park, the local housing price increased greatly, and thus the owner will obtain vast relocation compensation. Hence, in December 2006, Ma Haitao brought the case to the court and asked the court to declare the purchasing contract between them void and to ask Li Yulan to return his house. Besides, there were 13 similar cases at that time.

In 2004, the Beijing High People's Court issued the *Notice on the Printing and Issuing of the Minutes of the Seminar on the Principles of Affirmation and Management of the Validity of Rural Private House Transaction Contract in Dispute* according to the *Land Management Law* and relevant regulations of the State Council and the Ministry of Land and Resources, which became the basis for similar cases. The notice stipulated that the rural private house sales contract shall be in principle treated as invalid whereas being valid only as exception. Meanwhile, the interests of contracting parties shall be comprehensively balanced, and the buyer shall obtain the compensation according to the benefit from the compensation for demolition and the difference between original price and current worth. Besides, if the buyer has renovated and expanded the house, the buyer shall obtain the compensation on the added value.

The case was heard by Tongzhou District People's Court in accordance with the *Notice* above, and the plaintiff's claims were supported. In July 2007, the court decision invalidated the sale and purchase agreement, asking Li Yulan to return the house and requiring Ma Haitao to pay a compensation of RMB 93,808 Yuan to Li Yulan.

The court decision has aroused wide repercussions among painters in Painter Village and in the whole society, and many people criticized the behavior of Ma Haitao and the court decision to support Li Yulan. In December 2007, the Second Intermediate People's Court of Beijing issued the second instance decision, upholding the original decision and affirming that Ma Haitao is the main party liable for the invalidation of the contract and shall pay compensation for the losses of Li Yulan. On January 3, 2008, Li Yulan raised a counterclaim to the Songzhuang Village Tribunal of Tongzhou District Court, claiming an economic compensation of RMB 480,000 Yuan from Ma Haitao.

The case was heard and concluded by Tongzhou District Court. The court ruled that the economic losses of the buyer Li Yulan should be calculated in accordance with the profit obtained by the seller from land appreciation or demolition compensation, as well as the difference between the present worth and the original price of the house. After the mediation failed, the court judged that the property owner Ma Haitao should pay the total economic losses of RMB 185,290 Yuan to the buyer Li Yulan, accounting for 70% of the total estimated value of RMB 260,000 Yuan.

It was reported that after the court decision, Ma Haitao did not abide by the ruling, and he neither paid the compensation nor asked for the house.

The hearing and ruling of the case have not only revealed the obvious contradiction and conflict in current laws, but also have indicated the dilemma of the current judicial system.

Firstly, there is a conflict between the articles of the *Land Management Law* and the principles of the constitution. Article 63 of the *Land Management Law* provides that the use rights of the farmer's collective land shall not be sold, transferred or rented for non-agricultural construction. But this is not in accordance with the principles of the Constitution. Paragraph 4 of Article 14 in China's Constitution clearly specifies that the use right of land can be transferred according to law. Although it must be transferred according to law as required in the article, according to the system and interpretation method of legal hermeneutics and judged from the context, the law here should not be the limitation on the entity but be the law used for standardizing and adjusting the procedures for the transfer. The article is divided into four paragraphs from the article system. The first, second, third and fourth paragraphs govern the state land, collective land, land expropriation and land transaction respectively. Obviously, the lawmaker first makes a clear distinction between state land and collective land and makes separate provisions on them. Then he or she proposes the issue of land use rights that will not be distinguished covering state land and collective land, all of which are original meanings of the articles in the constitution. Consequently, the regulations of the *Land Management Law* deviate from the purpose of legislation of the constitution, and based on the basic principle of a higher rank law preceding a lower rank law and the regulations in Article 78 of the *Legislative Law*, the use right of farmers' collective land should be considered to be transferable.

Besides, there is also a conflict between the *Land Management Law* and the *Property Law*. The *Property Law* stipulates that if one building, structure and ancillary facilities are transferred, interchanged, financed or donated, the use right of construction land within the range shall be dealt simultaneously. Thus, according to the *Property Law*, the land is combined with the house, and the buyer should obtain corresponding land interests after burying the house, while the *Land Management Law* does not allow the collective land to be traded in the market. Certainly, this provision of the *Property Law* also contradicts Article 153. Accordingly, the implementation of the law is also in a dilemma.

Secondly, the hearing and ruling of the two instance trials are directly based on a meeting notice retransmitted by the Beijing High Court, which is in itself ridiculous. Conversely, the sale and purchase agreement of private housing should become the basis for the court decision, in which the party breaking the contract should lose the case according to the basic rule of law but not the discussion conclusions in a meeting that does not comply with the basic rule of law. We can even think that the court decision is to encourage the actor to violate the principle of good faith and to break the promise inconsiderately, so that it can only encourage the people to consider the law as a joke.

Thirdly, even on second thought, the current system is implemented by the principle of separated house and land, considering that the plaintiff has permanently left the village and come to the city and obviously he aims to obtain ill-gotten wealth, it is more reasonable to rule that the contract breaching party should pay the compensation to the buyer, the village collective can withdraw the homestead without compensation, and the seller should demolish the original house. Such ruling may better comply with the implementation of current laws and regulations.

Fourthly, the ruling of the case has also indicated the awkwardness and dilemma of the government to deal with such problems. The dispute of the case essentially focuses on who should obtain the incremental benefit from the second transaction of land. Obviously, the reason why the land in Songzhuang Village obtains large value appreciation is that the aggregation of painters makes Songzhuang Village become a world-famous brand and increases the land value greatly. In fact, villagers also saw this, e.g., JING Baisong, the secretary of the party committee of Xindian Village of Songzhuang Town, admitted that if artists did not come to Songzhuang Village and make the house price rise, the old house of Ma Haitao only can value RMB 20,000 Yuan. However, the decision of Tongzhou District Court based on current land management system holds that the original sale and purchase contract is invalid, accordingly both the use right and incremental benefit of homestead will still be owned by Ma Haitao. Obviously, in the ruling for the counterclaim by Li Yulan, the judge ruled that the incremental benefit of homestead should be owned by Li Yulan from fairness and common sense. However, it is contradictory that the original price of the house and the value of apposition were estimated to be over RMB 90,000 Yuan in the first instance judgment, but in the final judgment, the compensation for the economic losses of Li Yulan from Ma Haitao nearly doubled, and the painter Li Yulan will obtain most of incremental benefit of land, which leads to a question: Now that the legal owner of the use right of homestead is Ma Haitao, why does the court rule most of the incremental benefit of the homestead to Li Yulan?

Fifthly, if the case is ruled as the court of first instance in strict accordance with the current legal system, the losing party includes not only the painter Li Yulan but also all painters in Songzhuang, and once painters leave, the Painter Village will no longer exist. The cultural and artistic pioneer park will vanish into thin air, and villagers will suffer great losses, which are unfavorable outcomes for most parties. Fortunately, the court of second instance has supported the appeal of painters to some extent and the village has taken some new measures to retain painters, which allow the Painter Village to survive and further develop.

4. Worrying Signs in the Comprehensive Reform Experiment of Overall Planning for Urban and Rural Construction Lands: Is the Homestead Exchange for House a Breakthrough?

In the face of the increasingly serious situation of exhausted supply in urban construction land, lagging reform for rural construction land policy, worsening problem of the "sub-right" houses and even farmland occupation, as well as the social contradictions and conflicts aroused from contention over rural land, many local governments attempt to seek a breakthrough in the new round of reform. Thus, the contention has moved to those rural stock land for construction use with large area, the overall planning of urban and rural construction lands has become a breakthrough in this comprehensive reform for local governments, and some measures such as "homestead exchange for urban houses" and "two for one" scheme where farmers give up their houses and homestead for the guarantee of urban social security, have been eagerly taken in the implementation of overall planning.

4.1. *Blocking of government-led overall planning of urban and rural areas in Jiulongpo District, Chongqing City*

Jiulongpo District is located in the west of Chongqing, with an area of 432 sq. kms and a total permanent resident population of over 930,000 in 2005, including 660,000 urban populations and 270,000 rural migrants. As the pilot trial in the comprehensive reform of overall development of urban and rural areas in Chongqing, the overall plan was published and carried out on May 17, 2007. The planning area by 2011 is expected to reach 124 sq. kms, including 60 sq. kms of built up areas, which is planned to be carried out in three steps: The implementation scheme would be compiled within 3 months, the pilot projects would be carried out in key areas and fields within about one year, and the projects would be rolled out within 2 to 3 years. Among them, the 12 innovation bases for medium-sized and small enterprises and processing bases for agricultural and sideline products were expected to be constructed first. By the end of 2007, a total of 20,000 *mu* (13,333,333 m²) of land had been transferred in the whole district, of which 20% to 30% had not changed in ownership status and usage, while the other 60% to 70% had done so. At the beginning, the district planned to uniformly carry out planning, demolition and resettlement, investment invitation as well as construction and management in accordance with the procedure of urban construction regulations. But in fact, some villages and towns took some actions in advance, such as illegal construction, construction without approval and non-standard construction. In April 2007, an accident leading to a building worker's death caused by plant collapse in Hailong Village of Baishiyi Town occurred, and for this reason, the government began to conduct clean-up and rectification of the buildings (half standard ones and half unwillingly approved ones), forcibly removing over 100,000 m² of illegal buildings, while enterprises and farmers were resentful.

The reversal of the reform experiment was sparked off by the construction of Boshi Park in Jinfeng Town, with a planning area of 1,000 *mu* (666,667 m²). At the time the first phase of 200 *mu* (133,333 m²) was partly completed. According to the plan, 140 greenhouses would be constructed, and every two of them would be equipped with one management house covering 200 m² at a price of RMB 500,000 Yuan. These houses were nominally rented out, and yet they were actually sold. Soon after, the incident was reported to Premier Wen Jiabao, and on his instruction, the Ministry of Construction carried out a program of 100-day major law enforcement inspection, so the construction of 12 bases was stopped. The current situation is that two bases have not been constructed yet and will not be constructed for the time being; the Jiulong Textile Industrial Park in Taojia Town is quite successful and will be kept for continuous experiment; the Huachen base is located within the urban planning area and therefore also remains. The Bashiyi and Hangu bases have been constructed to some extent, but the other six bases have been shelved. Some of them have completed infrastructure construction, some of them are unlikely to be reclaimed, but as there are no profitable industries in suburban areas and they are located in hilly areas, farmers still have the urge to develop them. Faced with this, the government intends to resume the project after adjustment. Generally, we focus on two questions, one is whether the governments of Chongqing and Jiulong District actually realize their mistakes and have wised up from experience and lessons and seek some new ways in re-experiment, and the other is whether the central government can afford the second failure.

In the experiment of overall development of urban and rural areas in Jiulongpo, the Jiulong Textile Industrial Park is the only successful one, so we conducted further investigation.

Jiulong Textile Industrial Park, located in Taojia Town, with a planning land area of over 600 *mu* (400,000 m²), including 70 *mu* (46,667 m²) of homestead, was planned and designed from October 2006. The village collective signed a land lease with Chongqing Bicoo Science and Technology (Group) Co., Ltd., according to which the company will be responsible for construction and inviting investment. By now, the company has invested over RMB 200 million Yuan, constructed 55,200 m² of industrial factory buildings, attracted over 30 enterprises to achieve an annual production value of RMB 100 million Yuan and a total tax of RMB 3 million Yuan, and constructed 44,200 m² of villager's houses and 48,000 m² of worker's apartments. Besides all that, 50,000 m² of industrial factory buildings are being constructed. On November 22, 2008, some villagers began to move into the new houses, some workers' apartments were rented out, and the textile industrial park has taken initial shape.

One of the six reform targets of overall development of urban and rural areas in Jiulongpo is to seek a way of establishing a transfer system for trading the contractual rights over rural collective construction land and collective land, improve the support system and promote the scale and efficient management of rural land. According to the land transaction contract between Taojia Village and Bicoo, the buildings and attachments in the original land will be compensated by the enterprise according to the demolition resettlement standard in Chongqing, the villagers can purchase the residential building at a price of RMB 380 Yuan/m^2, and each household can generally purchase two houses with a per capita area of 55 m^2. Besides, the villagers can also purchase the apartment at a price of RMB 600 Yuan/m^2 for self-use or renting. The collective lands will also be rented by the enterprise at an annual rent of 500 kg rice per *mu* (667 m^2), which will be adjusted every three years, and the price of rice is counted at RMB 0.9 Yuan and RMB 1 Yuan in 2007 and 2008 respectively. Besides, the enterprise will pay a coordination fee of RMB 200 Yuan per *mu* (667 m^2) to the village collective every year.

According to the overall reform scheme in Jiulongpo, there are two objectives for deepening the reform and innovating the system, the first is to seek a road to break household registration barriers in the process of converting villagers' status from farmer to citizen, to gradually establish a uniform household registration system for both urban and rural areas and to take the lead in the reform experiment of the conversion from farmer to citizen in the whole city, and the second is to seek a road to establish and improve a multilevel social security system covering urban and rural areas, involving basic cost of living allowances, old-age security and medical security. The work has made some breakthroughs and progress. In total, there have been over 700 insured villagers for old-age security, the individuals and the collective will pay 8% of the current security standard RMB 300 Yuan respectively and will get a pension of RMB 156 Yuan every month after paying RMB 4,320 Yuan for 15 years. Accordingly, the integration in the social security system has been completed. Meanwhile, the rural cooperative medical service was comprehensively carried out, according to which there are two levels, namely a RMB 100 Yuan level and a RMB 200 Yuan level, including a subsidy of RMB 80 Yuan per person per year from the government. Those who pay

RMB 20 Yuan per year can get a reimbursement of RMB 30,000 Yuan to the maximum, while those who pay RMB 120 Yuan per year can get a reimbursement up to RMB 100,000 Yuan. The catalogue of reimbursable medicine is the same with the urban area.

There are some similarities and differences between the experiment in Taojia Town and that in Zhenggezhuang Village. Firstly, both of them are developed by the cooperation between the villages and the enterprises without the direct participation of governments, but the enterprises in Taojia Town are outsiders, while the enterprises in Zhenggezhuang Village are village-owned enterprises and have fewer conflicts than that in Taojia Town. Secondly, in the development of both places, the land is capitalized, actually sold and transferred, but the status of property and owners are not changed, the enterprise obtains the use right, while the villager collectives and villagers maintain the ownership and the long-term usufruct. Thirdly, due to the barriers against the experiment of overall development of urban and rural areas, the partnership in Taojia Town has also encountered many troubles, and at worst, the relatively successful reform may fall apart.

4.2.　The comprehensive supplementary reform in Huaming demonstration town in Tianjin led and financed by governments

Huaming Town is located in Dongli District of Tianjin, north of Jinghan Road and Tianjin Airport Logistics Processing Zone, south of Beihuan Railway and Beijing–Tianjin–Tangshan Expressway, west of Huamingxin Community and Donglihu Tourist Resort, and east of Huaming Economic Function District. It is 10 km from the downtown, 3 km from Tianjin International Airport, 30 km from Tianjin Port and 120 km to the 4th Ring Road of Beijing. The town has 14,000 households in 12 villages, including over 900 non-agricultural households, and a population of 40,000, including a labor force of 18,000. It covers more than 40,000 *mu* (26,666,667 m²) of land, of 12,000 *mu* (8,000,000 m²) are construction land. In 2005, as one of the demonstration sites for new village, farmer and agriculture, the town was approved by the Ministry of Land and Resources and the Tianjin Development and Reform Commission to implement the comprehensive supplementary reform. The Ministry of

Land and Resources allocated 8,000 *mu* (5,333,333 m²) of construction land for a three-year period of temporary use to the town government that is responsible for organizing and implementing new village construction, including farmer's move from one story houses to storied houses, village demolition and homestead reclamation. The planned land area and building area reached 5.618 sq. kms and 4.6 million m² respectively, of which 3.88 sq. kms and 3.2 million m² are for the housing land and building area respectively. The construction was started from April 2006, and by now, 380 apartment buildings have been constructed with a total area of 1,800,000 m² and 35,000 people in 12,000 households have moved in, and the relocation of another 2,000 households are ongoing.

The new village construction will be conducted by the government following the policy of "don't reduce arable land, don't change the system for contracted responsibility, respect farmer's will and implement homestead exchange for housing." The government will not force farmers but will actively carry out the project by providing incentives and guidance. The detailed implementation steps are as follows:

Step 1: Come to the village to promote policies and conduct opinion poll.

Step 2: Establish Tianjin Dongli Investment Co., Ltd., a company wholly financed by the district government, with a registered capital of RMB 200 million Yuan and cash flow of RMB 30 million Yuan.

Step 3: Apply for a 5-year mortgage loan of RMB 2.5 billion Yuan from the branch of Tianjin Development Bank with the 8,000 *mu* (5,333,333 m²) of land as collateral, and there is still over RMB 200 million Yuan of credit available.

Step 4: Establish relevant compensation and resettlement policies, including identity confirmation (agriculture population can enjoy preferential treatment, but the non-agriculture cannot, the latter only can replace their houses by the actual area), the standard for demolition compensation for different houses such as earth house, brick house, storied house and storied house with private courtyard and other facilities such as telephone, cable television and air conditioner, as well as the compensation standard for house replacement difference (the compensation for brick house is taken as the reference, the earth house should pay RMB 200 Yuan/m², the storied house can obtain a price difference according to the purchasing price, and the difference will be refunded at the level of over RMB 1,000 Yuan/m²), while the storied house with private courtyard will be compensated at 1.4 times.

Step 5: Arrange the order for house replacement, sign the contract for replacement, select the number for replacement, demolish old houses and move into the storied houses, and return the homestead to the government.

Step 6: Conduct reclamation. In total, in the first phase, reclamation has been completed for a total of 220.2 hectares of original lands, and the reclaimed lands in Yonghe and Zhangzhuang villages have been distributed for planting.

It is not easy for Huaming Demonstration Town to achieve the land balance, to complete such large scale construction and reclamation tasks within two years, and to complete large scale inhabitant relocation within two years. Generally, the experiment is conducted in the way of government-led organization and construction, financed by land mortgage, which is following the road of urbanization first, industrialization later, and construction first, industry development later. However, during the process, some problems occurred, some of them have been solved, some of them need to be solved in accordance with their further development, while some are potential. Thus, there are three major issues.

The first is the land balance. The experiment does not involve the farmland but only the replacement of 12,000 *mu* (8,000,000 m²) of construction land. The balance between occupation and compensation has been achieved as the project is carried out in accordance with the current policies. In total, 12,000 *mu* (8,000,000 m²) of rural construction land has been changed into urban construction land, farmers are removed from the storied house to improve their housing conditions, and the governments at all levels have obtained their own benefits from the experiment. Among the 12,000 *mu* (8,000,000 m²) of land, 8,000 *mu* (5,333,333 m²) is designated for the project, of which 3,600 *mu* (2,400,000 m²) are retained land. For the rest of 4400 *mu* (2,933,333 m²), 1984 *mu* (1,322,667 m²) is commercial land and 2,500 *mu* (1,666,667 m²) is industrial park land, which is the project land for the town and district governments respectively, and will be distributed by Dongli Investment Co., Ltd. The remaining 4,000 *mu* (2,666,667 m²) is owned by the municipal government. Besides, 120 million *mu* (8,000,000 m²) of land from reclamation is state-owned agricultural land, and will be owned by the government and managed by the investment company, and the land allocated for three years of temporary use has been returned to the Ministry of Land and Resources.

The second is the financing balance. According to the original estimation of the design, the expenses for assorted construction will reach RMB 3.7 billion Yuan, which will be slightly smaller than the land leasing income of RMB 3.8 billion Yuan. But, in fact, the actual income and expenses are quite different. The expenses have occurred, but the income has not been obtained. Besides, RMB 2.2 billion Yuan of mortgage loan from the Development Bank has begun to be repaid, and the repayment was RMB 400 and 600 million Yuan in 2008 and 2009 respectively. Meanwhile, in order to complete the demolition within the required time and meet the requirements of inspection and acceptance by the Ministry of Land and Resources, the government has implemented a series of incentives, e.g., for those moving in time, each household will obtain RMB 3,000 Yuan and will be supplied with a heater for winter of 2008 for free, which approximately needs RMB 50 million Yuan, so the demolition cost is estimated to be about RMB 300 million Yuan by adding other costs, and the operation cost of the demonstration zone is estimated to be RMB 60 to 80 million Yuan. In addition, the reclamation cost for 12,000 *mu* (8,000,000 m²) of construction land in the original village will reach RMB 800 million Yuan. All above are advanced by the district financial department. In terms of income, the state and municipal governments give a special fund of RMB 20 million Yuan, and 50,000 m² of public houses are estimated to obtain a total income of RMB 30 million Yuan at a rent of RMB 3 Yuan/m² per day, but the actual rent income is only RMB 8 million Yuan, so the income available is only RMB 28 million Yuan. Other incomes are from the transfer of land use rights. The financing balance would not be a problem under previous price for the transfer, but actually, the price for the transfer of land use rights has decreased greatly at present, and sometimes no transfer can be made. Fortunately, according to the officials from the district government, the district financial department can support the expenses in the coming one or two years.

The third is about the employment and long-term development for the farmers replacing their houses. During the relocation, the government issued a questionnaire for each household, and the satisfaction rate reached 97% according to statistics. The per capita living space increased from 26 to 37.46 m^2 before and after the house replacement, and therefore the farmers not only have their residential conditions improved but also get commercialized urban houses. However, farmers have nothing to do with 12,000 *mu* (8,000,000 m^2) of land from reclamation, as well as 8,400 *mu* (5,600,000 m^2) or 4400 *mu* (2,933,333 m^2) of land from replacement. They only own the use right of 3,600 *mu* (2,400,000 m^2) of land in retained areas. Among the labor force of 18,000 in Dongli Town, 10% are engaged in agriculture, 70% are engaged in the secondary and tertiary industries, and there are still 4,000 to 5,000 unemployed. Obviously, such concealed unemployment has been explicit. Although the project of the demonstration zone and subsequent development can solve the employment for some villagers, there are still 2,000 people left unemployed. Consequently, the construction of the demonstration town should not only solve the housing problem of farmers, but also the problem of land capitalization and long-term development. If no attention is paid to such problems, the current high rate of satisfaction will only serve to conceal the potential problem.

4.3. Comment on government-led overall development experiment of urban and rural areas

Certainly, these reform experiments all have a general planning or design, some of which strictly comply with current state policies and regulations, and some are conducted in a careful and detailed way. But, from the existing practices, these experiments are deviating from the original intention of overall development of urban and rural areas, and there are still some basic problems required to be discussed and thought about.

Firstly, the reform is conducted in the name of market-like land transaction but actually in the way of disguised land expropriation. Obviously, current arrangement of the reform is based on the lessons learned from previous instances where the governments' conduct resulted in a series of

social conflicts, farmer dissatisfaction and resistance due to an over-simpli-
fied and unfair operation in the process of requisition. On the surface, the
reform is not conducted in the way of forced acquisition and demolition.
Rather, it is done in the way of market-like transaction between the government and farmers, but actually, in such transaction, parties involved are
governments with authority and scattered farmers, the government can
establish the transaction conditions favorable to themselves, while farmers
cannot bargain with the government and their demands that exceed the
transaction limit will not be supported by the government.[9] Furthermore,
the reform merely solves the housing problems for farmers, but does not
ensure the rights of farmers and the village collective and their future development as all replaced lands become state-owned, which is actually a disguised way of land expropriation. Thus, if previous governments' conduct
in land requisition is a forced way to obtain land from farmers, the current
exercise can be regarded as a disguised equivalent that makes farmers confused and even happy to give their lands to the government under the prospect and immediate benefits given by the government and officials.

Secondly, under the current system, the urban governments cannot
really achieve their target of simultaneous development for both urban and
rural areas. Even not considering the rent-seeking and corruption of officials, there are needs for expansion of the city, enlargement of available
land and increase of investment, which are actually different aspects of
one issue: funding. If governments cannot control the benefits from land
appreciation, the development problem of urban areas still cannot be
solved. Thus, the government's land expropriation aims to obtain the benefits from land appreciation for financing their projects, which is actually
the primary purpose of the current exercise under the name of all comprehensive reforms of overall development of urban and rural areas. On the
other hand, farmers can move into the storied houses through house
replacement and even change their identity from farmer to citizen, but

---

[9]It was reported that in May 2008, a total of 866 households with 3,368 villagers from
Guanzhuang Village and Chitu Village of Huaming Town brought lawsuits through
Farmers' Right Law Firm, but the courts at all levels in Tianjin have not heard them up to
now, as reported in the *Tianjin: What is Brought from Homestead Exchange for House* in
20th edition of *China News* in 2009.

they will lose their land and can no longer share the benefits from land appreciation. The basic requirement for actual overall development of urban and rural areas, however, should be that while the replaced lands are used for urban construction, the major part of the benefits from land appreciation should be given to farmers for their long-term development.

Thirdly, the current practice has deprived farmers of their rights of participation and development. The so-called "overall development of urban and rural areas" is a government-led operation, and farmers are not actually participating in it, although some measures such as opinion polls and democratic discussions are taken in practice. They are only the recipients and target of the project. The key here is not about the selection rights in the process of house replacement for farmers, but about the relations between farmers and the land, or the issue about whether the land is the state-owned property or the collectively owned property. If the land becomes state-owned, farmers will undoubtedly lose their participation and development rights, but if the land is collectively owned, farmers will not only participate in the reform but also master the development right in the long term. Thus, whether the reform of overall development of urban and rural areas is successful depends on whether some kind of public trust fund can be set up, with the usufruct rights from land staying with farmers after the rights to use and own are transferred to the government. In other words, farmers should be the beneficiaries of that public trust fund, and if the government fails to implement this, the overall development of urban and rural areas will be undoubtedly another deprivation from farmers.

Fourthly, both homestead exchange for urban residence and rural housing land for social security are the deprivation of land from farmers. Obviously, the homestead exchange for urban houses is an unfair exchange, the homestead property rights of farmers should involve the property rights of both homestead and the corresponding houses, but the current overall development of urban and rural areas only ensures the housing right of farmers. Moreover, the collective homestead is usually nationalized by local governments through "bidding, auction and listing" during the process of house replacement, which is a deprivation of the homestead property rights from farmers. Similarly, the social security for rural housing land is also an unfair exchange. Obviously, it is irrational and unfair to replace the land or homestead property rights of farmers with the constitutional right (social security). After farmers lose their land and homestead, how will the government deal with the problem associated with the negligible social security payments that can only maintain farmers' livelihoods over a few years? That is a very short sighted policy and irresponsible government behavior.

5. Innovations and Experiments by Farmers, Collectives and Local Governments

Faced with the situation where local governments and developers collude with each other to plunder rural collective construction land, farmers and collectives in the villages surrounding urban areas take some tit-for-tat actions in building numerous houses for sale, and with which some incidents of farmland occupation do occur. Nonetheless, there is not much of a farmland left in the surrounding areas in any case. On the other hand, the current policies purported to see to it are in practice counterproductive due to their bad design. Meanwhile, the land expropriation becomes more and more difficult and unpopular, so local governments carry out the projects of overall development of urban and rural areas and the homestead exchange for urban houses, which makes the contention on rural homestead more complicated. The serious institutional defect, however, will undoubtedly create opportunities for innovative practices. Indeed, numerous breakthroughs and innovations created under such a chaotic environment can actually be potent and effective in our current and future reform. Thus, we should only need to turn them into the government's policies and regulations, which not only can solve the chaotic land problem and promote China's rural reform and development, but also are the path and the secret of success for us over the past 30 years.

5.1. *The land capitalization in Zhenggezhuang Village of Beijing with farmers as main players*[10]

Zhenggezhuang Village, located on the banks of the Wenyu River in the north of Beijing, 20 km from the downtown, has 318 households with a

---

[10]The data here is sourced from the *Research on the Phenomenon of Zhenggezhuang — A City on Collective Land* (printed edition), written by Liu Shouying *et al.* in 2008 and organized by the Research Group about the Transition of Beijing Village System.

population of 1,158 covering 4,332 *mu* (2,888,000 m²) of land. Before the reform and opening-up, it was a conventional village, in which 75% of villagers were engaged in agriculture, with an annual per capita income of RMB 182 Yuan, and the village collective and villagers were poor. However, after the reform and opening-up, especially since 1998, the village has been on a self-dependent development path of industrialization and urbanization. With a relatively independent village collective and enterprises that work together by way of specialization of their labor resources and capitalization of their land, the village has changed from a common suburban backwater to a developed urban community. In 2007, the total assets, total economic income and per capita income of the village reached RMB 3.2 Yuan billion, RMB 1.28 billion Yuan and RMB 21,000 Yuan respectively.

Before 1998, the village developed along a non-agricultural road and established a large quantity of township enterprises, most of which were eliminated under the environment of marketization. After that, as large-scale urban construction developed, the construction enterprises emerged and became the leading industry of the village collective. Through years of development, these construction enterprises were consolidated into the Beijing Hongfu Mechanized Construction Group (called Hongfu Group for short) in 1996. Moreover, a village-enterprise system where enterprises are based on the village while the village is depending on the enterprises was established to integrate economic organizations and resources in the whole village in order to capture the benefits of scale economy, laying the foundation for further land capitalization and great development.

With the expansion of enterprise scale, as of the end of 2007, over 90% of the Hongfu Group staff were from other villages and 51 of the group's backbone staff were from outside. These staff members work in the collective enterprise, but cannot enjoy the homestead benefits in the village. For this reason, providing housing for them becomes the key to retaining talent and developing the enterprise. Although the labor is not a problem, both the land and capital are indispensable. But, according to the original land utilization rules, the change of the land use of 2,000 *mu* (1,333,333 m²) of farmland should be approved, the transformation and development of 1,050 *mu* (700,000 m²) of homestead and 400 *mu* (266,667 m²) of barren land need funds, 1.000 *mu* (666,667 m²) of public land for roads, schools, etc. should not be changed in general, and the remaining 6 *mu* (4,000 m²) of office and factory land are utterly inadequate. In terms of the funding, the Hongfu Group is not in red on the balance sheet, but is mired in chain debts, causing huge problems in its cash flow. Thus, the enterprise decided to accept repayment in kind, thus obtained large quantities of building materials such as cement and steel, based on which the group opened the way toward business of village-rebuilding that has later on led to land commercialization and capitalization.

However, it is difficult to make farmers who live in the house with an exclusive yard move into an apartment building flat. For this reason, the village committee formed the written decision, established the plan and scheme and signed the demolition resettlement agreement with each household by following the principles of "Thinking of villagers in their position and not letting farmers suffer a loss" and based on democratic discussion and decision. Meanwhile, different purchasing rules and welfare sharing methods were formulated for five types of persons, including villagers, teachers, enterprise staff, and non-villagers with or without a house in the village. From 1998 to 2007, a total of 549,400 m² of houses were built, consisting of 1,130 resettlement houses with a total area of 101,700 m² and 120 reserve houses for villagers with a total area of 11,300 m² that account for 24.7% of total house construction area (391 households move into the house, the per capita housing area reached 70 m², which was 3 times of that before the reconstruction), 1,377 industry ancillary houses with a total area of 181,901 m² that were purchased by the enterprise staff and teachers at the cost price and 182 reserve houses with a total area of 181,215 m², both of which accounted for 30.8% of total construction area, as well as 3,075 houses for sale with a total area of 236,482.27 m², accounting for 44.5% of total construction area. The sales income of all houses reached RMB 1.378 billion Yuan.

The model of homestead commercialization and capitalization with farmers as the main players in Zhenggezhuang Village are of great significance. Firstly, it has made the residential land decrease from 1,050 *mu* (700,000 m²) to 250 *mu* (166,667 m²) and saved 800 *mu* (533,333 m²) of land. Secondly, it has greatly improved the living environment of villagers and made it change from a common village to a modern urban community.

Thirdly, it has accumulated a lot of capital for the industrialization of the village community enterprise. With a total income of RMB 1.378 billion Yuan, all of which has been used for business development, Hongfu Group has become a construction enterprise with grade 2 qualification that can undertake the Olympic Games project. Moreover, through the institutional innovation in homestead, the market-oriented transaction and transfer of rural construction land have been achieved and a new model for village reconstruction and real estate development has been created, which deserves more attention and discussion.

During the process of current city (village) reconstruction, the government is usually responsible for land expropriation and demolition, the developers are in charge of construction, and farmers move into apartment buildings and are changed into citizens. As a result, farmers lose their permanent land and the rights, their interests are impaired, and ceaseless disputes between farmers and developers and frequent conflicts between farmers and the government are caused. Indeed, the village reconstruction in Zhenggezhuang Village is completely self-invested, self-developed and self-managed without the participation of the government and developers, which will naturally neither increase the government's burden nor cause disputes of interests with developers. It has opened up a new route for free flow of production factors between urban and rural areas and the farmers' independent participation in the urbanization process, and has broken current pattern of deformedly developed real estate market and high housing price under current situation of state land monopoly.

At present, the legal development model for real estate approved by the government is a model involving several parties, and among them the developer is responsible for construction and operation and will obtain extra profit, the government monopolizes the benefits from land appreciation, but the rights and interests of farmers are deprived. However, the real estate development in Zhenggezhuang has created quite a different model, in which the saved rural collective homestead is activated and constructed by the village community enterprise. Parts of commodity houses are sold to the public, but all benefits are reserved for the village, community and village community enterprise, and villagers and the enterprise become the biggest beneficiaries.

The land utilization in Zhenggezhuang Village focuses not only on the change of farmers' dwellings and the village's environment, but also on the industrialization and urbanization of the village. Actually, the village has achieved the leasing management of land and has established a union trust fund through a clever contract among its enterprises, village and farmers by exploiting the loopholes of current policies and laws. During the process, the village compiled the Construction Planning of *21st-Century Ecological Manor of Zhenggezhuang Village* and the *Controlled Detailed Planning for Pingxifu Group in Zhenggezhuang District* formally approved by the Beijing Municipal Commission of Urban Planning in 2005, both of which become the basis and route map for urbanization in Zhenggezhuang Village. Under current land policies, the lands of the village can only be rented but not sold. Hence, a land transaction system that can ensure the rights, interests and profit of farmers was established through the contract between farmers and the village, and between the village and the enterprise. The Hongfu Group was authorized to be responsible for land leasing and operation at a price not below RMB 5,000 Yuan per *mu* (667 m²) per year, and those un-rented lands will be paid at a price of RMB 500 Yuan. That has brought many benefits, firstly, villagers and the village collective can obtain rent (RMB 36.499 million Yuan in 2007), which in turn becomes a common fund for all farmers, while the land becomes assets of the organization set up to manage the common fund; secondly, it rationalizes the land use where dwelling, public space of the community and industrial park are combined in an efficient way. On one hand, after the successful shift in land use from agricultural to industrial purposes, it further rationalizes its use by shifting it to that of services purpose, in which the lands for the secondary industry and service industry account for 13.5% and 62.4% respectively.[11] On the other hand, a highly-efficient and intensive land use pattern will be achieved, in which the lands for public facilities, offices of the enterprise and village and industry account for 0.3%, 0.08% and 80% respectively; thirdly, it has provided a large amount of land available and wide development space for the village-enterprise, which will greatly

---

[11]It is known that the transfer of farmland in Zhenggezhuang is conducted by ways of purchasing land use target and remote agency.

decrease the land costs for the enterprise development. On the whole, the farmer-led land capitalization model in Zhenggezhuang has provided the first-hand experience for effectively carrying out and achieving the relevant objectives of the land reform made by the Third Plenary Session of the 17th Central Committee.

5.2. A game over land property rights between villagers and the government in the project of "urban villages", Shenzhen

In the 30 years since China's reform and opening-up, Shenzhen has rapidly developed from a typical village in southern Guangdong to a modern city with a population of above 10 million and become China's 4th largest city in terms of economic size, which is miraculous in the history of global urbanization and industrialization. The project of "urban villages" in Shenzhen has developed under such context, which is also the secret of Shenzhen's miracle. However, urban villages are not a special phenomenon of Shenzhen but a common trend under China's special land property system. Nonetheless, the urban villages there stand out as more distinctive due to their unique development route and history.

People who have not been in urban villages will have rather abstract, unclear and imaginary ideas about what an urban village is, why an urban village should be formed and how to do it. They may think that urban villages just mean several villages, several rows of tile-roofed houses, some huts or several storied houses with broken walls with a dilapidated look, and the reconstruction of urban villages is to demolish these tile-roofed houses and huts and build numerous buildings, but that is not true.

In fact, the urban villages in Shenzhen are large and developed urban communities, in which adjoining high-rise buildings are common, most of which have more than seven or eight stories. Commonly, the first story is occupied by shops that can provide all kinds of goods and services, and the second story and above is basically the residence of villagers and migrant workers. Urban villages have no broken walls with dilapidated look, but a bustling, booming and prosperous scene, which have a lot of traffic and busy transactions in the daytime and are full of bright lights at night. For Gangsha Village, it has a total area of 96,000 m², in which there are 881 private buildings with a total construction area of 395,000 m² and 100,000 residents (Zhang Shuguang, 2008). Currently, Shenzhen has 320 urban villages (designated as administrative village) including 91 villages within the special zone. The villages cover a total land area of 93.5 sq. kms, including 8.5 sq. kms within the special zone and 85 sq. kms beyond the special zone. Besides, there are 350,000 private buildings with a total construction area of 106 million m², including 42,300 buildings within the special zone covering a total construction land of 21.39 million m². From the spatial distribution, urban villages within the special zone are unevenly distributed, most of which are close to the city center, district center or the port. However, urban villages beyond the special zone are the major part of urban built-up area, mainly distributed along the axis of urban development, most of which are located in the centers at district and group levels or around those important traffic arteries.

Urban villages in Shenzhen emerged in the 1980s, developed in the 1990s, underwent four periods of rush construction at large scale. The development can be divided into three stages, fraught throughout with intensive contentions between villagers and the government. The spatial distribution and construction pattern had generally taken shape in the early period of this century.

5.2.1. *Formation stage of urban villages*

In the early 1980s, as Shenzhen took the lead in opening to the outside world, the urban scale rapidly expanded and large quantities of farmland were changed into urban construction lands. For farmers' relocation, the government allowed original villagers to retain some land that can be used in urban commercial purposes and encouraged them to develop it themselves.

In 1982, the municipal government issued the *Interim Provisions of Construction Land for Rural Commune Members in Shenzhen Special Economic Zone*, which proposed the standard for new village construction, namely each household only has a land area of 150 m² for housing construction and should not have a homestead with an area larger than 80 m². This delimited the red line of land use for new villages, and nationalized all original residential lands from villagers. However, due to the lack of financial resources, the government was unable to pay the compensation for land expropriation at that time, and according to the *Interim Provisions*, the residential lands that are temporarily not expropriated by the government can still be used by villagers, which thus have resulted in the pattern of co-existence of new and original villages in Shenzhen.

Before 1984, original villagers built the new village in the delimited residential land essentially for their own use. Thus, the old building form of two or three stories with exclusive yards remained. However, with the rapid economic development of the special zone, numerous outsiders came, which resulted in a sharp increase of housing demand and the formation of low-rent housing market. Soon after, original villagers began to break the standard of land use specified by the government and built large quantities of houses. Meanwhile the state began to expropriate more and more farmland within the special zone. As a result, original villagers have gradually changed their production and living status from the traditional agriculture to house renting and collective real estate.

In 1986, the municipal government issued the *Notice on the Further Strengthening of Rural Planning in Shenzhen Special Economic Zone* and made clear provisions on the housing construction by farmers within the special zone, according to which the land for housing construction for each household should not exceed $200\,m^2$ (including the lands for roads, public facilities, grassland and cultural and sports activities), the projection area of house foundation should not exceed $80\,m^2$, each building principally should not exceed three stories, the per-capita construction area is $40\,m^2$, and the total construction area should not exceed 150 and $240\,m^2$ for the household with less than and more than three persons respectively. Meanwhile, the municipal Bureau of Land and Resources conducted a survey village by village and delineated the control line or the red line for land use of village land and the boundary of new villages within the special zone. Hence, the land scale and boundary of urban villages within the special zone have been basically determined and the pattern of urban villages has been formed.

As the regulations on original homestead and private housing construction are the government's unilateral behaviors, they do not constitute effective constraint on the behavior of original villagers. With the high-speed development of Shenzhen's economy and the rapid increase of its population, the permanent population within the special zone increased from less than 100,000 in 1980 to above 1,000,000 in 1989, and Shenzhen developed from a frontier town to a megacity. That has provided a chance for original villagers to participate in the process of urbanization and share the benefits of urbanization. Faced with the formation of a low-rent housing market and the rapid expansion of its scale, some villagers began to add stories to their building (generally three to five stories) and reduce the interval space between buildings; besides that some phenomena such as building beyond the red line of land use also occurred.

In response to the villagers' behavior above, the government first took some measures to stop the housing construction of original villagers that exceeds the red line. Secondly, it specified the right of the lands compliant with the rules and issued the land use certificate, and thirdly ordered original villagers to return those lands outside permission of the rules and regulations with economic and disciplinary penalties. However, these measures were basically not carried out for the following two reasons. The first was that until 1989, the municipal government had not paid the demolition compensation to original villagers, and original policies still remained in effect, so the government's behavior lacked legal basis. The second reason is that for local economic development, most district governments adopted a more tolerant attitude on the behavior of urban villages.

In 1988, the municipal government issued the first document to unilaterally declare that the private homesteads within the planned red line in the special zone are state-owned and commune members only have the use right of homestead. In 1989, the government issued the *Several Regulations on Land Expropriation in Shenzhen Special Economic Zone*, specifying that collective lands available for development within the special zone shall be uniformly expropriated and be nationalized, and original villagers will still have the use right of expropriated lands after signing the land use contract with the municipal Bureau of Land and Resources. Meanwhile, the government made some compromise by preferentially appropriating some part of land for free to original villagers for constructing properties for business operation and rent, etc. However, the government's unilateral declaration on land nationalization was not acknowledged by the original villagers, but caused a new rush for construction of private buildings, and the scale of urban villages further expanded.

5.2.2. Shaping stage of urban villages

Since the 1990s, Shenzhen has ushered in the upsurge of economic development and urban construction, and the permanent resident population within the special zone had increased to 2 million at the end of 1990s, which greatly stimulated the market demand of rental property. Accordingly, more and more housing construction in urban villages occurred, the density of building became higher and higher, and the buildings became taller and taller — even some seven to eight-story tall buildings appeared, and some phenomena such as illegal occupation of common land including roads within the collective land also occurred in large quantities. In addition, development of urban villages beyond the special zone also increased rapidly and spread out continuously, which almost became the main part of urban construction. For that, the government declared that all villages within the special zone will be urbanized and all lands will be nationalized, integrated urban villages into the management of urban state land, and attempted to control and restrain the behaviors of original villagers in land use and housing construction through land registration.

In 1993, the *Several Regulations on the Handling of Legacy Issues about Property Rights in Shenzhen Special Economic Zone* was issued, which divided the land in urban villages into four types. The first type is the land for industrial and commercial uses within the red line that can be transferred with compensation, for which the owner can apply for real estate registration after paying the land use fee; the second type is the land for industrial and commercial uses beyond the red line, for which no application for registration of property right shall be accepted unless it does not violate the urban planning and is for self-use; the third type is the land for private housing provided by the government, for which each household only can select one house for registration of property rights; and the fourth type is the land in original villages, for which no registration of property right will be granted. However, original villagers and collective organizations did not acknowledge the unilateral behavior of land nationalization by the government. They maintained the original social structure and relations and still held on to the property right of collective land. Accordingly, original villagers and collective organizations took some actions, including not actively applying for property right registration for self-use real estate except cooperating with other enterprises for industrial and commercial lands within the red line, and for those industrial and commercial lands beyond the red line, some village collectives used the rule of property registration for self-use, completing the procedures necessary to legalize them. Due to the hidden nature of the transactions of the private homestead and related house property in the old village, the government's registration regulation did not present much of a restraint. Thus, under the environment of marketization, the government's unilateral behavior on property rights registration without any appropriate transaction of property rights and contractual arrangement becomes invalid.

In addition to property rights registration, the government also tried to restrain the demand on so-called illegal rental houses through the management of the rental market, limit and stop the illegal housing construction by original villagers. In 1992, the municipal government issued the *Ordinances on the House Rent in Shenzhen Special Economic Zone* to specify that any house without property rights registration cannot be rented. But, due to large market demand, such regulations are nonbinding. In fact, there were two formal and informal rental markets, and the informal market had low level of rent and was more active than the formal market. With their low rent, superior location and relatively complete living ancillary facilities, rental houses in urban villages were popular in the rental market. According to the investigation by the Design Institute of Urban Planning, the monthly rent for a 100 m² house within the special zone was RMB 1,200 to 1,500 Yuan in urban villages and RMB 1,800 to 2,200 Yuan in common urban districts, and urban villages shared about 70% of the whole rental house market of the city and accommodated a total temporary population of about 5 million, accounting for about 50% of the whole temporary population.

Meanwhile, the municipal government issued the *Interim Measures on the Planning and Management of Land and Resources in Baoan District and Longgang District of Shenzhen* in accordance with the experience of the special zone to specify the standard of non-agricultural construction land in rural areas as follows: The area of industrial and commercial land is 100 m² for each person, the projection area of the foundation of rural house shall not exceed 100 m², and the land for public facilities is 200 m² for each household. But, the red line for rural construction land beyond the special zone had not been determined, so the construction of urban villages was basically out of control.

On March 15, 1999, the municipal People's Congress issued the *Decision on Resolute Investigation and Punishment on Illegal Buildings* to reaffirm relevant regulations of the municipal government on the management of urban villages (e.g., one house for one household) and to declare that some resolute investigations and punishments would be conducted for illegal buildings. That made original villagers rush their building activities before the deadline, which saw villagers expand and reconstruct their houses at an alarming rate, and a new round of illegal construction was formed. Commonly, the reconstructed private buildings were 8 stories or above, and even reached 12 stories, and the current spatial distribution and basic pattern of urban villages were formed.

In 2002, the municipal People's Congress issued the *Several Regulations on the Handling of Legacy Illegal Private Houses in Shenzhen Special Economic Zone* and the *Several Regulations on the Handling of Productive and Operational Illegal Buildings in Shenzhen Special Economic Zone*, specifying that those illegal private houses within the red line, constructed by original villagers in accordance with the principle of one building for one household, with a total construction area of 480 m² or less and a total number of stories of four or less, can be exempted from punishment and be registered in property right, and for those private houses above 480 m², constructed in accordance with the principle of one building for one household, can be registered after the owner pays the fine. The deadline was set at March 15, 1999.

The *Decision* in 1999 and the two *Decision*s in 2002 proved once more that the monopolistic government has to succumb to the market force by recognizing already formed property rights, which was well tested by the original villagers. As a result, those late-comers began to follow the deeds of their law-breaking predecessors and more villagers were racing to build private houses in large quantities, and a large number of high-rise buildings with over 15 stories and an area of 5,000 m² emerged. From 1999 to 2004, the construction area of newly constructed, reconstructed and expanded private houses had accounted for about 50% of total construction area of private houses in urban areas. After that, the urban village problem had become a real problem for the government.

5.2.3. *Comprehensive reconstruction stage of urban villages*

In 2003, the municipal government set the goal to build Shenzhen into a modern and international metropolis, and the urban village was on the agenda again. Citing urbanization as the reason, the municipal government nationalized the lands beyond the special zone, successively issued the *Opinion on Promoting Urbanization Process in Baoan District and Longgang District* and the *Land Management Measures for Urbanization in Baoan District and Longgang District*, declaring that after all members of rural collective economic organization become citizens, all lands collectively owned by original members will be nationalized. After that, the government issued the *Interim Provisions for Urban Villages (Original Villages) in Shenzhen* and corresponding *Implementation Opinion*. In May 2005, the government conducted the directional blasting for 16 tall buildings in Yunong Village, which marked the beginning of urban village transformation. Soon after, the government issued the *Urban Villages of Shenzhen (Overall Planning Outline (2005–2010) for Original Cities Transformation)*. However, the process of transformation was very slow and encountered great opposition, and it became doubtful whether they could achieve the expected objective of urban village transformation within and beyond the special zone within 5 years.

It can be seen from the formation and development of urban villages in Shenzhen that, with the rapid development of Shenzhen's economy and the acceleration of urbanization process, numerous foreigners poured in, which resulted in large demand in rental house market and fast appreciation of lands in urban villages. For the distribution and claiming of land rent, the repeated and drastic conflicts between original villagers or collective economic organizations and the government emerged. The former indeed participated in the process of urbanization and maximized the land rent through the original legal collective land property rights, the direct control ability and the active market transactions. But the latter denied the actual market transactions, unilaterally changed the actual land property rights and nationalized the lands through its administrative power. However, such behaviors obtained no acknowledgment and cooperation from opponents resulted in extremely high implementation costs, and had unbelievable threats. As large scale illegal land use and building become fact, the government has to make concessions over and over again to recognize the land property rights of original villagers and collectives.

The formation and development of urban villages are also the means for original villagers to participate in the urbanization and share the benefits through the land capitalization. The urban population in Shenzhen is characterized by high mobility, in which above 60% are temporary residents. This greatly stimulates the demand of the house rental market, and private houses of original villagers in urban villages provide effective supply for the market. Thus, a large low-rent housing market is formed in Shenzhen, creating a model of supplying low-rent houses with market means. As the cheap labor for the development of Shenzhen is stabilized and ensured, the wealth accumulation and social security for the farmers losing the land are also solved. Certainly, as the city develops, the diseconomy outside urban villages will become more and more glaring, which undoubtedly cannot be solved by way of market, but the government's way of solely strengthening land management will also come at a high price.

5.3. Several discussions

Obviously, the above-mentioned cases are the models of farmer self-participation in the process of urbanization using their lands (mainly homesteads) in the context of the government-led urbanization and land nationalization. We can draw following conclusions from them:

Firstly, it is commonly acknowledged by local governments that with the advancement of urbanization, farmers must actively participate in the sharing of benefits from land appreciation. Meanwhile, it has been demonstrated by practices and recognized by the people that the development of urbanization will undoubtedly increase the value of land, but the real problem is how to distribute the benefits from land appreciation.

Unfortunately, current Chinese policies and laws completely exclude farmers from the sharing of differential earnings from land. Although this was acceptable to the farmers at the beginning of the reform when the value of land was not so obvious, once the land value increased greatly and farmers' awareness of land property rights was awakened, those unfair laws were strongly challenged and boycotted by farmers, resulting in numerous mass uprisings caused by land in rural areas. If the government takes no action to change the situation, acts in a Procrustean way and maintains current laws that harm the rights and interests of farmers, it can only cause more serious conflicts, endanger social stability and break the social harmony.

Secondly, the distribution of differential earnings from land determines the way of urbanization. The prevailing view is that the increase of differential earnings from land is generated by the advancement of urbanization and the value of land will not increase without the government's investment in infrastructure. Obviously, the view above is superficial and is seemingly rational but practically wrong. Numerous cases have demonstrated that the land appreciation will not occur without the development of rural industry and the convergence of the population, and that the government will have no capital for urban infrastructure investment without the transfer of land ownership from farmers to the government and the subsequent capitalization on the land. If farmers' land property rights are compared to a hen, then the government's infrastructure investment should be an egg, which will not exist without the former. Thus, the distribution of differential earnings from land directly decides the road of urbanization, namely that, if it is distributed to the government, the urbanization will be government-led, and conversely, it will be the farmers' independent way.

Thirdly, farmers have enormous potential for institutional innovation. Faced with current unfair legal systems, instead of sitting back, they deal with the government and struggle against the developers, and make breakthroughs and innovations where they can strive for their benefits. Thus, it is rational for the government to get rid of the traditional view of omniscient and omnipotent government, and to change unfair legal systems that shackle the farmers.

6. The "Sub-Right" Houses[12]: Contention and Implementation of Property and Development Rights of Farmers

6.1. Definition and scope of sub-right houses

The sub-right house is relative of the complete property right house. The so-called complete property right house is the commodity house built on the state construction land, can be freely sold, transferred and mortgaged, and has relatively complete attributes of commodity so that its owner has relatively complete property rights. Correspondingly, the "commodity house" built on the rural collective construction land is prohibited from being sold to citizens in accordance with current laws and regulations and does not have the complete attributes of a commodity, and the property rights of its purchaser are not protected by current laws, and accordingly the rights of the owner of the house are in a sense lower in status (not complete) than that of the owner of the commodity house in urban areas. For this reason it is vividly called the sub-right house. In fact, such a phenomenon actually stems from the dual systems surrounding the real estate sector where residential land and houses on it belong to two separate systems. And thus it becomes clear that the sub-right houses are an institutional phenomenon.

Since a sub-right house is a commodity house built on the collective land, it will undoubtedly break the government's monopolistic position in the supply of land for commodity house development. Thus the government has given repeated orders to strictly prohibit the development and construction of these commodity houses and to prohibit citizens from purchasing the sub-right houses and farmers' houses, and the court has also ruled that the houses purchased by citizens from farmers are illegal.

---

[12]There are many English translations for minor property, such as informal property, partial property, limited property and minor property, but the former three can partially comply with its original meaning but cannot indicate Chinese characteristics and be interpreted into Chinese again. The fourth interpretation not only complies with the original meaning but also has Chinese characteristics. Similarly, the interpretation of peasant worker is also the same, as shown in the *Minor Property and Peasant Worker*, written by Feng Shigang and published in Volume 1 of *Reading* in 2009.

This way, all houses in rural areas have the attributes and characteristics of a sub-right house. Thus, the sub-right house has both broad and narrow meanings: Broadly speaking, all houses in China's rural areas are sub-right houses, but narrowly speaking, the sub-right house refers in particular to the rural house that is built on the rural collective construction land and is sold to non-rural citizens.

6.2. *Type and development pattern of sub-right houses*

At present there are various forms and types of sub-right houses with different development and construction patterns. According to the type of land used for development and construction, it can be divided into four types, which are built on rural homesteads, on other construction lands (e.g., township enterprise land), on four kinds of wastelands, and on the farmland respectively. Insofar as the trend of reform is concerned, the sub-right houses built on the first three types of lands should not be limited and prohibited but should be built as the real commodity houses like the complete property right houses, while those sub-right houses built on the farmland should be strictly managed and prohibited. However, any regulation will undoubtedly have loopholes. Thus, it is correct to make the best use of the circumstances to find a way to effectively protect the farmland.

In terms of the development pattern, the sub-right house can be divided into three types. The first type is the independent development pattern, which can be further divided into two cases; in the first case its construction land is supplied by the village, and it is developed by the village community enterprise and can be rented or sold after living requirements of farmers are satisfied and improved, e.g., Zhenggezhuang Village that has sufficient financial resources and construction teams; in the second case the house is constructed by villagers or construction teams and then is rented or sold — e.g., urban villages in Shenzhen and Fumin cooperative in Kunshan City. The second type is the cooperative development pattern, in which the village cooperates with external enterprises and rents the use rights of construction land to the enterprise. The external enterprise contributes to development and construction, which can not only meet the housing demand of farmers, but also meets the land use demand for the enterprise's development or can be sold — e.g., Chongqing Taojia Jiulong Textile

Industrial Park. The third type is the developer development pattern, in which the village collective transfers the construction land to the developer in a lump sum and promises to apply for the house property certificate, and farmers can move into the storied house and obtain one-off compensation, but will lose the land property rights. From previous experience, the former two patterns are more effective than the last one, in which the developer and a few principals of the village or town are the biggest winners. The biggest difference between them is that, in the first two patterns farmers still hold the capitalized land property rights and will share permanent benefits from land capitalization, while in the last pattern farmers lose the land property rights and may become vagrants with neither land nor job. This is the same as the government's development pattern by land expropriation and overall development of urban and rural areas. Fortunately, we have investigated and found that many farmers have understood the truth and will not pursue one-time benefits but ask for permanent benefits.

For example, just across the street from Jiulongpo Textile Industrial Park is a piece of land expropriated by the government. Both of them are in Taojia Village. Some households have two pieces of land, one is in the industrial park and is rented to the enterprise, while the other is located across the street and is expropriated by the government. During the interview, some farmers told us that they do not want to sell, but rather rent their land. And they have no way to resist the government's expropriation behavior.

In another example, in the farmland transaction in Chadian Town, Hangu District, Tianjin, a village secretary did not sell the facilities on the land (including reservoir, driven well, electric irrigation and drainage facilities, etc.) but converted them into the share, so that the village can have both capital and stock rights for their future development.

6.3. *Contention over sub-right houses*

The sub-right houses originate and develop after the implementation of urban housing reform. Before the reform, both urban land and house were communal, which are distributed with low rent according to the location, and the individual does not have ownership but has use rights. At this point, urban and rural housing systems were two different property rights systems, and the urban housing system was more ineffective than the rural one, which thus blocked the urban development and the improvement of the people's living standards. Apart from housing quality, the urban per capita housing area was only 6.7 m^2 in 1978, and some phenomena, such as three generations under one roof or two households living in one room, were common and many people lived in the office for a long time. For the author, one lived in the dormitory and was apart from his wife for 12 years, and lived in the office for another 6 years after his wife was transferred to Beijing.

At the end of the 1990s, the commercialization of township houses had been achieved in a short time with the advance of urban reform, and the construction of commodity houses had also developed greatly. This century, the real estate development investment has reached above 20% of urban fixed-asset investment, the percentage of real estate value-added in GDP has exceeded 5%, and the annual residential area under construction and completed residential areas have reached 1.398 billion and 597 million m^2 respectively, so that the real estate industry has become the major impetus for China's economic growth. The urban population in 2005 nearly doubled that in 1978, while the urban per capita housing area reached 26.1 m^2, which was nearly four times of the figure in 1978. Meanwhile, the price of commodity houses has also increased rapidly, which even resulted in the irrational exuberance and property-value bubble in recent two years, besides that the monthly growth rate of housing price has reached or exceeded 10%, and the increase of land price was even faster with some premium land reaching a price of RMB 10,000 Yuan/m^2 in many cities. Thus, it has stimulated the development of commodity houses in suburban areas.

The current so-called legal development pattern for real estate in suburban areas is as follows: The government expropriates the land from farmers at a low price, pays a compensation that is 30 times the average agricultural production value in the previous three years to farmers, and sells the land to the developers at a high price. All sales income will become the government's financial revenue and personal income of officials; then, the developers complete the housing construction and sell the house at a higher price to make huge profits. For example, the developers have made a profit of RMB 290 billion Yuan in 2007, increasing by 48.7% compared with the figure in the last year, but farmers and village collectives are excluded from the benefits from land appreciation.

With the advance of urbanization and the development of the real estate industry, the shortage and exhaustion of urban construction land have become more and more serious, and accordingly the sub-right houses in suburban rural areas has developed due to the rapid increase of house prices and the attraction of high profit. For this reason, on one hand, there are large quantities of cheap lands available in rural areas. On the other hand, due to the limitation of policies and the risk of purchasing houses in rural areas, the house price in rural areas is as low as 1/2 to 1/3 or even below the complete property right house.[13] So those that cannot afford a house in urban areas or long for the living environment of rural areas will purchase houses there and farmers can obtain many more benefits from the construction and development of sub-right houses than from agricultural production.[14] Consequently, the development of the sub-right houses is not only an important means for farmers and village collectives to obtain benefits from land appreciation with both the government and developers, but also a way for farmers' independent participation in the process of urbanization. Accordingly, although prohibited by the state, the sub-right houses have still mushroomed in the suburban areas of all cities. According to incomplete statistics from the departments of land and resources, until the first half of 2007, the total area of the sub-right houses

---

[13]The average sales price of a self-built house in East Community, Longgang District, Shenzhen ranges from RMB 1,000 Yuan/m^2 to RMB 2,000 Yuan/m^2, but the average sales price of adjoining commodity house reaches above RMB 4,500 Yuan/m^2. In other communities including Minle Garden and Minlecuiyuan where sales of self-built houses are concentrated, the average price reaches about RMB 2,500 Yuan/m^2, while the sales price of adjoining second-hand commodity house reaches about RMB 7,500 Yuan/m^2 and even reached above RMB 10,000 Yuan/m^2 in the last year. The sales price of commodity house within the special zone always lead the country, but the difference in price between self-built houses and commodity houses is greater, e.g., the sales price of one 100 m^2 villager's house at Xinzhou Village in Futian District is RMB 300,000 Yuan, but the sales price of one commodity house in the same location is not less than RMB 1,000,000 Yuan. Similarly, the sales price of a minor property right house in Tongzhou District of Beijing is about RMB 3,000 Yuan/m^2, but the sales price of adjoining commodity house within the East 4th Ring reached above RMB 20,000 Yuan/m^2 last year.
[14]Calculated by the average sales price of minor property right house in Tongzhou District of Beijing, the income of 667 sq. m of land is RMB 6 million Yuan, which is equivalent to 200 times of the compensation for land expropriation.

in China had reached 6.6 billion m², accounting for more than one half of the total area of the complete property right houses of 12 billion m². According to the survey by the Shenzhen Land Resources and Real Estate Authority, there are 350,000 sub-right houses with a total area of 120 million m² that are built by original villagers in urban villages in Shenzhen, accounting for 49% of the total housing area of the whole city. It is said that in Tongzhou District, one of the most intense areas for the sub-right houses in Beijing, the area of the sub-right houses accounts for about 55% of the total housing area.

6.4. Analysis on the ability to exercise property right in the perspective of the development of sub-right houses

The development of sub-right houses has formed a large and obvious paradox. Originally, as a monopolistic organization with authority, the government had responsibilities to define and protect property rights, which was also the most efficient institutional arrangement. However, the development of sub-right houses has demonstrated that, faced with unarmed and unorganized farmers, the strong government with authority a very weak ability to respect property rights. That raises a series of questions: Which factors determine the ability of exercising property rights? Compared with scattered farmers, why is the government's ability to respect land property rights so weak? Why is an institutional arrangement that is seemingly the most efficient only able to obtain the most inefficient results? And why is the rigid legal system so weak and vulnerable? Thus, it can be seen that it is not important at all whether the property right ownership is legally regulated or nominal, public ownership or private ownership, and national ownership or collective ownership, but the most important is the actual control and abilities of exercising property rights.

Firstly, the ability to exercise property rights depends on whether the property right system is fair and rational, which is the basis of the effectiveness and enforceability of the property rights system. Commonly, only the fair land property rights system and property rights implementation behavior can be effective as it should be, and conversely, the unfair one will undoubtedly encounter enormous resistance, or even cannot be implemented at all. Even if the government can enforce by power, which will not only be costly but in the end will have to return to a fair and rational track. Obviously, the current rural construction land system is unfair, and the government's policies to limit and ban the sub-right houses are an irrational limitation and deprivation of farmers' and village collectives' property rights. So, the current institutional arrangement and government behaviors on land property rights lacks the foundations for legality. For this reason, the government's policies and behaviors are resisted by farmers, and the government cannot enforce them. Thus, the formulation and implementation of the legal system and policy should be on the basis of fairness and legitimacy, and should not adopt some discriminatory regulations and unfair behaviors.

Secondarily, the effectiveness of the formal land property rights arrangement depends on its adaptability to the traditional land property rights, which is a key factor that can influence the ability of exercising. Past experience shows that the traditional customs and rules are not the only source of a formal system or rule, but also influence and determine the scope and flexibility of formal rules, and the rural land system will be no exception. Because current policies and regulations on rural homesteads and sub-right houses violate the traditional custom and rule on the delimitation and implementation of land and housing property rights, they will undoubtedly be rejected and resisted by tradition and cannot be implemented. Especially in rural societies with deep historical origins, the traditional system and rule on land property rights is certainly not backward but will move forward with the times, and is not indispensable but will play the role all the time and constitute an important basis and conditions for a formal property rights system. Obviously, for the sub-right house problem, farmers use the traditional rule to resist current formal rules and the government's implementation behaviors on land property rights.

Thirdly, the ability to exercise property rights is directly determined by the implementation cost under the condition of fixed benefit from property rights. Meanwhile, major factors that influence the cost of exercising property rights include the related knowledge and information, the directness and scope of influence, the degree to which the owners of property rights are organized, the scale of their coordinated actions, the level of resistance in the process of implementation, and the credibility of threats. Generally, the knowledge of land property rights and its implementation is typical local knowledge, which is dispersedly grasped by farmers who directly use the land, and so the cost for exercising the property rights of the government will increase due to proxy characteristics of governmental agencies and serious information asymmetry. Besides, farmers and village collectives directly control the land use and their behavior toward property rights is characterized by promptness. When their common interests are at stake, such a promptness would lead to some coordinated action, and with that, social scale emerges, which will not only strengthen farmers' or collectives' bargaining power in the exercising of property rights, but also will increase the difficulty and cost for the implementation of governmental policies. Moreover, the formulation and implementation of the government's policy usually has a time lag and should depend on the administrative hierarchy. If the government cannot in time guide farmers' movement but only formulate and implement some out of date policies in the hope of suppressing it, it will undoubtedly fail. Moreover, there are interest conflicts between governments at different levels, no policy can thus be implemented if the interests between the governments at different levels contradict each other. What is more, if the local government makes a threat regarding the implementation of property rights and that bluff is called by farmers, it actually encourages farmers' illegal behavior that poses a huge social cost. In such a process, the government's ability of exercising property rights will be greatly impaired, but the farmer's ability will increase to the highest level, which has been demonstrated by the case of urban villages in Shenzhen.

Finally, during urbanization, the farmer's ability of implementation on land property rights will increase with the development of land markets and the appreciation of land. For this reason, the ability to exercise land property rights of farmers in suburban areas is stronger than that in outer suburban areas and common rural areas, and the ability of farmers in the south is stronger than in the north.

Consequently, the emergence and development of sub-right houses shows that the ability of exercising and bargaining power of farmers and village collectives on the land property rights of rural collective construction land are much stronger than those of the government.

From a legal perspective, all houses built by farmers and village collectives on their own homesteads are private properties, which can be legally and rationally sold or rented. Just like purchasing food and vegetables from farmers, urban citizens do not steal or rob but purchase sub-right houses from farmers, which is a fair transaction that is in everyone's interests. Therefore, the government should not limit and deprive the property and development rights of farmers and village collectives through its monopolized enforcement power, but eliminate the difference between sub-right houses and full-right or normal commodity houses through institutional reform and policy adjustment. Only in this way can the property and development rights of farmers and collectives be guaranteed and the urban–rural construction and urbanization process be brought into the path of positive development, which can not only achieve the goals of farmland protection and farmer's prosperity, but also promote urbanization.

Last but not the least, of all market transactions, interests' relationship behind can be quite different. The selling of agricultural and sideline products is a mutual competition between farmers, but the selling of sub-right houses is a direct competition between farmers and developers. Thus, the development of sub-right houses by farmers and village collectives has touched the raw nerves of developers who are powerful groups in society due to the real estate industry's important role in the national economy and its promotion of economic growth. Meanwhile, the real estate sector is a profitable one supported by the authorities, and the collusion between urban governments and developers will not only ensure the government's achievements in economic growth but also gain enormous benefits, which have been demonstrated by land finance and recent rescue policies issued by local governments.[15] But the real problem is that, for the purpose of food security and farmland protection, the central government formulates a series of limitations and banning policies on sub-right houses,[16] and the

---

[15]On September 4, 2008, the government of Xi'an City took the lead in issuing some policies to rescue the real estate market. After that, the government of Nanjing City formulated 16 articles and the government of Hangzhou City issued 24 articles. By now, over 10 municipal governments have issued relevant policies in the name of rescuing the real estate market, but actually these policies aim to rescue the government.

[16]It should affirm that the case certainly exits and may be quite common.

General Office of the State Council issues a series of notices and regulations to prohibit the construction and the selling of sub-right houses. In that way, the government not only places itself on the wrong side of the constitution and farmers and plays a role of shielding powerful groups, but also ignores the fact that sub-right houses emerge in large quantities and have no law to depend on to ban those so-called illegal sub-right houses. This policy has not only damaged the government's reputation and harmed the seriousness of law, but also has promoted the unordered development of the sub-right housing market and directly endangered the implementation of basic farmland protection policy and the sound development of urban construction.

7. Way to Go in the Reform and Policy Suggestions

7.1. *Urgency of current problems*

Due to the expansion of urban construction and the widespread sub-right houses, it is imperative and urgent to regulate the market for rural collective construction land. For this reason, the Central Committee of the Communist Party of China issues the *Decision on Several Major Problems about Advance of Rural Reform and Development*, which aims at promoting urban–rural integration, focuses on the elimination of the urban–rural dual system, and takes it as the key task, trying to make some breakthrough so a platform for further reform can be set up. Therefore, we should now fully seize the reform opportunity created by the Third Plenary Session, conduct in-depth research, and clarify and unify our thinking to promote urban–rural integration, to guarantee farmers' land right, and to complete China's urbanization and industrialization.

7.2. *Way to go*

Firstly, rural collective construction land is an important part of all land. During urbanization, due to the limitation on space, the amount of construction land depends not only on the demand of construction, but also on the amount of agricultural land — especially food production land. Meanwhile, the effective transfer and transaction of rural collective construction land should be based on the protection of basic farmland. Thus, the construction land problem should not be considered alone but linked to the farmland issues, or it undoubtedly cannot be solved.

Secondly, the trading and transfer of rural construction land should be based on the actual implementation and strict protection of 1.8 billion *mu* (1,200,000,000,000 m²) of basic farmland, conducted in the way of promoting urbanization, and focus on the maintenance of farmers' property and development rights. Actually, the so-called comprehensive reform for overall development of urban and rural areas is aimed at solving problems relating to the three aspects mentioned above. A breakdown in any them would result in bad consequences. Therefore, mere policy tinkering when problems arise will not work.

Thirdly, given that the market-based reform of rural construction land is an essential way to change land management from extensive use to intensive operation, the reform in the system of farmland protection becomes the key in the whole process. If it fails, the subsequent market-based reform for construction land could hardly proceed. This is because the boundary between farmland and construction land can only be distinguished in theory but cannot in practice, even though it can be distinguished, the government also has difficulty controlling the behavior of farmers and village collectives to overstep the boundary. Once markets for rural collective construction land are opened, farmers and village collectives will have great impulse to convert farmland into construction land due to the large difference in benefits between them. This is what the government worries about, because the government can do nothing for these behaviors that may occur in about 700,000 administrative villages in China. Therefore, the premise and key to promote the marketization reform of rural collective construction land is to reform current basic farmland protection system, without which the government will not actively promote the marketization reform of land.

7.3. Fundamental way and specific method for implementation and protection of basic farmland

The current basic farmland protection system may be the most ridiculous institutional arrangement. Despite its clear and definite objectives and tasks, the relevant policies and measures are improper and their implementation will generate results opposite to the objectives of basic farmland protection with an extremely high cost and low efficiency. Under such an institutional arrangement, interests of all parties involved are in conflict or not compatible with each other. Obviously, the farmland protection is only the objective of the central government in Beijing but not for farmers, although local governments and developers have similar interests and objectives, which are quite in conflict with the objective of the central government as well. Therefore, interest incompatibility occurs not only between the central government and local governments, but also between local governments and farmers.

Besides a direct grain subsidy policy, the central government mainly conducts strict land use control and plans target management for the purpose of food security and social stability. The management not only focuses on farmers and collectives but also local governments, which results in the most obvious contradiction and conflict in land plan target management between local governments and the central government. However, the central government cannot manage the land by itself but has to depend on local governments, so that it should be careful of local government's hope for local development. Moreover, because the most relevant knowledge about land is typically local knowledge, the central government is at an absolute disadvantage in information. Therefore, the central government's objectives for land protection amount to nothing in the game.

On the other hand, the conflicts between local governments and farmers focus on land expropriation. Under the current tax system, local governments certainly will lower the land expropriation compensation as much as possible to develop the economy and deal with the problem of inadequate construction capital, while due to the advantage given by regulations to original residents, farmers will increase the land expropriation compensation as much as possible. Because of bundled transaction in many areas where parts of land are adjacent to each other, the land will be sold at the highest price, and the charges by farmers will be higher and higher, especially after they receive a signal of land protection from the central government. Thus, local governments will get into trouble under the pressures from both sides. For this reason, the scheme comes into being of the overall development of urban and rural areas by local governments as a disguised form of land expropriation.

In short, current systems and policies cannot actually protect farmland but are in effect moving in the opposite direction. It is thus essential to establish a mechanism where different interests are compatible so that all players, especially farmers and village collectives, will have incentives to protect their own farmlands. In a sense, all valuable things in the world should be treasured and protected. A failure to do so is normally due to two reasons. One is market imperfection where precious things are undervalued by the market. The other is due to unclear property rights such that owners actually cannot form rational expectations as to the values of properties they own like that of the public goods. Under the current land system, two problems above all exist in farmland protection. Since the farmland protection is an important national policy, the farmland will accordingly have the attributes of public goods, and the state should be responsible and pay the bill. Meanwhile, modern property rights theory demonstrates that the abuse and waste of resources is inevitable when the private value is smaller than the social value. Thus, an effective way is to increase the benefit of farmland to farmers as an incentive and make it equal to social benefit. Specifically, it is to increase the comparative gains from the land for agricultural use, to make the income from grain production in the basic farmland protection zone not lower than the average income of the province or even the state, and to let local governments have their own sources of revenue and not obtain income through land expropriation or disguised land expropriation. The detailed measures are as follows:

The first measure is to establish a mechanism where the responsibility of protecting farmland is divided between central and local governments. The central government can designate special zones and draw the red-line boundary to establish some national basic farmland protection zones in those granary provinces such as Heilongjiang, Jilin, Inner Mongolia, Henan, Shandong and Hubei, which will be directly managed by the central government with the assistance of local governments. Through the price subsidy, the price of grain from the national basic farmland protection zones will increase, which will certainly result in the rise of grain prices in the whole grain market, so that the comparative interest of land for agricultural use will increase. The land will be more valuable, and farmers will naturally cherish their lands. For large agriculture counties, the provincial governments will be responsible for agriculture and farmland management. The current system, in which all counties are managed by the municipal governments such that they actually provide the systemic conditions for urban governments' occupation of farmland, will be changed. In other words, urban governments' management of farmland will mainly focus on food supply for urban citizens while protecting basic farmland will be the responsibility of county authorities.

The second measure is to upgrade the ranking of county government in the basic farmland protection zone, to give the prefecture-level rank and treatment to large agriculture counties, to make officials concretely fulfill their basic farmland protection responsibility, and to take the grain output as an indicator for performance appraisal for officials from large agriculture counties. Besides, it should implement the decision about agriculture management formed in the Third Plenary Session of the 17th Central Committee, namely that, the first secretary of provinces and counties in the basic farmland protection zone should be responsible for agriculture management while provincial or county heads are actually in charge. In other words, the responsibility between the political party and the civil services should be separated.

The third measure is to establish the basic farmland protection fund and food security risk fund. Certainly, food security assurance and basic farmland protection are both national strategic targets and the responsibilities of the governments at all levels and the entire nation, which should be jointly undertaken by the central government, all local governments and all the people, as well as developed areas and cities — not merely those grain farmers and grain-producing areas. For this reason, the responsibilities and benefits for basic farmland assurance should be specified according to the principle of cost distribution and benefit sharing. That is to say that cities and developed areas should take the responsibility for basic farmland protection as well. To do so, the first is to determine the amount of basic farmland required to be protected that will be done according to the size of population (including foreign population with more than half a year of permanent resistance), and the second is to determine the cost required for basic farmland protection that will be carried out in accordance with the difference between the amount of basic farmland requested for protection and the amount that they actually owned, and also the degree of economic development (e.g., per capita GDP). Based on that, a protection fund and a food security risk fund can be established. Generally, the former can provide farmers with incentives for farmland protection, while the latter can offer incentives for grain production.

7.4. Reform fiscal and tax system, eliminate the revenue source from land financing

As for the land problem, one of the primary causes for the failed implementation of basic farmland protection policy and the conflicts in collective construction of land between local governments and farmers or collectives is the defect of the current fiscal and tax system, in which local governments have too many responsibilities but too little fiscal power, namely, local governments take too many economic responsibilities but are lacking an independent revenue source and cannot collect funds independently to maintain public functions. Thus, the solution is to reform the current fiscal and tax system, which not only reduces economic burden of local governments, but also can ensure an independent source of income for local governments. The most important is to establish the land property tax system in which all revenues will be retained in local governments, so that the current pattern of relying on land financing can be completely changed.

Land tax includes land occupation tax, ownership tax and transaction tax. Among them, land occupation tax is a tax collected from the farmland changing into non-agricultural land, which includes farmland occupation tax, farmland reclamation fees and the land use fee for new construction, and aims to protect farmland. Land ownership tax is a tax imposed on the owner of construction land, which is determined by the tax department in accordance with the appreciation of land compared with the land price in a certain area at certain time that is published by the neutral land appraisal organization based on the non-renewable property of land and inevitable appreciation caused by economic development. Land transaction tax is a tax imposed on transactions of construction land, which can not only make local governments obtain stable tax, but also is favorable for the optimal use of land. It is estimated that land property tax will not reduce but increase the financial income of local governments (Macroeconomic Group of China Center for Economic Research in Peking University, 2006), so local governments have an incentive to collect the tax.

7.5. Implement the permanent status in farmers' land contract rights and ensure farmers' rights in land ownership, use and future gains

The Third Plenary Session ensures permanent stability and full implementation of farmers' relevant rights, which makes farmers' consciousness of their rights stronger and clearer. Therefore, the government should take some policy and legal measures in response. Specifically, we provide the following suggestions: (i) Specify the time point (or starting point) of members' rights. As the contractual relation has become permanent, the farmers in collective economic organizations will compare with each other the time points when they got their members' rights. Therefore, it is suggested that agricultural authorities should issue measures for defining the members' rights of rural collective economic organizations; (ii) Specify the main body and boundary of the ownership, set up registration and issue the license. Considering that 90% of rural lands are owned by production teams, the ownership boundary and functions are always defined "based on the production team." Thus it is suggested to specify the natural village as the owner of collective land and carry out an experiment for land registration and certification based on the four boundaries, land area, ownership situation and members of natural villages; and (iii) Carry out an experiment in rural land registration and certification based on land block rather than farmer household.

7.6. Deepen the marketization reform of rural collective construction land and establish urban–rural land market

If the basic farmland is protected, the trading and transfer of rural collective construction land will become easy. Fundamentally, the house can be independently developed by farmers and village community enterprises, or cooperatively developed by farmers, collectives and external enterprises, or through the overall planning of urban and rural development by the local governments, but it should not be carried out through land expropriation, disguised land expropriation or land nationalization. Conversely, it should be carried out through land capitalization to make the capitalized construction land become the asset and common fund for farmers and village community, so that farmers can enjoy the land rent permanently and share the benefits from land appreciation. The detailed suggestions are as follows:

I. Establish Urban–Rural Construction Land Market and set up rules for Collective Construction Land Transaction

(I) Under the precondition that land use meets the requirement of planning, collective construction land should be allowed to be rented, sold, transferred and mortgaged; (II) Carry out pilot projects in the collective construction land market; (III) Carry out pilot projects for collective construction land index trading between areas within the province; (IV) Implement a selling system for collective construction land that is the same as the national construction land, including the transaction by agreement or by bidding, auction and listing; and (V) Grant certificates for land use rights and ownership rights to the land and properties lawfully entering the collective construction land market.

II. Establish Strict rules for Rural Construction Land and Carry out a Pilot Program for efficient use in Collective Construction Land

(I) All idle collective construction land, waste common land and land from village renovation and old village transformation should be consolidated as farmland; (II) The newly established construction land index can be traded between different areas; (III) The newly designated construction land should remain the property of collective ownership and be used by farmers; (IV) The pilot program should be carried out in the closed area.

III. Implement the Principles of Same Price and Rights for the Same Collective Land and National Land, and Implement Policies concerning the collectively owned construction land used for Non-agricultural purposes.

(I) When expropriating farmers' collective land within the urban planning range, the government should reserve some construction land at a proper proportion for those expropriated villages, which can be utilized by collective economic organizations to construct standard factories, shop fronts and other facilities for renting, and all rental incomes should be distributed to villagers in the form of shares. Meanwhile, those retained lands that may affect urban planning can be traded through bidding, auction and listing, and the net land income should be mainly returned to village collectives. Besides, the departments of land and resources should issue some special policies to specify the proportion, nature of ownership, way of use and principle of income distribution concerning retained lands; (II) Those stock collective construction lands within the range of urban planning can be owned by rural collectives, should be used by farmers, or become state-owned and be used by farmers for a long time, under the precondition that the planning is satisfied; (III) Rural collective lands beyond the range of urban construction that are used for non-agricultural construction can be partly distributed to collectives under certain use regulation and planning conditions; (IV) Historical problem of collective construction land should be practically solved and sorted in a case by case manner.

IV. Issue Measures for Differential Income Distribution of any Gains from Rural Collective Construction Land

(I) Specify farmer collectives as the major gainer of differential income of land, and farmer collectives have the right to obtain the differential income from the renting and trading of homestead and collective construction land; (II) Allow the enterprise and farmer collectives to develop the collective construction land in the form of joint stock and cooperative development, but the enterprise only can obtain the profit from property sale and industrial investment. Meanwhile, a certain proportion of properties should be given to farmer collectives for renting, and the permanent income can be used for common investment and villagers' welfare; (III) Establish measures for the management of differential income of collective construction land, which is mainly to ensure farmers' land rights and interests; (IV) Carry out a pilot program to let local governments collect collective construction of land tax in accordance with relevant tax laws on the ownership, use and benefit of national construction land.

V. Management of Existing Sub-Right Houses

    (I) Collect land use fees from purchasers as one source of income for collective common funds; (II) The state should collect corresponding taxes from collectives and rural constructors and give them to local governments.

8. Revision of Related Laws

  I. The Standing Committee of the National People's Congress should issue an announcement to declare the equal price and right for the same land regardless of ownership, and specify that all of it can be traded and transferred in the market. Meanwhile, it should specify that farmers' houses are private property and the individual has the full rights to deal with them.

  II. Revise the Article 63 in the *Land Management Law* from "The use right of all rural collective lands cannot be sold, transferred or rented for non-agricultural construction" to "Rural collective construction land can be sold, transferred, rented or pledged".

  III. Revise Article 153 of the *Property Law* as "Allow rural construction land to be freely transferred and traded, and farmers have the real right for usufruct."

  IV. Abolish relevant laws and regulations that restrain the transfer of collective construction land.

  V. Establish relevant laws and regulations concerning the transfer of rural homestead.

Bibliography

The *Decision on Several Major Problems on the Promotion of Rural Reform and Development*, approved by the Central Committee of the Communist Party of China in the 3rd plenary session on October 12, 2008.

Constitution of the People's Republic of China, approved by the National People's Congress in the 2nd meeting on March 14, 2004.

Gao Shengping, Liu Shouying, 2007, Research on Initial Obtaining System of Use Right of Homestead — Comment Related Rules in Chapter 13 of *Property Law*, *China Land Science* (Volume 2), 2007.

Land Management Law of the People's Republic of China, revised by the 9th Standing Committee of the National People's Congress in the 5th meeting on August 29, 1998.

Macroeconomic Group of China Center for Economic Research from Peking University (2006), Property Tax Reform and Local Public Finance, *Economic Research*, Volume 3.

Marx, *Das Kapital* (Volume 1), People's Publishing House, 1963.

Property Law of the People's Republic of China, approved by the 10th Standing Committee of the National People's Congress in the 5th meeting on March 16, 2007.

Research group about *China Land Problem* from Beijing Unirule Institute of Economics, Implementation and Protection of Land Property Right under the Background of Urbanization, *Management World*, Volume 12, 2007.

Research group about the transition of Beijing village system (written by LIU Shouying *et al.*), 2008, Research on the Phenomenon of Zhenggezhuang — A City on Collective Land (printed edition).

Research group of Beijing rural research center, 2008, Perfect Rural Homestead System and Advance Land Registration and Certification-Research Report on the Policy for Beijing Homestead Registration (printed edition).

Sub-right House: Final Madness, CCTV.com, October 29, 2008.

Zhang Shuguang, Secret of Urban Village Transformation, *Scientific Decision*, Volume 3, 2008.

Chapter 3

Land Transfer and Agricultural Modernization[*,†]

This research provides a detailed account on the evolution of the policies concerning land transfer and large-scale production, and sums up the phasic idiosyncrasies and regional differentials in such operations. Six cases in Tongzhou District of Beijing, Ningyang County of Shandong Province, Pixian Country and Chongzhou City of Chengdu City are analyzed, revealing the fact that the land transfer and the subsequent scale of operation are the basis or the premise for agricultural modernization, as well as

---

[*]The report is organized by Beijing Unirule Institute of Economics, mainly written by Zhang Shuguang, followed by Liu Shaoying, Zhang Chi, *et al.* Zhang Shuguang has given a speech on the topic in the 406th biweekly forum of the Unirule Institute of Economics and in the seminars held in Zhongshan University and South China Agricultural University. Besides that other scholars such as Li Guoxiang, Tan Shuhao, Liao Hongle, Zhao Nong, Sheng Hong *et al.* have given wonderful discussions. The research is funded by German Foundation, Boyuan Foundation and the *Research on the Existing Rural Land Transfer System and Peasant Right Protection*, a significant research topic of social science organized by the Ministry of Education. The investigation has also obtained substantial support and help from relevant departments of Tongzhou District of Beijing, Ningyang County of Shandong Province, Chengdu City, Pixian Country and Chongzhou City. We thank all of the above here. The author takes sole responsibility for his views.
[†]Originally published in *Management World*, the 7th edition in 2010.

the source of significant changes in rural areas. The research also conducts a comparative analysis on the exiting methods of land transfer, illustrating the essential distinction between quota transaction and land transfer. Finally, it discusses the role of government and rural finance in the process, and presents related policy recommendations.

1. Introduction

China is still a country mainly composed of rural population. With the rapid industrialization and urbanization, the rural population has constantly decreased, causing a series of significant social and economic transitions. The most important of them is a shift in the relationship between rural population and land, the fundamental structural change in rural areas.

Against the background of urbanization and based on the current institutional conditions, farmer households can be divided into three types in accordance with their relation to land or attitude toward land. The first type consists of those rural migrant workers in the city, especially 20-to-30-year-old youths. They are unwilling or unable to return to the village, but at the same time they still occupy contracted land. So the question is what institutional arrangement can make them completely leave their hometown and fully integrate into urban life. The second type consists of farmers that live in suburb areas. With the progress of urbanization, land in suburban areas is appreciating fast, and this land will necessarily be occupied in the process of urbanization. Therefore, the conflict between these farmers, the government and developers on the benefit from the rapid land appreciation has now reached a white-hot state. If they can fairly share the benefit from land appreciation, the lands in suburban areas will be smoothly utilized for urban construction, and problems such as the urbanization of rural populations and sub-right housing in suburban areas will be properly solved. The third type of farmer households consist of farmers who live in the traditional agricultural areas and are far from the radiant areas of urbanization, especially the farmers growing grain that are unable and unwilling to abandon their land to come to the city and become workers. But they can only obtain a small income from grain growing and cannot feel comfortable. So for these farmers, great efforts should be made to solve the problem of comparative earnings from agricultural production and the development prospects of agricultural industry. Consequently, to solve the land problem and promote urbanization, it is actually required to address the needs of these three types of farmers, and to this end we need a general solution and framework for action.

In order to solve the problem, we have conducted some investigations and research since 2006, and we have completed two research reports, namely the *Implementation and Protection of Land Property Right under the Background of Urbanization*, and the *Implementation and Protection of Property Right of Rural Construction Land-Involving the Problem of Sub-Right House*. This paper is the third in the research results and is mainly to answer the questions of how to carry out land transaction and scale management in rural areas; which practices are successful or logically rational in both theory and practice; which practices have problems and how to solve them; and what other problems should be solved during further development.

2. Evolution and Characteristics of Policies over Land Transfer and Large-Scale Management

2.1. Evolution of policies of land transfer and large-scale management

The rural household contract responsibility system emerged in the late 1970s and early 1980s and was first carried out secretly in poverty-stricken areas. Among the most famous is Xiaogang Village in Fengyang County of Anhui Province, which was protected and supported by local officials. After debate and discussion at the Central Working Conference in 1981, the system was approved by the No. 1 document for rural work issued by the Central Committee of the CPC, and thus came to light and was legitimized across the whole country. After two years of vigorous promotion, the policy was implemented throughout the whole country in 1984, and the household contract responsibility system was implemented for 99% of production teams and 96.6% of households by the end of that year.

With the implementation of the household contract responsibility system, farmers' spontaneous land transaction began to emerge. In 1984, the Central Committee of the CPC issued the third No. 1 document for rural work, specifying that "before extending the contract period, the collective can uniformly adjust the land allocation at the request of farmers after adequate negotiations by following the principle of major stability with minor adjustment," and that "the gradual concentration of land to those skilled farmers shall be encouraged, and within the contract period, the commune member who is unable cultivate or requests to contract no or a small amount of land due to business variation, can return the land to the collective or transfer the land to others." In 1986, the fifth No. 1 document for rural work clearly suggested developing moderate scale management and specified that "with the shift of farmers to non-agricultural industries, it is encouraged to distribute more farmland to skilled farmers and to develop specialized households at a certain scale."

Since the mid-1980s, township enterprises have grown in developed areas and suburban areas of large cities and have rapidly spread. However, in these areas, a large proportion of rural labor forces have shifted to non-agricultural industries but still live in their hometowns, which results in the disjunction between land occupation and utilization. That is, some households do not want to grow crops and are unwilling to lose their land, while other households want to grow more crops but cannot obtain land. Meanwhile, in 1987, the Political Bureau of the Central Committee issued a document about the advance of rural reform, specifying that "one or two counties in suburban areas of Beijing, Tianjin and Shanghai, Southern Jiangsu Province and the Pearl River Delta can be selected to develop home farms or cooperative farms of a certain scale or organize other forms of specialized contracting, in order to explore the experience of intensive land management." For this reason, the State Council decided to establish pilot sites for rural reform to moderate scale management in Suzhou, Wuxi and Changzhou of Jiangsu Province, Shunyi District of Beijing and Nanhai of Guangdong, and to carry out the Two Cropland Tillage System experiment in Pingdu City of Shandong Province. The documents issued by the Central Committee and the State Council in this stage also proposed that "based on the stability and improvement of the household contract responsibility system, moderate scale management can be conducted in rural areas of developed regions and the suburbs of large cities".

Since the 1990s, discussions on the defects of the household contract responsibility system and the proposals to promote the scale management of the collective economy have heated up. Meanwhile, the collectives in some areas began to reduce or reclaim farmers' contracted land in the name of more land reservation, the development of Two Cropland Tillage System and the structural adjustment of agriculture. While correcting these deviations, the central government has always adhered to policies to promote land transaction and develop moderate scale management. In November 1993, the Central Committee of the CPC and the State Council issued the *Several Policies on Current Agricultural and Rural Economic Development*, clearly specifying that the household contract responsibility system and the dual management system based on the combination of centralization and decentralization in operation are a basic rural system of China and should be insisted on for a long time and continuously improved; and in order to stabilize the land contract relationships and encourage farmers to increase agricultural input, original contract periods would be extended by 30 years after expiration. The document also advocated the policy of "Do not increase farmland when population grows and do not reduce farmland when population decreases." Meanwhile, the document further pointed out that on the premise that the collective ownership and the use of land are ensured, the land use rights can be transferred with compensation with the agreement of the contract-issuing party. Besides, according to the actual situation and farmers' desire, some necessary adjustments and moderate scale management can be carried out in a few areas where the second and third industries are developed and most labor forces have shifted to non-agricultural industry. At that time, the moderate scale management can be achieved by village-based farmland operation, or by large households through the Two Cropland Tillage System, or through the free transfer of land use right.

The *Decision on Several Problems to Establish a Socialist Market Economy System* approved by the Third Plenary Session of the 14th CPC Central Committee proposed that on the premise that the collective land ownership is insisted upon, the land contract period can be extended, and that the government admits the contractual management right for developmental production projects to be inherited, allows the land use rights to be transferred with compensation, and allows a few developed areas to develop moderate scale management by way of subcontracting, shares, etc. in accordance with the principle of farmers' willingness.

In order to prevent local governments and collective organizations from depriving the farmers of their contractual management right in the name of Two Cropland Tillage System and scale management, the State Council endorsed the *Notice on Proposal to Stabilize and Perfect Land Contract Relation by the Ministry of Agriculture* in March 1995, clearly specifying that when conducting land adjustment, the government shall strictly prohibit relevant parties from changing land ownership or changing the land owned by the collective economic organizations into village-owned land, and strictly prohibits the contract-issuing party to retain excessive reserved land in the name of land adjustment. The notice required that the reserved land is not necessary in principle. If need be, it should not exceed 5% of total farmland area. The notice also required establishing a transfer mechanism for land contractual management rights and allowed contractors to legally subcontract, transfer, exchange and securitize on contracted land within the contract period under the agreement of the outsourcer and on the premise that the collective land ownership is insisted upon and the agricultural use of land is not changed. Considering the symptom of overhasty development of moderate scale management in some areas, the central leadership clearly proposed that it is a long-term process for the transition to land moderate scale management through land use rights transfer. In 1997, the central government's documents proposed that the policy of major stabilization and minor adjustment can only be adopted as required and the minor adjustment is only suitable for a few households with a clear dilemma between household business and land cultivation, but not for all households, and that it is definitely not allowed to use administrative orders to adjust the land contract relation in the whole village every few years. Meanwhile, the central government did not advocate the Two Cropland Tillage System and required that reserved land should be strictly controlled. Meanwhile the central leadership pointed out in the central rural work conference that the land contract relationship should be stabilized and the land transaction is admitted and should be based on farmer's free-will, and the development of moderate scale management should be based on the principle of mature conditions, moderation, diversity, guidance and service. In August of the same year, there were problems occurring in a few areas, such as the land contract period being extended after the deadline of the first round and some local governments changing the land contract relationship at will in different names and forcibly reclaiming or partly reclaiming farmers' contracted land. Furthermore, some local governments forcibly promoted land scale management against the will of farmers. So the central government proposed some guiding opinions to further stabilize and improve the rural land contract relationship. The opinions required carefully rectifying the Two Cropland Tillage System, clearly stating that the System should not be advocated and required strict control and management on the reserved land for unforeseen use.

In 2001, the central government issued the No. 18 document *Regulation for the Transfer of Land Contractual Management Right*, proposing stricter regulations on the principle of land transaction, as well as the main contracting body. It clearly specified that farmers are the main body of rural land transaction, and that land transactions should be carried out according to farmers' will and the law with compensation. The Two Cropland Tillage System should not be adopted. The document also proposed strict limitation on the proportion of land reserved by rural collectives for unforeseen use and discouraged enterprise's large-scale land contracting in rural areas for the prevention of the enterprise's land enclosure in rural areas. In 2002, the *Rural Land Contract Law* was issued, which insisted upon all regulations on land transaction above and clearly specified that the land contractual management right obtained by household contracts can be legally transferred by way of subcontracting, renting, exchange, transfer, etc. The transfer of land contractual management rights should be carried out in accordance with the principles of equal consultation, willingness and with compensation. No organization or individual should force or block the contractor from transferring the land contractual management right. The law stressed that the contractor is the owner of the transfer of contractual land management rights and has the right to determine whether and how the contractual land management rights will be transferred.

In January 2005, the Ministry of Agriculture issued the *Measures for the Management of Rural Land Contractual Management Rights Transfer*, giving some operative regulations on the transfer principle, party right, transfer method, transfer contract, transfer management, etc. for rural land contractual management rights. After that, the transfer of rural land contractual management rights became normative and legal.

In 2008, the Third Plenary Session of the Seventeenth CPC Central Committee approved the *Decision on Several Major Problems to Improve Rural Reform and Development*, giving more systemic specification on the transfer market of land contract rights. The decision continued to insist upon the principles pursuant to the law, willingness and compensation, to allow farmers to transfer the land contractual management right by way of subcontracting, renting, exchange, transfer and stock cooperation etc., and to allow developing moderate scale management in several forms. Meanwhile, it proposed strengthening the management and service for the transfer of land contractual management rights, to establish and perfect the transfer market of land contractual management rights, and to develop some scale management in those conditional areas, such as specialized large households, family farms and farmer specialized cooperatives. Besides that it stressed that the transfer of land contractual management rights should follow the principle of "Three Prohibitions," namely the prohibitions against changing the collective ownership of land, changing the use of land or harming farmers' land contract rights and interests.

It can be seen from all above statements that, over the past 20 to 30 years, the policies on contractual management rights transfer and land scale management have been continuously improved and specified with the advance of rural reform and the adjustment of agricultural structure, which not only stress the stability and protection of farmland contractual management right in most of areas, but also take into consideration the actual demands of rural labor mobility and transfer and the promotion of moderate scale management of land in some areas, and have provided the policy standard for land scale management and agricultural modernization under the change of agricultural structure. Consequently, all policies are generated from practices and are full of the wisdom and creativity of grass-roots cadres and farmers.

2.2. *Phasic characteristics and regional difference of land transfer and scale management*

A policy is always used to standardize and guide practice, and its evolution is not only the indication but also the requirement of practice. Thus, from the view of the correlation between theory and reality or policy and practice, the evolution of land transaction and scale management policies and the development of corresponding practices have undergone three stages and shown the following characteristics.

The first stage was a spontaneous implementation stage that occurred in the mid-to-late 1980s. At that time, land transaction mainly occurred in coastal developed areas and suburban areas of large cities. With the increase of grain production, the problem of food and clothing had been basically resolved, and township enterprises in developed areas and suburban areas of cities provided conditions in both supply and demand for land transactions. Meanwhile, with the development of township enterprises, most rural labor forces in these areas became workers of township enterprises, but due to the national grain ordering task, the village collective still undertook the task from the state, so that the village collective began to concentrate farmers' contracted land and developed scale management with certain subsidies, namely that, the village collective concentrated above 80% of the land in the village and contracted it to several large households. Each large household could have about 50–100 *mu* (33,333 to 66,667 m^2) of land for cultivation. At this stage, the village collectively provided the land to large households without land rent. It collected little or no service charges for agricultural machinery and agricultural technology, and provided a certain amount of subsidies for means of production, while the larger households completed the state's grain delivering task for the village collective. The land transaction at this stage had the following characteristics: Due to the fact that farmer households took land contracts as a burden and were more than happy to shed them, the village collective subsequently reduced its cost in land collection and became the main player in land concentration and transfer; and most households for scale management depended on subsidies. Due to the existence of the grain delivery task, the government and collective had strong administrative intervention in land management rights transfer, and the scale and range of land transactions were generally confined to collective organizations.

The second stage was an exploratory stage. It started from 1987 when some pilot reform areas were established in Suzhou, Wuxi and Changzhou in Jiangsu, Nanhai of Guangdong and Shunyi District of Beijing for the development of moderate scale management, and ended at the beginning of the century when the tax reform was implemented in rural areas and the No. 18 document and the *Land Contract Law* were issued and put into effect. At this stage, the general scale of land transaction was still not large. According to the sample survey by the Ministry of Agriculture, in 1992, there were 4.733 million farmer households that subcontracted and transferred 774,000 hectares of farmland in 1992, which accounted for 2.3% and 0.9% of total contracted farmer households and total contracted land areas respectively. Meanwhile, the results of a sample survey on 30,000 farmer households by the research center of the Ministry of Agriculture indicated that 4.09% of farmer households subcontracted parts of their contracted lands, 1.99% of them subcontracted all of the lands, and 10.68% of them subcontracted others' farmland.

Compared with that in the first stage, the land transaction in this stage was not only continuously popularized in developed areas, but also was implemented in some villages of central and western regions. However, the land transaction at this stage had obvious regional characteristics and there was a large difference between central and western grain-producing areas and the areas with many exported labor forces and suburban areas of coastal or large cities. In the traditional farming areas, on one hand, the land burden became more and more serious due to the implementation of the policy of "Three Withdraws and Five Collections," which resulted in excessively high tax, negative net earnings and a great reduction of farmer's incentives in farming. On the other hand, a large number of township enterprises in rural areas of non-coastal regions went bankrupt and the business model of working in the hometown was difficult to continue, so numerous surplus rural laborers went to work in enterprises in the Pearl River Delta, Yangtze River Delta and other large cities. As a result, large quantities of lands were abandoned, and even in some central farming areas, over 30% of the land was abandoned. At this stage, the land transactions in these areas were diversified by type. The first type was farmers' spontaneous transfer in which the lessor's contracts were leased without any rent, but the lessee shouldered most or all of the land burden. In the second type, the village collective reclaimed these abandoned lands (without the agreement of the original contractor in most cases) and then subcontracted them to other contractors and the lessee would directly pay rent to the village collective. However, even the central government had issued repeated orders to prohibit the Two Cropland Tillage System and subcontracting, but both of them were still common in these areas. Actually, the Two Cropland Tillage System had become the most common pattern since 1986, and by 1992, a total of 1.7 million village groups adopted the Two Cropland Tillage System, accounting for 32.3% of total village communities and increasing by 42.6% since 1990. A total of 39.597 million hectares of land was covered by the Two Cropland Tillage System, increasing by 7.3% from 1990.

Meanwhile, in coastal areas and suburban areas of large cities, the land revenue had greatly increased due to high-speed industrialization and urbanization, and large areas of lands were utilized for industrial and urban construction. Farmers and collectives also utilized their own lands to build factories or houses for renting. The farmland area, agriculture production value and employment share had also greatly decreased, and thus agriculture had become a subsidiary business. The remaining farmlands were generally contracted by farmers or village collective to foreigners, which resulted in the gradual formation of scale management households who mainly grew commercial crops with high value and the crops that could serve the city. The central government made it clear for the first time in 1987 that the intensive land management could be explored in a planned way in those areas with conditions, but the progress of land moderate scale management was still slow until 1991. Since 1992, the land transaction and moderate scale management have obviously been accelerated, especially in the coastal areas. In 1993, there were 2,816 scale management units with above 1 hectare of land for per laborer in Wuxi County, Changshu City and Wuxian County, with a total management area of 15,000 hectares, and the proportion of the land under scale management in the total contracted land increased from 1.1% in 1988 to 22.4%.

According to the practices in this stage, related departments formulated some guidance documents on land transaction, and the National People's Congress approved the *Land Contract Law* in 2002. Faced with the phenomenon of land scale management, the government's policies not only continued to reaffirm support on moderate scale management of land, but also enhanced rules on farmer's contracting rights so that farmers' interests would be protected during the land transaction, which aimed at ensuring the stability of the land contract relation, the prosperity of rural areas and the stability of the whole society.

The third stage of land transaction evolution was a stage for standardization and development, emerging in many rural areas since the beginning of this century. The event in the stage that caused the largest effect on land transaction was the advance of rural tax reform, especially the removal of agricultural taxes in 2003. After that, the contracted households no longer needed to pay agricultural tax, but more importantly, the charges by both county and township governments became baseless, and the institutional conditions and cost structure for farming were greatly changed. Owing to the land burden removal and the direct subsidy generated from preferential policies for farmers, those who abandoned their land before thinking that farming was profitable returned to the village to reclaim their contracted land. At this stage, the land transaction showed different characteristics in different areas. For example, in most traditional farming areas, the farmland transaction still depended on the spontaneous transfer between farmers, but it was different with the previous stage in that, in addition to a farming subsidy, the lessor could also collect some rent from the lessee. Meanwhile, some cooperative economic organizations founded by capable farmers emerged. Another important phenomenon at this stage was that in the farming areas with large labor force outflow, coastal developed rural areas and suburban areas of large cities, a large number of agriculture-related enterprises come to rural areas to contract large tracts of land, ranging from tens to hundreds of hectares. These enterprises obtained the land mainly in two ways. In the first way they signed the land transaction contract with each household, but in most cases the land was obtained in the second way which the village collective organizations played an important role. Some of the organizations provided the platform of land information as the bridge between farmers and enterprises and collected some agency fees, while most of them first concentrated the lands originally contracted to farmers through administrative power and then signed the land transaction contract with the enterprises. These enterprises generally delivered the rent to the village collective that would distribute part of the rent to each contracted household and the rest for public facilities.

All cases in the next section are basically stories that occurred in this stage.

3. Cases on Land Transfer and Scale Management

3.1. Case in Tongzhou District of Beijing[1]

3.1.1. Land transfer and scale management in Qianfu Village of Yujiawu Town

Yujiawu Town is located in the south of Tongzhou District, 19 km from the new town of Tongzhou. It consists of 23 administrative villages and is the only town with ethnic minorities in Tongzhou District (i.e., Hui) and also a traditionally large agriculture town. The town has abundant land resources with a total area of 65.7 km², implemented the land registration and certification in 2004, has registered a total of 54,718 mu (36,478,667 m²) of land and 23,913 people (per capita land area reaches 2.29 mu (1527 m²), and has signed contracts of operation right and usufruct and issued 8793 certificates of operation right and usufruct. As of September 2009, the total area of transferred land reached 11,699 mu (7,779,333 m²), accounting for 21.4% of total registration area.

After 2002, land transaction began to emerge in Yujiawu Town. In 2007, with the development of urban agricultural projects such as a pumpkin-themed agricultural park and a Taiwan boutique tourist park on the southern bank of Fenggang Alkali River, and the implementation of comprehensive treatment projects for agricultural rivers and roads, the scale land transaction and modernized agricultural management had started. At the beginning of 2009, Qianfu Village cooperated with Shennonghegu Rice Fragrance Agriculture Development Ltd. and transferred 2,000 mu (1,333,333 m²) of land at a time, in which the Shennonghegu Company would plant sweet sorghum with aerospace breeding and would consider establishing the land transaction service center. Thus, the land transaction and agricultural modernization have been expanded.

Qianfu Village has a total area of 1.08 sq. kms, including 2,000 mu (1,333,333 m²) of farmland. It has 207 farmer households and 481

---

[1]Zhang Shuguang and Liu Shouying conducted a field investigation on August 26, 2009.

villagers, of which 417 are agricultural population. Before the scale land transaction, the village mainly planted corn, wheat and vegetables. In 2008, the total grain output reached 1.35 million kilograms, the net return of per *mu* (667 m²) of land reached RMB 600 Yuan (including the direct grain subsidy), the total income was RMB 1.2 million Yuan, with the per capita net agricultural income less than RMB 3,000 Yuan. The village had a debt of RMB 867,000 Yuan, and only RMB 10,000 Yuan left in its account. At that time, the village had a weak economic foundation, bad relationship between the villagers and cadres and was divided in villager's opinions. So administrative affairs of the village were difficult to carry out. Thus, the construction experience of Pumpkin Park indicates that farmers can be enriched through land transaction and the develop ment of facility, ecological tourism and high-efficiency agriculture.

The organizations at township and village levels had established a 5-person working group for land transactions before the investment invitation and related farmland transaction contracts were finally signed after three months of hard work, since which the large-scale agricultural planting and management have been formed. However, at the beginning, farmers had some concerns about land transaction, the first of which being that the contract would not be permanent. They also felt uneasy making any deals with large enterprises and were afraid that the contracted enterprises would not focus on farming and quit if they could not make money from country-side hotels and growing fields which destroyed the land. The second concern was how to coordinate with those farmers who were reluctant to lose all lands and the third was how to deal with the purchased chemical fertilizers, pesticides and seeds. The fourth was that farmers worried the village collective would underpay rent through subcontracting. Not only that, farmers were unwilling to communicate with the enterprises for fear of lacking any guarantee, while the enterprises were also unwilling to directly communicate with farmers because the direct communication would be troublesome and would cause problems that were potentially unsolvable.

For this reason, cadres at township and village levels asked for each household's opinion and proposed that the purchased chemical fertilizers, pesticides and seeds could be returned as far as possible or could be transferred to relatives if they couldn't be returned. Meanwhile, those farmers who wanted to farm could keep some of their land, and the land within the transfer range could be exchanged and adjusted. Furthermore, all land transferred to the enterprise could only be utilized for agriculture but not for turf planting, so that the land could continue to be used for farming if the enterprise quit. While the subcontracting violated the principle of willingness, the existing land transaction was completely voluntary. Besides, in order to relieve the worry of farmers, the land transaction working group fully utilized the rural land transaction platform and network of Tongzhou District, issued the land transaction and investment invitation information to the community, and actively mobilized social resources to introduce the land transaction project. Through repeated selections, the village selected Shennonghegu Rice Fragrance Agriculture Development Ltd. as the cooperation object. Before signing the contract, the minister of organization of the town's party committee, the deputy township head in charge of agriculture, the branch secretary and related members of the working group conducted a field investigation on the target company and received the Feasibility Study Report on Biological Energy Source R&D and Planting Base compiled by the company. All investigators agreed that the company's qualifications, capital, strength and scale complied with the cooperative conditions. In the first negotiation, the rent for per *mu* (667 m^2) of land was suggested by the company to be RMB 700 Yuan, which was agreed to by 50% of the households, and in the second negotiation, the rent was increased to RMB 800 Yuan, which was agreed to by 70% of households, and a progressive increase was arranged. Considering that farmers can make money without capital input, risk and concerns, and that most youths go out for work leaving only 40-to-60-year-old villagers to do farm work, all households finally agreed to land transaction.

In order to solve the difficulty in direct communication between the company and households, all land transaction contracts were signed between the village collective and the company or the household. On June 4, all villager representatives and party members signed the Land Transfer Agency Contract with the village committee and the party branch respectively. After that, the village collective signed the contract with each household, and finally the village committee singed the contract agreement with the company. According to the agreement, all land would be transferred to Shennonghegu Company at one time, with a total area of 2,000 *mu* (1,333,33 m^2), a period of 18 years, an expense of RMB 1,000

Yuan/*mu* (667 m²), including RMB 800 Yuan/*mu* (667 m²) rent for each household and a RMB 200 Yuan/*mu* (667 m²) service fee for agricultural facility. The contract was signed with the participation of the Economic Management Station of the town and under the supervision of the law office and notarization organization.

The complete transfer of land has also solved some historical problems. It created an increase of over 100 *mu* (66,667 m²) of farmland through land consolidation, and the land income for over 50 households (with no contracted farmland) who obtained the usufruct in 2004 obtained a subsidy of RMB 130 Yuan per capita paid at one time.

The management pattern after the complete land transaction is as follows: The company entrusts the village committee to be responsible for field management, the village committee will organize all agricultural machines and labor forces to participate in all steps of field operation, including seeding, weeding, watering, fertilizing, and harvesting, while villagers can work in their originally contracted lands and obtain wages from the company. Thus, the management pattern cannot only reduce its production cost and save the management expenses, house rent and traffic expense, but also can increase villagers' income. Both parties can gain profit. Given that the sweet sorghum has a growing period of 100 days and can be planted in two seasons, it was assumed that the service income could reach RMB 400 to 500 Yuan/*mu* (667 m²), the total income of all villagers can increase by RMB 0.8 to 1 million Yuan, the yearly income can be doubled with the consideration of the rent of RMB 1.6 million, the per capita net income can increase by RMB 2,877, the income per labor force can increase by RMB 4,026 Yuan, and the per capita income of the agricultural labor force can increase by RMB 11,320 Yuan.

Obviously, the complete land transaction and scale management have promoted the modernization of agriculture. Generally, separated land management can only meet the needs for food and clothing but not for becoming rich. The contract based on separated fields can only depend on small blocks, small machines and physical labor, but does not need large machines, scientific and technological input and no scientific training and guidance. But the intensive transfer of land to the large company can not only obtain land rent and labor income, but also can solve the problem of employment, increase scientific and technological input and achieve mechanized operation.

The introduction of the project has especially promoted the adjustment of agricultural production structure and formed a vertical industrial chain, in which the sweet sorghum and its straw can be used as basic material to produce sugar, bioethanol, newtol, medium and high-grade papers, the fourth generation of biological compound fertilizer, and protein feed. This can lead to the development of industries within 50 km to 100 km of the area.

3.1.2. *Land cooperative in Aoxiaoying Village of Yongledian Town*

Aoxiaoying Village of Yongledian Town, located in east of Yujiawu Town, with a total of over 300 households, 1,300 villagers and 2,300 *mu* (1,533,333 m²) of land, is named after its business of nitrate production. Before the land transaction, the village had no industrial enterprise or collective income and adopted an extensive management pattern. Farmers originally planted wheat and later corn, which brought very little income. Meanwhile, some farmer households had no land. They could obtain a subsidy of over RMB 100 Yuan every year after the land registration in 2004, for which the village should pay a total of RMB 5,200 and should pay about RMB 20,000 Yuan with the consideration of a RMB 50 Yuan subsidy per *mu* (667 m²) after the land transaction, but the village could not afford it.

The land transaction in Aoxiaoying Village was quite different than in Qianfu Village. It was based on the land cooperative founded by 74 farmer households who agreed to land transaction and had a total of 500 *mu* (333,333 m²) of land. This land would be used for planting vegetables and fruit through the cooperation with the aviation service company, and they would also be used as the teaching and experiment base for the university due to the location in a university town.

The land cooperative of Aoxiaoying Village is a corporate organization separated from the village committee, which will communicate with both the enterprise and farmer households, and will obtain the lands transferred from farmers and then contract them to the enterprise. The cooperation pattern between the cooperative and the enterprise is that the cooperative assigns a special person to supervise the production and operation statuses of the enterprise, but does not directly participate in the management. Both parties have an individual financial management system and there is an institutional arrangement of minimum income and dividends. Namely, that the minimum income means that the enterprise will pay a land transaction fee of RMB 1,000 Yuan/*mu* (667 m²) to the cooperative, which will increase every five years; while the dividends mean that the enterprise will pay 20% of the profit to the cooperative, and the latter does not need to take the responsibility for the enterprise's deficit. This forms a community interest between them. Similarly, the institutional arrangement of minimum income and dividends is also adopted between the cooperative and farmer households and the minimum income and dividends represent land transaction fees and profit respectively. The cooperative will utilize 70% profit as the fund and 30% as operation expenses, and 30% of the total fund will be used as dividends. Among all households joining the cooperative, 73 of them are individual households and one is the collective household. Besides, over 100 *mu* (66,667 m²) of land from land consolidation will be distributed to the collective household, but parts of it will be used as the subsidy for the household with no land.

Compared to the pattern in Qianfu Village, the land transaction in Aoxiaoying Village has many advantages. Firstly, it does not only avoid the awkward role of the village collective that plays the role of both party A and party B or both defendant and plaintiff, but it also has proper subject qualification and equal rights and liabilities. Secondly, the cooperative will replace the village committee to solve possible disputes, which can solve the confounded functions of government and enterprise. Thirdly, it can avoid the possibility of subcontracting. Fourthly, the economic relationship within the contract has changed from a land tenancy relationship to a community, in which the village collective has performance stock, while farmer's income will consist of three parts, including rental income, income though wages and dividends.

3.2. *Organic vegetable specialized cooperative in Zhenglong Village, Jiangji Town, Ningyang County, Shandong Province*[2]

Ningyang County, located in Southwestern Shandong Province, is under the jurisdiction of Tai'an City. Jiangji Town, located in the central part of

---

[2]Zhang Shuguang gave a speech and conducted an investigation in Ningyang County of Shandong Province on March 15 to 18, 2009.

Ningyang County, with a total area of 83 sq. kms and a total farmland area of 62,000 *mu* (41,333,333 m²). It has 40 administrative villages, 13,000 households and 52,000 people, and is a traditional agricultural town. During the land transaction and scale management, Zhenglong Village adopts the model of stock holding mechanism combined with cooperation with the aim of all-round benefits, and farmers can use the land shares to participate in the cooperative, so that the scale, intensification and standardization of the production can be achieved.

3.2.1. *Land share cooperative in Zhenglong Village*

Zhenglong Village, located north of the Yiwen River, has fertile land and a total of 320 households and 1,260 villagers. The per capita land area reaches 1 *mu* (667 m²). After becoming the secretary of the village, Tian Wenwu, who has a talent for becoming rich, planned with the members of both village and party committees and aroused masses to discuss how to develop the collective economy and to become rich under a new strategy. In the discussion meeting involving village cadres, party member representatives and the representatives from the discussion group of villagers held in September 2007, a veteran party member Zheng Xiudong, known as the Mushroom King, proposed to jointly grow mushrooms, for which he can provide the technology and the village can use idle land to build the greenhouses. His proposal was agreed to by all representatives, and after that, the village built 8 greenhouses to grow oyster mushrooms and *Coprinus comatus*. An order contract with Tai'an Honghai Company was signed, which attained a net profit of RMB 50,000 Yuan at the end of this year.

During the cooperation with Honghai Company, Tian Wenwu guided all cadres to visit the company and other vegetable planting bases. After returning to the village, he began to think about establishing a cooperative to plant organic vegetables with high value. However, his proposals were opposed by many villagers, and voices came out, such as "I've grown grain for a long time, and how should I deal with the possible loss caused by planting vegetables?", "The intensive land management is actually a behavior of egalitarian practice and a form of retrogress", and "Can the village collective pay for land transaction after signing the contract?"

Faced with villagers' queries and concerns, the village formulated the principle of "Willingness, pooling of land as share, intensive management and income dividends", gave detailed instructions to each household, and collected the land of cadres. Besides that, Tian Wenwu contributed RMB 80,000 Yuan in his name to sign the contract with households. For this reason, 110 households agreed to transfer nearly 20 years of the contractual management right on the premise that the project was led by cadres and guaranteed by the secretary, with a total area of 300 *mu* (200,000 m^2). After that, the cooperative established and improved various management systems, such as a financial management system, and elected the Council and the Board of Supervisors through the general meeting of shareholders, and elected Tian Wenwu as the president. The cooperative adopted the unified management and operation pattern and divided stock into many shares (667 m^2 for one share). In addition to enjoying the share capital per *mu* (667 m^2) of land (increasing from the original RMB 400 Yuan/*mu* (667 m^2) to later RMB 700 Yuan/*mu* (667 m^2), the shareholder can earn money at the base of the cooperative and obtain the dividends at the end of the year. The detailed distribution pattern is as follows: 10% of the surplus will be extracted as accumulation fund and public welfare fund for expanding the production service ability and loss subsidy and for developing the business and commune member's welfare, while another 10% of the surplus will be extracted as risk fee and be used as the subsidy for the cooperative if its operation suffers great economic loss.

After planting one season of green beans, the cooperative obtained a net income of RMB 360,000 Yuan, and the dividends for per *mu* (667 m^2) of land reached above RMB 1,000 Yuan. The visible and sensible high profit made those villagers who had not participated in the cooperative before regret their mistake and ask Tian Wenwu to adsorb them into the cooperative. In September 2007, the remaining 150 households signed the contract for the transfer of the contractual land management right and became the second batch of shareholders in the cooperative. By that time, the cooperative's lands had reached 920 *mu* (613,333 m^2), including 120 *mu* (80,000 m^2) from 260 households of an adjacent village. In 2008, the village collective's economic income reached above RMB 400,000

Yuan, and the farmer's per capita net income reached RMB 5,700 Yuan, increasing by about three fold and 50% more than those in 2006.

3.2.2. *Management pattern of the cooperative*
in Zhenglong Village

After the cooperative was established, the village took advantage of the good relationship with Honghai Company that was formed during mushroom planting and signed a cooperative contract with the Company. Thus, the management pattern combining the company, the cooperative (base), the farmer household and the collective was formed. According to the contract, Honghai Company would assign a representative to be responsible for seeds, technology, marketing, conservation expenses and the guidance and monitoring of the whole production process, while the cooperative would be in charge of production management, unified planting for seed variety arrangement, unified planting in management and unified management service by orders. Production bases were established for different planting varieties, including broccoli, green sword bean, asparagus, etc., in which production groups were set according to the scale of production to be responsible for the labor utilization and the control of product quality. On the whole, most young villagers had gone to the city, and the remaining villagers, mainly old people and women, worked in the cooperative.

The cooperative has changed the dilemma of single-household-based marketing strategy, solved the contradiction between small-scale farmer economy and large market, and improved the farmer's strength on market competition. It is known that according to the acquisition agreement on broccoli signed with Honghai Company, the procurement price is RMB 1.6 Yuan/kg at first, but due to the rise of vegetable prices in the market, it increases to RMB 2.2 Yuan/kg after several rounds of negotiation with Honghai Company, by which the cooperative can gain an incremental profit of RMB 180,000 Yuan. However, the sales price in the market reached RMB 4 Yuan/kg. Faced with the difference in price, Tian Wenwu thought that the village adopted the collective management pattern but not a single-household-based operation pattern, so the village should not breach the contract to sell vegetables to the market, and the village would rather lose benefit than lose integrity and market share.

Because organic fertilizer and biopesticides are indispensable for planting organic vegetables, the village cooperates with Honghai Company to establish an organic fertilizer factory to produce the organic fertilizer and develop ecological agriculture and a circular economy. By coincidence, adjacent Xiaohu Village had been beset by time and labor consuming treatment problems relating to stinking cow dung generated from over 1,000 milk cows raised by about 30 households. So the cooperative signed an exchange contract with Xiaohu Village, according to which one truck of broccoli leaf can be exchanged for the equivalent cow dung to produce organic fertilizer. The powdery organic fertilizer from the factory would be the cooperative's use, while the granular fertilizer would be sold to other bases that signed a contract with Honghai Company.

The vegetable planting in Zhenglong Village has already been on a road of standardization, in which precise measurement is conducted in line spacing, spacing and height and the fertilizing is conducted in accordance with regulations in time, type and dosage. As vividly described by villagers, the village adopts the accurate management pattern, the fertilizing is conducted in accordance with related regulations, and villagers plant vegetables while adopting standardization. Meanwhile, in order to master the planting technique of organic vegetables more skillfully, the cooperative establishes the business connection with some R&D institutions such as Shandong Agricultural University and China Asparagus Association, invites related experts to give lectures at regular intervals, and strengthens the technical training for commune members. The village has carried out over 1,000 training sessions and popularized 10 new technologies and 8 new species. Thanks to its standardized production pattern, the cooperative's organic vegetables have gained the certification for organic food, and the village has submitted an application to the State Administration for Industry & Commerce for *Longyuquan* trademark, and has not only signed direct supply contracts with supermarkets in Tai'an City and Jinan City but also has obtained a permit to sell on the international market, by which its organic vegetables can be sold to several foreign countries like America and Japan.

3.3. *Case of western flower world in Lingyun Village, Xinminchang Town, Pixian County, Chengdu City*[3]

Lingyun Village is located in Xinmingchang Town, Pixian County and about a 40 minute drive northwest of Chengdu. It has a total of 16 cooperatives, 767 households, 2,432 villagers and 4,249 *mu* (2,832,667 m²) of land. Since 2008, the village has begun to conduct large-scale land transaction and consolidation to promote the industrialization of agriculture, and to construct a comprehensive industry base combining production, sales exhibition, tourism and relaxation.

3.3.1. *Lay the foundation for industrialization of agriculture by implementing land consolidation*

In 2008, approved by the Sichuan Department of Land and Resources, Pixian County implemented a comprehensive land consolidation project in Xinminchang Town, including farmland consolidation and rural land acquisition for urban development. More specifically, the first step is to conduct farmland gridding and consolidation, which can yield a 224.3 *mu* (149,533 m²) increase of farmland. The second step is to build a concentrated residential district with a land area of 160 *mu* (106,667 m²) and a building area of about 100,000 m². The third step is to conduct reclaimation for the courtyards after the centralized dwelling, which can yield a 375.2 *mu* (250,133 m²) increase of farmland. The fourth step is to replace 364.8 *mu* (243,200 m²) of construction land to Pitong Town as urban construction land. The project has a total investment of RMB 402.34 million Yuan, of which RMB 185.65 million is for new dwelling area construction, compensation for farmers' demolition and land consolidation, and RMB 216.69 million Yuan for new town construction in Pitong Town. The land auction price in Pitong Town in 2008 reached RMB 1,730,000 Yuan/ *mu* (667 m²), based on which the prospective earnings from 364.8 *mu* (243,200 m²) of land replaced to new town construction in Pitong Town

---

[3]On August 23 and 25, 2009, Zhang Shuguang, Liu Shouying, Liao Bingguang *et al.* participated in the Research Group of Rural Reform organized by the Development Research Center of the State Council and conducted two times of investigations in Western Flower World.

will reach RMB 410.22 million Yuan (it should be RMB 631.104 million Yuan based on correction). Thus, the Small Urban Development Investment Company from Chengdu is introduced to solve the problem of capital investment and rural infrastructure construction.

Through the comprehensive land consolidation described above, Lingyun Village has incremental farmland of 599.5 *mu* (399,667 m^2), a newly constructed 1,400 m long road, and 1,926 m long U-shaped ditch. The replaced 135 *mu* (90,000 m^2) of construction land is used to develop tertiary industries. Meanwhile, the effective large-scale land transaction is achieved, a tight interest community is formed under the model of industrialization of an agriculture integration base, and a 4,500 *mu* (3,000,000 m^2) core area of flowers and plants is constructed with Lingyun Village at the center.

3.3.2. Large-scale land transfer creates institutional conditions for agriculture modernization

Spontaneous land transaction emerged four to five years ago, and the local owners and villagers utilized or rented the contracted land to plant flowers and plants. In the past two or three years, an early form of the industry has emerged on both sides of the road, but most of the participants in the industry have only 8 to 10 *mu* (5,333 to 6,667 m^2) of land and are small scale, weak, and have poor technology and low quality. In order to help farmers make the industry larger and stronger, the governments at county and town levels actively introduced large foreign enterprises and promoted the large-scale land transaction while conducting land consolidation. Some villagers disagreed with the land transaction at the beginning. Before land transaction the villagers could only obtain a net income of about RMB 100 Yuan per *mu* (667 m^2) after deducting the expenses of chemical fertilizer, pesticide and seed from the income of RMB 1,200 Yuan from a yield of 300 kg (value of RMB 400 Yuan) of wheat and 500 kg (value of RMB 800 Yuan) of rice, and in addition one laborer is required for farming for a family of three, but after the land transaction, they can obtain a salary of RMB 800 Yuan to RMB 1,000 Yuan per month in addition to land rent and need not to worry and take risks. After being presented with the above facts, all farmers agreed to carry out large-scale land transaction.

During the large-scale land transaction, the village collective first signs a land rental agreement with farmers (See Annex 5) and then signs a land transaction contract with the enterprise. The contract regulates the rights and duties of both parties, as well as the payment and distribution of rent. The rent of each 1 *mu* (667 m²) patch of land values 500 kg of medium-grade rice at a market price in the middle and end of September, which will be paid by the enterprise to the village collective in two payments, including 50% before May 30 and 50% before September 30, and will be paid by the village collective to farmers, including 40% before June 30 and 60% before September 30.

There are also other two important agreements that are not expressly specified in the contract: The first is, for the purpose of investment attraction, the contracted enterprises are exempted from rent in the first three years, which will be afforded by the government. Specifically, the rent will first be paid by the enterprise to farmers, and then paid by government to the enterprise as a subsidy; and the second is about the collection of a coordination fee of RMB 100 Yuan per *mu* (667 m²) of land, which will be used to pay public security and sanitation workers and to pay for households in hardship or as festival and holiday allowances.

3.3.3. *Modern agriculture management of Senhe company*

After the large-scale land transaction, some leading enterprises and large planting households are introduced and modern management is achieved. The village now has over 60 enterprises, with an annual production of 150 million units of potted flowers and a sales income of RMB 120 million Yuan, shifting over 700 laborers or over 400 farmer households from traditional farming to the project. This increases income by over RMB 1,000 Yuan for each farmer. Among these enterprises, Chengdu Senhe Modern Agriculture Science and Technology Ltd., Chengdu Miaofu Modern Nursery Stock Science & Technology Co., Ltd. and Shanghai Jinwin Greening Art Development Ltd. are the most famous.

Chengdu Senhe Company, a wholly-owned subsidiary of Zhejiang Senhe Seed Industry Co., Ltd., with a registered capital of RMB 6 million, plans to invest RMB 50 million Yuan to rent 1,000 *mu* (666,667 m²) of land in Xinminchang Town, is mainly engaged in the breeding and cultivation of new variety, the new technology research and development and the new product promotion of the best flowers and colored-leaf ornamental plants, and mainly plants colored-leaf trees and shrubs such as *Photinia serrulata* and howardii, as well as rare flowers such as *Dendrobium nobile*, cymbidium, butterfly orchid and cyclamen. The company has a production capacity of 15 million germchits, 8 million small container-grown seedlings, 50,000 large container-grown seedlings and 200,000 pots of rare flowers. It will construct over 20,000 m² of intelligent greenhouses, 1,600 m² of steel-structure operating houses and 27 *mu* (18,000 m²) of flower and nursery stock hypermarkets. It achieves a production value of RMB 70 million Yuan and obtains a sales income of RMB 30 million Yuan per year. The company had 300 workers in 2008, paid salaries totaling over RMB 2 million Yuan — 95% of which was paid to local farmers.

The company adopted the plastic film mulching and aggregate cultivation technique, in which land (but no earth) is required and ground fabric and containers are used. The container is put on the ground fabric and is filled with organic matters generated from various mushroom dregs (peanut shell, rice husk and other wastes), and finally the nursery stock is planted. There are two types of germchits, one of which takes waste plastics as female parent and is snipped from female parent for cultivation, and the other of which adopts the mesh bag to culture seedlings that are planted in the container. In order to improve the cultivation quality, the company selects and trains a team of technicians there, from which local technicians and administrators are trained, and recruits two college graduates. Meanwhile, the company provides the technical guidance for local farmers and is responsible for research and development, recovery and marketing for scattered households, while the households are responsible for intermediate planting.

The operation and development of the company have greatly changed Xinminchang Town in many aspects. Firstly, the environment quality has been improved due to the construction of Flowery Park and the holding of Flowery Festival that result in bright red blossoms and green willows throughout the four seasons. Secondly, farmer's income has increased. The labor income ranges from RMB 800 Yuan per month to over RMB 1,000 Yuan per month, the per capita income can reach RMB 15,000 Yuan, and farmer's material life has been improved. Thirdly, the production mode has been changed, farmers become industry workers engaged in mulching film, greenhouse, industry agriculture and industrialization operations. They usually work for eight hours every day but from 4:00–08:00 and 18:00–22:00 in the summer, and they have some welfare like a summer cooling subsidy and festival and holiday rest.

3.4. Case of High-Tech Modern Agricultural Industry Park in Qiquan Town, Chongzhou City, Chengdu[4]

Qiquan Town, located in the southwest of Chongzhou City, about 10 km from the urban area of Chongzhou City, with four administrative villages and one neighborhood district, has a land area of 18.09 sq. kms, a farmland area of 18,200 *mu* (12,133,333 m²), a population of over 14,000 (98% are farmers), and belongs to a typical agriculture town. Before 2003, Qiquan Town was mainly engaged in traditional agriculture, small enterprise and primitive commerce and trade, had a weak basis of agriculture, lagged rural development, and it was difficult to increase farmer's income. The per capita net income was only RMB 3,000 Yuan.

In 2003, as a pilot town for a comprehensive demonstration project of overall planning of urban and rural development in Chengdu, Qiquan Town depended on High-Tech Modern Agricultural Industry Park. It gave great impetus to promote land transaction, develop a modern agriculture industry, innovate in the agricultural service system and make breakthroughs in solving agricultural issues. It promoted developing city and countryside integration, made the agricultural output go from small to large, shifted from traditional techniques to modern technology, grew from small farmer operation to scale integration, and went from single cultivation to including ecological tourism. By 2008, the per capita net income for farmers reached RMB 5,935 Yuan, about RMB 400 Yuan higher than the average level of the whole city, increasing by 73% over the level in 2003. Besides, rural infrastructure and housing conditions have been obviously improved and the new urban–rural form has been gradually formed.

---

[4]On September 26, 2009, Zhang Shuguang, Liu Shouying, *et al.* participated in the Research Group of Rural Reform organized by the Development Research Center of the State Council and conducted an investigation in Qiquan Town of Chongzhou City.

3.4.1. *Promote large-scale land transfer and develop new organization for economic cooperation*

In order to promote land transaction and develop modern agriculture, Qiquan Town started with property rights reform, conducted land registration and certification and property rights return, by which the ownership of rural collective land, the use right of collective construction land (including homesteads), the ownership of housing on the collective land, the contractual management right of farmland and the collective forest rights are certificated ("entitled property right") to the village collective economic organization and farmer households, and the property rights become substantial. Based on all the above, the village strives for support from national policy and project, conducts land consolidation and courtyard demolition and combination based on Gold Land project and land consolidation project, and guides some farmers to separate from the land. Besides, the village constructs a high-tech modern agricultural industry park, vigorously attracts investment, cultivates, introduces and fosters leading enterprises and special cooperative organizations, and actively promotes land transaction and scale management. The specific measures are as follows:

(1) **Land (share) cooperative:** Some land cooperatives are established based on village, including Zhonghe Community, Shengjian Village Community, Lindong Village Community, Qiangong Village and Qun'an Village Community, having a total of over 3,900 households. Entrusted by households that participate in the cooperative, the land is uniformly transferred to the owner through investment attraction. Currently, 49 companies and business owners have been successfully introduced and 12,300 *mu* (8,200,000 m^2) of land has been transferred. Huhui Group and Yingmalong Company have established 6,100 *mu* (4,066,667 m^2) for a production base. According to the contract between both parties, the cooperative uniformly collects the rent from the owner, 95% of which is distributed to farmers in accordance with the transferred land after the certification, and another 5% is used as the cooperative's income to collect land transaction information, introduce business owners for the land transaction, sign the land transaction contract and maintain the commune members' income.

(2) **Farmers' specialized cooperative:** In accordance with the principles of civilian-run, civilian-managed, civilian-owned and civilian-benefited, larger households and able farmers engaged in the breeding industry take the lead to establish some special Farmer Specialized Cooperatives, such as Runhe Fruit and Vegetable Specialized Cooperative, Qiangong Village Pig Raising Specialized Cooperative, Tianci Pig Raising Specialized Cooperative, Zhikang Pig Raising Specialized Cooperative, Wenfang Pig Raising Specialized Cooperative, Pig Brother Pig Raising Specialized Cooperative, Qun'an Pig Raising Specialized Cooperative and Hongfa Pig Raising Specialized Cooperative, which have a total of 226 member households.

(3) **New farmer innovation park:** 20 agriculture cooperatives from Shengjian Village invested RMB 200,000 Yuan to establish Chongzhou Xincheng Agriculture Development Ltd., which has the property management rights of new farmer centralized residential area in Zhonghe community in Qiquan Town, has the rights to operational proceeds in kindergarten, 25 shops, 2,400 m² of management housing and 17 houses for production management. It has the operation rights for 500 *mu* (333,333 m²) of increased land from land consolidation of collective economic organization, and has established 500 *mu* (333,333 m²) of new farmer innovation parks in accordance with the pattern of small owners and large parks. The park plans to establish 6 standardized cultivation units with an area of 30 *mu* (20,000 m²) and 470 *mu* (313,333 m²) toward a special planting base to develop the cyclic agriculture of planting and breeding. Currently, 7 owners have moved to the park, and mainly engage in the planting of vegetables and red grapes and the cultivation of pigs.

3.4.2. *Establish new agriculture service system and develop the service before, during and after the agricultural production*

Large-scale land transaction and centralized management of ownership not only require some professional industry services involving agricultural machinery, crop protection, advisory and proxies that can solve or reduce operation risks, but also require professional, skilled and organized labor services. This allows weak labor forces to increase their income without leaving their land and their hometown. Thus, the establishment and development of modern an agricultural service system becomes the inevitable choice.

The first measure is to establish the agricultural machine service company and the agricultural implements service platform. In March 2008, 5, frontline agricultural technicians established Chongzhou Dadi Agricultural Service Company, with 90 m² of office space, 15 3W-950 type mobile sprayers, 4 plunger pump sprayers, 1 thermal fogger, 4 rice planters, 2 large tractors and mating operating machines and tools, 8 small tractors and 1 transportation tricycle. The company is mainly engaged in providing plant disease and pest prevention treatment service, agricultural machine operation service with equipped personnel, technical agricultural advisory service and grain planting. Since its inception, the company has developed three core businesses: (1) **Crop specialty and green prevention and control:** The biological missile (trichogramma and special virus) has been popularized and applied in sweet corn production, and some IPM technologies such as pyrethrum, BT, azadirachtin, gyplure, insecticidal lamp and palette have been popularized in vegetable planting. In 2008, the Dadi Company provided the all-round crop protection service for 11,000 *mu* (7,333,333 m²) of crops and vegetables for Rice Base of Chongzhou Company of State Grain Reserve Warehouse, Yingmalong and Huhui Farms and Tianying Planting Cooperative. The vice general manager of Chongzhou Company said: "The prevention of rice stem borer required over 200 persons and about 10 supervisors at one time. The whole process lasted for over 10 days, but the effects were not ensured. Workers just wanted to earn money. They did not care about the prevention effect. If some problems occur, the company only had itself to blame. But this year we have signed the prevention and control contract with Dadi Company. We only need to pay a maintenance fee of RMB 6 Yuan per *mu* (667 m²) and contract all works to them, and they will ensure the prevention effect of 95%. If there is a problem in the prevention effect, someone will be responsible to deal with it. So we do not need to be concerned over when to use what pesticide to prevent what disease or pest, and we get efficient service with lower costs." Meanwhile, Huhui Company will continue to order new service and plans to integrate and move its planting bases in other cities to Chongzhou; (2) **Practical characteristic agricultural machine service:** Dadi Company takes the lead to conduct ridging operation by large machinery in Chengdu and has conquered several problems in vegetable planting in clayey areas at a stroke. If there is no high ridge, then the plant will be vulnerable to rain and flood, while artificial ridging costs as much as RMB 250 to 300 Yuan per *mu* (667 m^2) every time. But the ridging by large machinery only needs RMB 60 to 70 Yuan per *mu* (667 m^2). In 2008, the company provided mechanical rice transplanting for 650 *mu* (433,333 m^2) of land for Chongzhou Grain Storehouse Company, and provided mechanical ploughing and ridging operations for 2,600 *mu* (1,733,333 m^2) of land for Huhui and Yingmalong farms, two watermelon planting households to Chongzhou and some enterprises such as Jindalin Agriculture and Lvsheng Agriculture; (3) **Breeding, raising seedling, entrusted cultivation and management:** In 2008, the company provided mechanical rice seedlings for 400 *mu* (266,667 m^2) of land for Huhui Farm, as well as a 160 *mu* (106,667 m^2) plantation of temporary barren land. It is estimated that the company's services in unified seedlings, unified prevention of plant diseases and insect pests, tractor ploughing, mechanical transplanting, mechanical prevention and harvesting saved a total of RMB 21,000 Yuan and generated a net income of over RMB 5,000 Yuan for rice scale management of Chongzhou State Grain Storehouse. Besides, the company's services in tractor ploughing, ridging, greenhouse disinfection and the prevention of plant diseases and insect pests for the vegetable base of Huhui Group have achieved the scale, facility and standardization production. By now, the company has 6 fixed base customers with a service area of about 4,500 *mu* (3,000,000 m^2).

The second is to establish the labor service cooperative and agricultural labor service platform. In 2008, Chongzhou Qiquan Limin Agricultural Labor Service Cooperative was established, mainly composed of 40-to-60-year-old farmers (who have lost land and still stay) from Qiquan Agricultural Industry Park. The cooperative now has 120 members, including 95 females and 15 males, 62 farmers of 40-to-50-years-old, 40 farmers of 50-to-60-years-old and 8 farmers below 30-years-old or above 60-years-old, 36 students of primary school education, 72 students of middle school education and 2 illiterates. The cooperative is mainly engaged in the following businesses: (1) Export of labor service: It provides the export of labor service for the owners engaged in crop farming, the breeding industry and the processing industry to solve the shortage of labor power and technologies during the production management; (2) Labor service technical contract: The company takes advantage of its own technological and mechanical strengths to provide the owners with ploughing service before production, management service during the production and service after production; (3) Labor training: Depending on the cooperation with research institutions and its own agricultural equipment, the cooperative can provide suitable skill training and certification service. Currently, 70 of the 120 members have mastered relevant vegetable planting techniques through the training and have become workers in the agricultural industry. Meanwhile, the cooperative has signed the agricultural labor service contract with 23 owners of land scale management or agricultural industrialization enterprises, according to which a total of 102 members will be employed to work for over 220 days every year. Their salary will be increased from RMB 25 Yuan/day to RMB 35–40 Yuan/day.

The third measure is to introduce Sichuan Wenjing Modern Agriculture Base Management Ltd., and to innovate the management method of agricultural bases. The Wenjing company that settled in Qiquan High-Tech Modern Agricultural Industry Park in 2009 can provide service like the hotel or nanny industries to manage the production base in view of problems in modern agriculture, such as technical and labor management, production cost accounting, marketing management, normalization, standardization and mechanization of production procedures, etc. It is specially engaged in some base services, such as agricultural park planning, agricultural investment planning, labor service and technical management contract, agricultural products marketing, distribution and export, facility agriculture construction, rural migrant worker training, popularization and application of new technologies and products. Meanwhile, the company has signed a contract with Kangzhuang Farming Company to provide the whole course labor and management service for $200\,mu$ ($133,333\,m^2$) of sweet corn, for which the company will only charge RMB 360 Yuan per *mu* ($667\,m^2$) as the fee for labor service, machine tools and management service. This is RMB 80 Yuan less than the cost of management by the Kangzhuang company itself.

3.4.3. *Establish specialist house and science and technology center for commercializing research findings; implement agricultural standardization production and industrialization management*

Cooperating with Sichuan Agriculture Academy of Science and Sichuan University, the Chongzhou Qiquan Park establishes the Agricultural Expert House, implements the chief expert responsibility system, employs 36 permanent experts including 16 agricultural experts at the provincial level, and establishes the commercialization center of agricultural science and technology findings to focus on the pilot scale test of agricultural science and technology findings and the popularization of agricultural science and technology. The park has established the scientific research demonstration base for new varieties, materials and technologies and is equipped with an agricultural laboratory, detection room and relevant equipment. Over the past year, the park has introduced 168 new crop varieties, has conducted some experiments and demonstration research, such as soil-less cultivation, Baishikang microbial fertilizer and Xinpinchuan healthy cultivation techniques. It has introduced over 20 new demonstration and popularization farming technologies and over 40 new varieties. It has implemented the planting of over 10,000 *mu* (6,666,667 m^2) of super sweet corn, rice transplantation by seedling puller for over 3,000 *mu* (2,000,000 m^2) of land and the autumn pepper cultivation technique for 3,500 *mu* (2,333,333 m^2) of land. The park has also established a standardized vegetable greenhouse for factory-like vegetable seedling raising, which covers an area of 1,060 *mu* (706,667 m^2). In addition, the park has developed some agricultural science growth-type enterprises such as Wan'an Agricultural Science & Technology and Yiyou Biochemistry, as well as some intensive agricultural product processing enterprises and new-type logistics enterprises, such as Yingmalong, Chuanqi Food and Hulida Grain and Oil. This not only has improved the technological content of agricultural products, deepened and lengthened the chain of agricultural industry, but has also developed a new sales model of agricultural products, connected agricultural products with supermarkets, schools and restaurants, and has increased the export of agricultural products. Meanwhile, the park has promoted brand building for agricultural products and has developed agricultural standardized management. The park established the Provincial-Level Agricultural Standardization Edible Mushrooms Production Base in 2007 and the Provincial-Level Agricultural Standardization Red Grape Production Base in 2008, implemented the detection and certification for pollution-free products, green and organic agricultural products such as red grapes, hot peppers and balsam pear, focused on the building of Wenjingyuan brand, and registered the Qiquan trademark. Moreover, the park supports its leading enterprises to create well-known brands and famous trademarks, e.g., Yingmalong Company has exported its canned vegetable to the European Union, and Runhe Fruit and Vegetable Cooperative has registered the "Runhe" trademark.

3.5. Case of scale planting of Sichuan Chongzhou Grain and Oil Reserve LLC[5]

Sichuan Chongzhou Grain and Oil Reserve LLC, also called Sichuan Chongzhou State Grain Storehouse, is a state-owned grain enterprise engaged in grain and oil purchasing, preservation, processing, sales and agricultural planting registered in No. 163, Jinpen Avenue, Chongyang Town, Chongzhou City. It is a leading enterprise of agricultural industrialization and the biggest grain grower in Chengdu. The company now has one processing line producing 30,000 tons/year of rice, one producing 5,000 tons/year of flour and noodles, and one producing 2,000 tons/year of colza oil. It has a planting area of 2,000 *mu* (1,333,333 m²), has an annual production of 1,000 tons of Dachun rice (grown in spring or summer) and 600 tons of Xiaochun wheat (grown in autumn or winter), and owns "Luweng" series agricultural products.

In 2003, the company took lead in the system to implement land transaction and order-form agriculture and other planting patterns. In 2007, the company relied on the town government and the village committee to

---

[5]On September 26, 2009, Zhang Shuguang, Liu Shouying, *et al.* participated in the Research Group of Rural Reform organized by the Development Research Center of the State Council and conducted an investigation in Chongzhou City.

mobilize farmers to entrust their lands to the collective economic organization for uniform transfer and established the grain production base in Qiquan Town. In the transfer transaction, the company will give farmers 300 kilograms of rice for per *mu* (667 m^2) of land every year, which is equivalent to about RMB 800 at market price and will be paid to farmer households through the village collective organization or the cooperative.

The company adopts the cooperative pattern combining the company, farmer household, the collective and R&D institution to conduct the production and operation, in which local villagers are employed as workers and the company will sign the labor contract with administrative staff and common staff. The company is mainly engaged in rice, flour, noodle and vegetable oil processing, as well as rice, wheat and vegetable planting. All grains planted by the company will be used for state reserves and will be placed for sale on the market after the rotation period expires, but all produced commercial crops will be directly placed on the market.

It is estimated that the costs for seed purchasing, tractor ploughing, seeding, fertilizing, spraying insecticide, insect pest and disease prevention, field management, harvesting, transportation and tending etc. are RMB 497 Yuan per *mu* (667 m^2) for Dachun rice and RMB 300 Yuan per *mu* (667 m^2) for Xiaochun wheat, and the total cost is RMB 1,597 Yuan per *mu* (667 m^2) after considering rent, while the average sales income of rice and wheat is RMB 1,600 Yuan per *mu* (667 m^2), so the cost is basically equal to the profit and the net income is zero. After the implementation of infrastructure, fine breeding and uniform tractor ploughing, the labor cost greatly decreases, and RMB 200 Yuan per *mu* (667 m^2) is saved. The company mainly obtains profit through intensive processing and brand building.

Recently, the state has gradually increased its investment in grain planting, and the government of Chengdu has also issued several benefit subsidies, such as a direct grain subsidy, fine breed subsidy and farmland protection fund, all of which will be given to farmers but not to planting enterprises and owners. However, the government will give the land transaction subsidy of RMB 100 to 200 Yuan per *mu* (667 m^2) to the planting enterprises who plant continuously for more than three years.

4. Land Transfer, Organizational Transition and Agricultural Modernization: Analysis and Discussion Based on Cases

4.1. *Business crisis facing traditional agriculture*

China's reform and opening up started from rural areas, while rural reform centered on abandoning the original commune system. It shifted to the household contract responsibility system based on the collective ownership of rural land. This was a large liberation of social productive forces in rural areas. Moreover, due to the adjustment and increase of grain prices, China's agricultural economy rapidly increased in the first half of the 1980s, and the problem of food and clothing that had not been solved for the previous 30 years was solved. Over the past 30 years of reform and opening-up, in order to consolidate the achievements of rural institutional reform, to protect farmer's land property rights and to ensure the stability of rural areas, the central government has continued to insist on keeping the rural basic economic system unchanged while strengthening farmers' status as the main player. In the rural land system, the central government has extended the contract period from 15 years to 30 years and proposed the permanent stability of the system in 2008 to stabilize the relationship between farmer and land. In order to prevent land adjustment within the village or community, using the pretext of major stability and minor adjustment is not allowed, and the relationship between farmer and land is specified as the matching relationship between person and the field. All systemic improvements have laid a foundation for changing farmers' land contract rights to property rights.

However, since the mid-1980s, farmers' employment situation has changed greatly, which has resulted in the change of the economic importance of farmland to farmer and the relationship between farmer and land. Farmers' property rights then mainly include farmers' contracting, management and transfer rights. At the beginning of the reform, farmers had no other job opportunities and could gain higher benefit in agriculture, so they were mainly engaged in farming and land contracting and management rights were combined. However, with the development of township enterprises, parts of rural labor forces shifted to local non-agricultural industry and the land contracting rights began to be separated from management rights. In the 1990s, with the formation of coastal industrial zones and the emergence of world factories, inland township enterprises began to decline. As a result, numerous farmers from central and western rural areas went to coastal areas to work, and the separation between land contracting rights and management rights became more common and permanent. Unfortunately, due to the lack of rural migrant policies and the lagged development of inland farmland transaction market, China's urbanization has been distorted to an uncompleted urbanization due to the disjunction between population mobility and resources flow. According to statistics, 150 million farmers come to the city and work there all the year round, but the percentage of transferred farmland only reaches 4% to 8%, most of rural migrant workers subcontract their lands to neighbors or relatives, or leave it to the women and old villagers back at home. It can be seen from the data of the second agricultural census that after most rural male labor forces go to coastal areas to work, women become the major laborers and operators for agricultural production. The first agricultural census in 1996 showed that the percentage of woman laborers among the total labor force in the whole country, central and western areas were 47.55%, 36.93% and 38.49% respectively, but in the second agricultural census in 2006, the figures increased to 53.2%, 54.3% and 51.4% respectively. In the seven provinces with the largest exported labor forces, the proportions were are all above 50%. As most young laborers go out for work and show a tendency for becoming younger, agricultural practitioners and laborers become older and older. It can be seen that the percentages of agricultural laborers above 51-years-old among total laborers in the whole country, central and western areas have increased from 18.5%, 17.3% and 17.69% in 1996 respectively to 32.5%, 33.3% and 31.2% in 2006 respectively. For the seven provinces with the most exported labor, including Chongqing, Sichuan, Anhui, Hunan, Hubei, Jiangxi and Henan, the percentages were 46.2%, 41.9%, 37.5%, 37.2%, 37%, 32.5% and 28.2% respectively. The feminization and aging of agricultural practitioners and laborers have posed a challenge to traditional agricultural management and have created a bad prospect for the agricultural industry.

The household contract responsibility system is a type of small-scale farmer economy involving single households and equalization. Although it can meet the needs for food and clothing for farmers, it cannot help rural areas become rich. Indeed, the system activated farmers' enthusiasm in production compared to the commune system, but it cannot continuously arouse the enthusiasm, as demonstrated in the agricultural fluctuation of the late 1980s and the first half of the 1990s. Especially, with the advance of marketization, industrialization and urbanization, the scattered household-based management pattern cannot meet the requirements of economic and social developments, and becomes the obstacle for development and makes rural areas the backwater of the economy. Moreover, due to the faults of other rural policies, the so-called problems in agriculture, farmer and rural areas have become more and more serious. Thus, the farmland transaction and scale management are not subjective wills, but the inevitable choice for the traditional agriculture in the face of a crisis.

4.2. *Land transfer and moderate scale management becoming the premise of agricultural modernization*

Land transfer and scale management are actually two sides of the same coin, as the land transaction is indispensable for relative land concentration and the enlargement of agricultural management scale. Thus, land transaction and scale management are the basis and premise of agricultural modernization. Although there is a difference in the growth rate of agricultural modernizations in different stages, most of them are in the initial stage, which can be seen in all cases.

Firstly, modern agriculture needs both division of labor and specialized production, which certainly cannot be achieved in the decentralized operation by single households. At the decentralized operation stage, there only exists natural division but no social division. Farmers cannot conduct the specialized production but several types of operations for their own needs, and due to the collective ownership and the household contract responsibility system, the land becomes very scattered, one household can generally have 3–5 *mu* (2,000 to 3,333 m^2) of land scattered in several blocks to plant several crops, so the fragmentation of land is inevitable under small-scale farmer economy. Conversely, after the implementation of land transaction and scale management, social division and specialized production naturally become common and a series of specialized production bases are formed, which are demonstrated by all cases above. For example, after the complete transfer of 2,000 *mu* (1,333,333 m²) of land in Qianfu Village, the sweet sorghum from aerospace breeding is planted in all lands, which has changed the original state of planting wheat and corn; Aoxiaoying Village has planted vegetables and fruits and carried out tour agriculture; Zhenglong Village has become the specialized vegetable base with a scale of over 1,000 *mu* (666,667 m²); Lingyun Village specializes in planting various kinds of flowers and plants and nursery stocks and has become a veritable Western Flower World; the High-Tech Modern Agricultural Industry Park in Qiquan Town has large area and adopts several types of operation and comprehensive development patterns, but it has a finer social division and higher degree of specialization. It has not only formed the specialized vegetable base and red grape base, but also has established the specialized organization or institution to provide specialized machinery service and labor service.

Secondly, agricultural modernization requires science and technology input for the advance of scientific farming, which cannot be implemented under a small-scale farmer economy. The field-based contracting is conducted based on small land, small scale, small machine, scattered and single-operated pattern, physical labor and previous experiences, which require neither large machines nor scientific and technological input and training. So, the small-scale farmer economy is only the traditional and experienced agriculture, but not the modern scientific and technological agriculture. However, after the implementation of land transaction and scale management, most have been changed and continuously varied, which is demonstrated by all cases above. For example, sweet sorghum planted in Qianfu Village adopts the aerospace breeding, and large agricultural machinery can be used at a large scale for the plant and harvest. Although there are no significant changes in other operations, the processing technique of sweet corn of Shennonghegu Company is completely high-tech. The vegetable planting in Zhenglong Village has specialized technical guidance and supervision, and its technical training also has been paid attention to and gained great achievements. Similarly, the planting of flowers and plants and nursery stocks in Western Flower World is also on a road of scientific development, which has conducted technical training for local farmer workers to improve their cultural quality and technical capacity and has trained its own technicians and administrative staff. In addition, the plastic film mulching technique, aggregate cultivation technique, cell cultivation technique, facility agriculture and the industrialized production of the company have shown the advantage of agricultural modern development. The High-Tech Modern Agricultural Industry Park in Qiquan Town has obtained impressive achievements in science and technology agriculture. The large-scale mechanical farming, the insect pest and disease prevention, the standardized vegetable production base, the red grape base, the high-quality pig cultivation base, the construction of other characteristic agricultural production bases, the building of Wenjingyuan brand and the registration of Qiquan trademark have all shown the scientific spirit of modern agriculture — especially the establishment of Agricultural Expert Building, the activation of agricultural science and technology innovation and the commercialization of science and technology results have shown the good prospect of agricultural science and technology development.

Thirdly, the standardization and industrialization of the production and operation are another important symbol of modern agriculture. Commonly, the standardization of industrial production has become common sense, while the standardization of agricultural production is still an unsolved problem, but it actually cannot be expected or achieved under the single household-based production pattern, because the small scale and manual operation do not need and cannot implement the standardized production and industrialized operation. However, after the development of land transaction and scale management, the standardized production has been put on the agenda. Although there is a difference in the specified standard and implementation method between different agricultural industries, as well as in the stage of development, all cases above still have revealed the tendency of development for us. It is especially obvious in the standardization of vegetable planting in Zhenglong Village, as described above, the precise measurement is conducted in line spacing and the fertilizing is conducted in accordance with regulations in time, type and dosage. As vividly described by villagers that plant vegetables while striving toward standardization, the village's objectives are to conduct comprehensive course control from field to dining table for agricultural products and establish a standardized pattern of production with standardization, product with mark, quality with detection, authentication with procedure and market with supervision. In another case, the standardization in Western Flower World is enterprise-led. All containers have certain dimensions ranging from 12*12 cm to 12*15 cm, and the breeding and cultivation of flower, plant and nursery stock and the popularization and application of new technologies all have a set of clear standards and strict procedures. The High-Tech Modern Agricultural Industry Park in Qiquan Town focuses on the construction of standardized production base, the implementation of various production and service standards and the accomplishment of scale, facility and standardization production. It has established the Provincial-Level Agriculture Standardization Edible Mushrooms Production Base and the Provincial-Level Agriculture Standardization Red Grape Production Base, implemented hotel-type management and one-stop service, adopted the management pattern of unifying brands. It has also specified production standards, quality, rebates for over-fulfilling production targets, profit sharing, technical contract and labor service contract, and is amenable to exploring feasible routes for different agriculture standardizations.

Fourthly, ecologicalization is the direction of modern agriculture. Traditional agriculture involves some natural ecological factors, such as the application of organic fertilizer and crop rotation of cultivated land, but the management on small scale not only limits its development, but also reduces its action and effect. Fortunately, the implementation of land transaction and scale management has provided wide space and huge possibilities for the development of ecological agriculture and circular economy, which is demonstrated by all cases above. For example, the planting of sweet corn in Qianfu Village has provided basic raw materials for adjusting the agricultural production structure and forming circular agriculture and industrial chain, e.g., the seed and straw of sweet sorghum can be used to produce sugar, bioethanol, newtol, medium to high-class paper, the 4th generation of biological compound fertilizer, protein feed, etc. The ecological agriculture and circular economy are also developed in Zhenglong Village, in which the leaf of broccoli is exchanged with cow dung from Xiaohu Village that is used to produce organic fertilizer, by which waste of both parties are utilized to meet their requirements, save costs and greatly increase economic and environmental benefits. The aggregate cultivation technique in Senhe Company in Western Flower World adopts such waste as rice husks and peanut shells. The construction of agricultural product processing park in Qiquan Town not only has developed export-oriented agriculture with high added value and long processing chain, but also has produced microbial fertilizer and biodiesel using leftovers and waste from agricultural production. Meanwhile, the common development direction of all cases above is to combine the primary and tertiary industries to develop tourism, picking, adventure travel and leisure agriculture.

Finally, modern agriculture is marketization agriculture, which highly depends on market construction and the development of logistics and distribution channels that cannot be achieved in traditional agriculture. The scattered individual agriculture, mainly self-sufficient agriculture, has less agricultural surplus and extremely low commodity rate, pays no attention on product sales and is unable to expand the market, and naturally cannot endure the risks caused by market fluctuations. Conversely, modern agriculture developed based on large-scale land transaction is commercial agriculture that serves the market and other participants, in which the products should be rapidly distributed and sold to achieve product value and complete the circulation of reproduction. All cases in this paper are related to this aspect. For example, Zhenglong Village adopts the pattern of combining both company and base, developing contract farming, signing a purchasing contract with Tai'an Honghai Company to ensure market outlet, and participating in the determination of agricultural product price relying on its economic strength. In addition, its supply contract with supermarkets in Tai'an and Jinan is favorable for the direct distribution of vegetables to the market and can not only reduce intermediate links but also can meet social demands. Several companies in Western Flower World will establish their own flower and tree hypermarkets and will be responsible for purchasing and selling the products from local flower growers under the pattern of company and household combination. The agricultural industry park in Qiquan Town pays more attention to market expansion and mechanism construction. In addition to establishing the Qiquan Agricultural Product Logistics Center and Exhibition and Selling Center, it has established the specialized cooperative for agricultural product marketing and has developed new marketing patterns, such as the connection between agricultural products, supermarkets, schools and restaurants. The park was named by the Department of Agriculture as the "Pilot Base for the Connection between Agricultural Product, Supermarket and School." Lvsheng Agricultural Science & Technology Development Ltd., is also listed by the Department of Education as the Direct Supply Base of Agricultural Product to Canteen of Colleges and Universities in Sichuan Province; and Runhe Vegetable and Fruit Cooperative has signed a direct supply contract for high-end agricultural products with Jinniu Hotel and has formed an industrial chain integrating raw material production, product processing and product distribution.

4.3. Great changes caused by land transfer and scale management

Large-scale land transaction and agricultural modern management have obviously changed the production mode of agriculture and the living pattern of farmers and have injected new dynamics into rural development. These changes are different in breadth and depth, but great attention should be paid on these changes.

The first change is about the entry of external enterprise into agriculture and the change of the operators in agriculture. For all cases in this paper, such as Qianfu Village and Aoxiaoying Village in Tongzhou District of Beijing, Western Flower World in Pixian County of Chengdu, the High-Tech Modern Agricultural Industry Park in Qiquan Town of Chongzhou City and the grain planting base of Chongzhou Grain Reserve Storehouse, an obvious change is the entry of external enterprise into the agriculture, which has changed the operators in agricultural production. As for Zhenglong Village in Ningyang of Shandong Province, it does not introduce any external enterprise but has established the economic cooperative organization, which has also caused similar changes in operators, and the management pattern has changed from original small farmer management to enterprise management, and farmers are no longer operators but property right owners and agricultural workers. Meanwhile, the change in the role of operator has not only caused the change of farmer's identity and position, but also has solved the feminization and aging problems of management under traditional agriculture to some extent, which will become the leading force for rural revolution.

However, the most contentious is the attitude toward the introduction of external enterprise. For this, the government's documents propose that enterprises are not encouraged to contract land in rural areas, and some people worry that the external enterprises will violate farmers' benefits. But we think that the introduction of external enterprises into the agriculture has a positive role, which can bring technology and funding for those areas with large rural labor mobility and the urgent need for structural adjustment. Aside from that it also has obvious contributions in the transformation of traditional agriculture. Thus, it is questionable for the government to issue prohibitions without considering specific reasons and circumstances. In the process, the following aspects should be carefully examined: Firstly is whether the enterprise obtains the land by voluntary transfer from farmers. If local governments are keen to accelerate land transaction and attract investment, so the land transfers are under duress. Under such circumstances, it should be clearly prohibited. Second is whether the land rent given by the enterprise is determined based on the negotiation between both parties, and whether the land rent can be ensured to be fair after the land management right is transferred from farmer to the enterprise. Third is whether the enterprise actually utilizes the land from rural areas for agricultural use, and whether there is some executable supervision and punishment when the enterprise does not apply them for agricultural use. Fourthly, whether the enterprise's utilization on land may destroy the arable layer is a problem that should be supervised and constrained by the administrative department.

The second change is about the transition of farmer's identity and position, which can be seen in all cases above; namely farmers have become shareholders, commune members or agricultural workers. Meanwhile, the composition of farmers' income has also been changed, and farmers usually have two or three types of income, including rental income plus labor income, or rental income, labor income and dividend income. The current situation of this change looks quite good and farmers' income does not decrease but obviously increases after the land transaction. For example, the per capita net income of Qianfu Village has increased from RMB 3,000 Yuan before the transfer to RMB 5,877 Yuan after the transfer, which is nearly doubled; over two years after the implementation of land transaction and scale management in Zhenglong Village, the per capita net income has increased by more than RMB 2,000 Yuan; the monthly labor income of a villager in Lingyun Village has reached RMB 800 to 1,000 Yuan, and the annual salary can reach as high as RMB 15,000 Yuan. The net income of a farmer in Qiquan Town has also increased from RMB 2,500 Yuan in 2003 to RMB 5,935 Yuan in 2008. Moreover, farmers have more spare time to develop and meet various other demands. In Qianfu Village and Western Flower World, farmers can even freely arrange their work time. Thus, we think that the change in farmers' identity will undoubtedly lead to separation of farmland's contractor from its operator. The state policies should focus on the trend and scope of this change, and some efforts should be paid to the possible impact on the rural households, farmers' income and possible policy arrangements.

The third change is about rural industrial structure and grain management. It is indicated from cases in this paper that the scale transfer of land has promoted the adjustment of rural industrial structure, has changed the production and management pattern of traditional agriculture, and has been on a road of intensification, industrialization and standardization. The industrial structure of traditional agriculture usually has a single development pattern that mainly focuses on grain planting, but after the land transaction and scale management, the professional level has been greatly improved, besides that the variety of planting or cultivation has greatly increased. As we see in the existing cases, most villagers plant various vegetables, flowers, plants, nursery stocks and raw materials for biological energy sources and cultivate different types of livestock and fowls. Moreover, the degree of mechanization in the whole production process has been improved, the science and technology investment and market coconsciousness have been increased, and the service systems before, during and after the production have been established. Meanwhile, due to the intensive utilization and industrial management of land, the output capacity of land has been doubled, which can be seen in all cases of land transaction and scale management. For example, the development of agricultural industry park in Qiquan Town had a regional GDP of RMB 352 million and a financial income of RMB 10.8 million in 2008, which was an increase of 32% and RMB 6.8 million respectively over 2003. The ratio of three industries has also changed from 49:27:24 to 33:37:30.

Unfortunately, it was difficult for us to find the cases about specialized grain production during our investigation. This is obviously caused by the low comparative benefit of grain growing. For new agricultural operators, the target of profit maximization will undoubtedly make them allocate their resources to those crops with higher added value. Thus, how to solve the problem of grain production under modern agriculture may need special policy guidance and practical and effective policy measures.

The last change is regarding the development of new cooperative economy. After the implementation of the household contract responsibility system, rural areas still adopt the collective economy system, but the collective economy actually has become an empty shell in many areas. For example, the village collective of Qianfu Village has a liability of RMB 860,700 Yuan and less than RMB 10,000 Yuan in its account. In the traditional collective economy, all farmer households make their own decisions and do not take a uniform action. Their income and living basically have nothing to do with the village collective, and they are only connected with each other by the collective ownership of land and the membership right of each household. Such a collective economy has no element of a cooperative economy and has changed into the economy of cadres at town and village levels to a large extent. However, after the land transaction and scale management, some villages have established the land (share) cooperative, some have developed various specialized cooperatives, some have constructed facility agriculture and various specialized production bases, some have introduced external funds, technologies and enterprises, and in this way the element of cooperative economy has actually been introduced and generated by adopting the cooperation pattern integrating both company and farmer households. A new cooperative economic organization has been formed, and originally scattered farmer households are combined into a community. Meanwhile, the original collective economy has been strengthened. The organizations and cadres at town and village levels have wherewithal and incentives to increase investment in public undertakings, and the relation between village collective and villager has been improved. Some cooperatives are completely separated from the organizations at town and village levels and are operated in accordance with the regulations of cooperative economic organization, and through common interests. Villagers who participate in the cooperative economic organization become the master of the organization and can participate in the decision-making and management of the organization. Given the fact that the *Property Right Law* has confirmed the nature of land contractual management right as a property right in law, the land transaction and scale management will undoubtedly play important role for such a change. Especially, with the income growth brought by land transaction and scale management, some areas began to change the living pattern from scattered to intensive, to construct settlements and new residential quarters for farmers and to conduct the construction for rural infrastructure, which has greatly improved the housing conditions of farmers. Meanwhile, the government of Chengdu has further put forward and carried out an urbanization standard that is quite different from the current standard, so that farmers' thoughts and living pattern have been greatly changed.

4.4. *Choices over patterns of land transfer and scale management*

So far land transaction and scale management are still tentative and are being created and innovated by all governments and farmers. They are implemented in various patterns, which are worth careful summary.

The land transaction can be divided into two types by transferors, the first of which is the direct transfer between households, the second is the secondary transfer through the cooperative organization or the village collective. In other words, farmer households transfer their land to the cooperative organization or village collective, who will then transfer this land to enterprises. Generally, many farmer households participate in the first type of transfer, but each household only transfers small pieces of land, usually to large households, and the large household-based management pattern is formed. Meanwhile, quite a few farmer households participate in the second type of transfer. Each action transfers large tracts of land, mostly to enterprises, and the management pattern integrating both enterprises and production bases is formed. Comparatively, the latter has larger management scale and higher degree of modernization.

By recipients, land transaction can be divided into three types, including farmer households (especially large ones), cooperative organizations and external enterprises. Here, the village collective is usually considered as the intermediary for the second outflow and can be treated as a non-receiver. It can be seen from the existing situation that the inflow amount of land to common household is small, the one to large household has an upper limit of $100\,mu$ ($66,667\,m^2$), the one to the cooperative organization is about $1,000\,mu$ ($666,667\,m^2$), while the one to the enterprise is different in scale, sometimes can reach as high as several thousand mu ($1\,mu$ = $666,667\,m^2$). The inflow to large household requires some skilled farmers, while the one to the cooperative organization requires the entrepreneur or foregoer to cooperate, and the one to the enterprise mainly depends on agricultural enterprises and agricultural product processing enterprises. Among three patterns above, the one that can best reflect and protect the interests of households who transfer their land is the cooperative economic organization for the following reasons: In the transfer to large households, the transferors can only obtain land rent and might not continue to labor on their land. All profits will go to the large household, but labor forces liberated from the land can seek other work, such migrant work. In the transfer to the enterprise, each household will obtain both rental and labor incomes, but the enterprise other than transferors will obtain the profit; while in the transfer to the cooperative organization, the organization will obtain the profit, and each household will obtain dividend income in addition to rental and labor incomes. For example, Huang Shiyou, a share-holder of the land share cooperative in Zhenglong Village, bought into a share using his $5\,mu$ ($3,333\,m^2$) of land, and obtained a salary of RMB 15 Yuan/day, a share capital of RMB 3,500 Yuan and a dividend of RMB 5,000 Yuan in 2008. Unfortunately, entrepreneurs are rare, especially in rural areas, and we do not pay any attention to protect[6] them, so the existing land transaction and scale management basically depends on large households and enterprises.

---

[6]In the process of China's reform, there numerous entrepreneurs have fallen, such as Zhu Shijian from Yunnan Province, the first urban entrepreneur to fall, and Huang Guangyu, who was caught recently. Meanwhile, in the case of Dongsandao Village in Haicheng City of Liaoning Province (discussed in Implementation and Protection of Land Property Right under the Background of Urbanization), Ma Yuying, a local farmer entrepreneur known as the head of the village was caught and expelled from the Party.

By the type of operation after land transaction, the scale management can be divided into five types, including grain planting, vegetable and fruit planting, flower, plant and nursery stock planting, the breeding industry and the planting of other commercial crops. As we see in the existing situation, the transfer to large household mainly focuses on grain planting and the one to the cooperative organization mainly focuses on the breeding industry and the planting of vegetables and fruit. The one to the enterprise mainly focuses on the planting of flowers and plants, nursery stocks and other commercial crops. However, there is no case of enterprise-led grain planting. The grain planting of Chongzhou Grain Storehouse is related to its own function and further processing. In other words, the enterprise's specialty is in grain production. The difference between them is not only related to the production and management conditions of inflow party (i.e., the one at the receiving end of land transfer) and the inflow scale, but also is related to entrepreneur ability and some external conditions such as market and capital. Consequently, how to ensure grain planting during the processes of land transaction and scale management is worth further discussion.

From the degree of participation of transferors, the transfer to large household has the lowest degree of participation, followed by the transfer to the enterprise, while the transfer to the cooperative organization has the highest degree, which is well demonstrated in the case of Zhenglong Village. From the existing institutional conditions, the transfer to the enterprise may become the major transfer pattern for following reasons: Firstly, entrepreneur resources are rare in rural areas. Secondly, rural areas are relatively poor and lack investment. Thirdly, enterprises can bring external resources. However, transfer to the enterprise may not be optimal, but the one that is based on the transfer to the cooperative organization and combines several transfer patterns may be optimal, which can be well indicated in the case of High-Tech Modern Agricultural Industry Park in Qiquan Town of Chongzhou. There, a mutually coordinated institutional arrangement was formed by adopting the advantages of all transfer patterns.

After conducting some separate investigations, we can conduct a general analysis and discussion. It is obvious that theoretically, the existing pattern of land transaction and scale management can be summarized into two types: The share cooperative management of land and the leasing management or tenant farming of land. However, we should see the difference between the pooling of land as shares or cooperative management and the general joint-stock enterprise in the following aspects. Firstly, the share based on land contracting rights is not an actual financing share but has its leasing attribute, which can obtain the rental income. Especially at the present stage, land share cannot be transferred, sold or mortgaged, while the stock of general joint-stock enterprise can be traded, obtain dividends and bonuses, but cannot obtain rental income. But whether the land share will go through further marketization and finally move towards stockholding system still needs to be answered in practice. Secondly, the stockholders of the joint-stock enterprise have the right to sell their stock equity based on their own decisions, while in the land share cooperative, the members cannot sell their stocks but have the right to quit within a fixed time. Thirdly, in the bankruptcy liquidation of the stock-joint enterprise, stockholders should pay by using their investments, while if the cooperative goes bankrupt, the members can still own the land. Fourthly, the regional characteristics of the cooperative make the members' direct participation in the affairs of the cooperative active and the participation in the management, while the stockholders of the joint-stock enterprise can only put forward their views in the general meeting of stockholders, but have no other direct effects on the enterprise.

Meanwhile, there are also some obvious differences between the land share cooperative system and land rental system. Firstly, in the land share cooperative system, farmer's transfer on land contracting rights is not thorough or complete, and if the household owns the contractual management right individually before the transfer, the household will still collectively own the right after the transfer and still has the usufruct right. But the transfer of the contractual management right under rental system is thorough and complete, the household only has the usufruct right. The contractual management right can be reclaimed after the expiration of tenancy, but from the degree of marketization of property rights, the share cooperative system is lower than the rental system. Secondly, in the rental system, the household can only obtain rental income, but can obtain labor income from the lessee or other parties in accordance with the difference of employer, while the lessee will undoubtedly own the profit. But in the share cooperative system, the household can participate in the cooperative's work and obtain labor income in addition to rental income, besides that the members will share the profit. Thus, in view of ensuring farmer's rights and interests, the stockholding cooperative system is better than the rental system. Thirdly, from the growth of income, the rental system adopts the contractual arrangement and contractual (fixed) income, while the share cooperative system will generate the residual income or variable income.

All discussions above aim at explaining that a perfect land transaction pattern does not exist, and the selection of transfer pattern should be conducted in accordance with specific conditions and future development, or through competition in practices.

4.5. Roles of the governments and collective economic organizations in land transfer and scale management

All cases above indicate that the governments and collective economic organizations have played quite an important role in land transaction and scale management. For example, in Qianfu Village, the village committee is actually the main player in land transactions. It plays the roles of both inflow and outflow parties, both party A and party B of transfer contracts, and both plaintiff and defendant if contract disputes occur. Meanwhile, the officials from the government conduct an investigation of the target company before the transfer, and the village committee becomes manager of farming activities after the transfer. Similarly, in the implementation measure for construction of Western Flower World in Lingyun Village of Pixian County, the first article is "government leadership, coordination by departments and standardized operation". The government not only completes the construction of road and water supply and drainage pipe networks, but also is responsible for investment invitation activities in which officials take multiple trips to Shanghai to complete their tasks. It exempts enterprises from the land rent for three years for the reason of attracting external investors, and besides it also provides a connection bridge between villagers and enterprises. In the construction of agricultural industry park in Qiquan Town of Chongzhou City, the government also plays a leading or promoting role. In the cooperative organization in Zhenglong Village, Jiangji Town, Shandong Province, Tian Wenwu holds the position of both party secretary and the chairman of the cooperative, and the government of Jiangji Town has formulated the *Measures for the Transfer of Contractual Management Right of Rural Land in Jiangji Town, has established the Jiangji Office of Rural Land Transfer*, and has established and implemented a series of procedures for the application and review of land transactions. We can draw a conclusion from all cases in this paper that land transfer is impossible to develop or cannot develop rapidly without the government's leading role, so the existing land transfers and scale management in China are a government-led process to a large extent.

The leading role of the government and collective economic organizations in land transaction and scale management is not a product of officials generated on a whim but has its objective basis and conditions. Firstly, China adopts the centralization system, in which both the party and central government have strong administrative and mobilization abilities. So, when the central government wants to promote land transaction and scale management, all party organizations and governmental departments will naturally take positive action, because the success of land transaction and scale management are related not only to the development of agriculture and the stability of rural areas, but also the achievements and benefits of officials at lower levels. Secondly, China adopts the collective ownership of land in rural areas, which is not an originally cooperative economy but an administrative power-led economy. In this system, the village collective organization and its agents are the subjects of property rights, and organizations at the village level are not only economic organizations and nominally voluntary but actually agencies of township government at the basic level. Meanwhile, the contractual management right other than the ownership of land is transferred, but the owner's will is usually decisive. Besides, the selection of transfer pattern and the decision of successful transfer usually reflect the combination but not the separation between the ownership and management rights. Moreover, the central government forbids the Two Cropland Tillage System and subcontracting while discouraging enterprises from contracting land in rural areas. But actually, both systems are common in the early stage of transfer, while the transfer to an enterprise becomes the major pattern in the middle stage of transfer.

Thirdly, after the implementation of the household contract responsibility system, China's rural economy has returned to the scattered and single-household-based small-scale farmer economy to a large extent. Farmers' negative memories of the commune movement makes them worry and boycott the re-collectivization, so worries from farmers in Qianfu Village and Zhenglong Village are not uncommon. Under such a background, land transaction and scale management are difficult to carry out or may be implemented slowly without the leadership and promotion by the government. Generally, Chinese farmers have a special relationship with government officials. They fear but have to depend on or need the officials, so the government-led pattern is inevitable. Finally, in rural society of China, the government and its officials are the most creditworthy organization. While the communication between farmers does not need the participation of government, once the communication goes beyond the person-to-person scope, individual reputation will be ineffective without the participation of the government. For example, the communication between farmers and external society (including enterprises and other organizations) needs the government and the financing from financial institution also needs the guarantees of the government or officials.

On the whole, the government plays a necessary and important role in land transaction and scale management, but sometimes farmer's interests are violated owing to the strong position and interference of government officials. Fortunately, the central government has repeatedly stressed the protection on farmer's land contractual management right and has clearly specified that land transaction should be decided by the contractor and be conducted at the contractor's will, and farmers have also boycotted the simple and crude actions of cadres, and therefore the situation is now being gradually improved. All transferors have signed a contract with each farmer household, most of which need a democratic process of mobilization and discussion. For example, in the land transaction of Zhenglong Village, the second batch of households firmly applied to join the cooperative because of the demonstration effect. In the land transaction of Chengdu, households who want to join the cooperative should fill out an application form (See Annex 10). We should realize that the land transaction in this stage has the highest degree of spontaneous farmer participation in the 60-year history of Chinese rural reform.

However, there are also some problems, which mainly occur during the processes of comprehensive land consolidation and urban–rural replacement. For Chengdu, the government does well in land transaction and scale management that has a large scale. It not only has actively promoted and implemented the work on a large scale and has explored a set of operational procedures in accordance with its own situation to make the work on a normative path, but also has thought about how to protect farmers' interests and has identified and solved some important problems, such as establishing a farmland protection fund and presenting a set of standards for urbanization. All of these have been put into practice.

But there are still some problems and disadvantages. As an important part of overall-planning of urban–rural development, land transaction and scale management in Chengdu are usually bound with land replacement and the construction of farmer's concentrated residential areas. For this reason, the land consolidation should be first conducted and the gullies of farmland should be filled to increase farmland. Meanwhile, the scattered farmer households are concentrated in the new residential areas and the homestead is reclaimed as farmland, and finally all construction land quotas are sold to the city for raising capital for new residence construction and land consolidation. On the whole, such action is rational, and even an innovation or breakthrough, in eliminating the dilemmas under current institutional conditions. This is mainly because it can change fixed assets into valuable things and put them into circulation and transaction. But the question is whether such transactions are led by government officials without the participation of farmers. On the surface, farmers may be glad to own a new house with a per capita area of $35\,m^2$, but actually they suffer losses in this transaction. Among cases in Chengdu, such transactions are only explained in the case of Lingyun Village, Xinminchang Town, Pixian County. The village obtains an incremental $375.2\,mu$ $(250,133\,m^2)$ of farmland through land consolidation and homestead reclamation, $364.8\,mu$ $(243,200\,m^2)$ of which is replaced as construction land for urban construction of Pitong Town, so that the village would obtain an income of RMB 631.104 million Yuan in accordance with the average auction price of RMB 1.73 million Yuan/mu $(667\,m^2)$ in 2008, but it only obtains RMB 410.22 million Yuan, which is more than RMB 200 million Yuan lower than the income it deserved. Moreover, the total investment is RMB

402.34 million Yuan, including RMB 185.65 million Yuan for new community construction, demolition compensation and land consolidation (including a farmer repurchase fund of RMB 23.60 million Yuan) and RMB 216.69 million Yuan for new residential quarters construction of Pitong Town. Yet it is doubtful whether the Lingyun Village should pay for the construction of new residential quarters of Pitong Town in addition to the investment in the construction of its own new residential quarters. More puzzling is that it is known from officials of Chengdu that the average land price for quota replacement is RMB 80,000 Yuan/*mu* (667 m²). Why is there so large a difference between them? What is the basis for such a calculation? Why cannot such transaction be more transparent? All these questions still need to be answered for farmers.

4.6. *Land transfer versus quota transaction*

The problems regarding land transfer and land quota transaction arise from the cases in Chengdu in the section above, which are important because many people confuse their different characteristics and consider quota transaction as an important method of land transfer. But, they actually have both similarities and principled differences.

Land transfer is basically a market transaction behavior with the participation of the government, which takes land contractual management rights as the target of transaction and farmer households who contract the land as the main traders. Even the secondary transfer in which government is involved and plays a decisive role represents the will of the contractor to some extent and needs to obtain the authorization from the property owner, to which the agreement on the first transfer can be seen as evidence. Thus, the development of land transaction and scale management is the further development and deepening of rural marketization reform and is an inevitable course of modernization for rural areas.

In the process of China's reform, quota transaction is common and usually is considered new. The earliest quota transaction was the foreign exchange quota transaction of the late 1980s and early 1990s. Owing to foreign exchange control and retention system, some units had foreign exchange quotas that were not utilized temporarily, but some units had no foreign exchange quotas but were badly in need of it, while the foreign exchange control resulted in separate official prices and black market prices. For this reason, the government established the foreign exchange transaction center, in which both parties of supply and demand could conduct quota transaction at the official price, and then the purchasing party could make up for the selling party at the black market price. However, with the enlargement of transaction scale, the dual-track system of exchange rates ended in 1994 (Sheng Hong, 1996). The second case of quota transaction was regarding cigarette quota transactions. Because cigarettes had a high price, high profit and high tax, all regions wanted to establish cigarette factories. However, some regions had raw materials and some had no quotas. Owing to the cigarette monopolization system and the special distribution mechanism of cigarette production quotas, cutthroat competition emerged. In order to solve this problem, the State Development Planning Commission and the State Tobacco Monopoly Bureau carried out the quota transaction in each region. Those regions with quotas but no raw materials could sell their production quotas to those regions lacking them but with raw materials. Then the selling regions could get part of the profits and taxes from the purchasing regions (Jiang Xiaojuan and Liu Shijin, 1999). There are other examples of quota transaction, which will not be listed here.

The existing overall planning of urban–rural development is actually a large-scale land quota transaction. However, there is an obvious difference between land quota transaction and foreign exchange quota transaction or cigarette quota transaction. The foreign exchange quota transaction was completed through the foreign exchange transaction center, but it was a direct behavior between both parties of demand and supply, even if it was agents of both parties that participated in the transaction. In the cigarette quota transaction, the main player was local governments and the transaction price was actually tax revenue, which is one type of rationing transactions as described by Commons (1983) in which the property owner is the main player in the transaction because the major property right of the government is the right to collect taxes. But it is quite different for land quota transaction, which is a kind of simulation under the current land system and a mechanism intentionally created by the government, which can achieve various objectives. The transaction is not that of construction land but merely the quota. After obtaining the quota, the party possessing it will have to actually buy land necessary for construction. Meanwhile, the player with the construction land quota transaction is not actually the owner of construction land; rather the local government and its officials are. Unfortunately, in such a transaction, the owners of property rights cannot participate in the determination of the transaction price. They do not even know who they are dealing with, let alone being able to choose their business partners. Therefore, it is not so much a commission agency relationship as administrative coercion. It is not so much a market transaction as a black box operation without the participation of the subject of rights. And it is not so much an equivalent exchange as it is the government's secret occupation over farmers' rights and interests. Thus, the land replacement or quota transaction is different from land transaction. As we know, in the land transaction in Qianfu Village, villagers participated in the determination of price and increased the rent from RMB 700 Yuan/*mu* (667 m^2) to RMB 800 Yuan/*mu* (667 m^2). In addition, the cooperation with Shennonghegu Company was also agreed upon by villagers after the investigation by cadres. Thus, the land replacement or quota transaction cannot be confused with land transfer. If the government intended to confuse them, the problem would seem more serious.

Although there are large differences between them, there are still similarities. Namely, if the quota transaction can be decided by farmers and can provide most income to them like farmland transfer does, the problem regarding the transfer of construction land will be properly solved.

4.7. Financing land transfer and development of rural finance

Financing is important for land transaction and scale management, which to a large extent determines the selection of transfer patterns, decisions regarding transfer scale, and the size of transfer deals. With the land transaction and scale management in Qianfu Village and Aoxiaoying Village, the former introduced the Shennonghegu Company, while the latter cooperated with an aerospace service company. But both aimed to solve the financing problem with land transaction — namely how to pay land rent. Similarly, in the case of Western Flower World, some external enterprises were introduced, which not only solved the source of land rent but also introduced external funds. For instance, Senhe Company invested RMB 50 million Yuan, Miaofu Modern Nursery Stock Company invested RMB 106 million Yuan, and Jingwen Greening Arts Company plans to invest RMB 50 million Yuan, with RMB 30 million Yuan in the first stage. Just like solving the financing issue in rural areas of Chengdu's Lingyun Village, the land replacement based on land consolidation mainly aims to meet the financing need for new residential quarter construction, while the concentrated residence is closely related to land consolidation and land transaction. However, the High-Tech Modern Agricultural Industry Park in Qiquan Town has developed rapidly and has various sources of funding, including RMB 35 million Yuan from fiscal investment, RMB 10 million from governmental investment companies, RMB 90 million Yuan from social funds and others from external enterprises. For example, since 2003, the park has introduced 41 agricultural projects with a total investment of RMB 593.46 million Yuan and introduced 12 processing enterprises for agricultural industrialization, including Yingmalong Company with a RMB 60 million Yuan investment and Huhui Company with a RMB 23 million Yuan investment. It has also introduced the logistics enterprise Chengdu Dahao Agriculture Ltd., that invested RMB 5 million Yuan. Zhenglong Village does not introduce external funds, but in order to dispel villagers' worries and concerns regarding the establishment of the cooperative, secretary Tian Wenwu took out RMB 80,000 Yuan as security money. Therefore, solving the financial problem is an important method to promote land transaction and scale management and is among the key areas for rural development.

However, owing to the lack of financial institutions and narrow financing channels, the financing for rural areas is always difficult. The rural credit cooperative is the main supplier of rural finance, which is not just nominally a credit cooperative organization but is actually a financial institution controlled by local governments. Although town banks have developed for years, there are only about 100 banks in the whole country, which are inadequate for rural financing. Therefore, in reality, informal financing is undoubtedly common in rural areas.

At present, there are two major ways to solve the financial problem in land transaction and scale management. The first of which is introducing investment from external enterprises, which has become the most common one, as described in the cases above. Even if the central government did not encourage enterprises to contract land in rural areas, it has become one of the most important ways for land transaction, as local governments should depend on it to solve the financing problem for land transaction and scale management. The second way is financing through the investment company established and controlled by the government, which is also common, especially in the construction of small towns in Chengdu. The loan can be obtained from financial institutions through the investment company established and controlled by the government, by the governmental reputation, or through a bank mortgage after land is obtained through new residential quarter construction and land replacement. So the price of RMB 80,000 Yuan per *mu* ($667\,m^2$) of construction land quota occurs. However, farmers still cannot directly obtain loans from financial institutions using their property rights (including land contractual management right and homestead use right) as mortgage. It is reported that the pilot project for state-owned insurance companies is starting to be carried out in Chengdu.[7] Due to the participation of the government or officials, the financing through external enterprises or government-controlled investment companies have become two major methods of financing in rural land transaction and scale management. Obviously, under such institutional conditions in which the government lays strict restriction on rural finance, only the governmental credit is effective, but the non-governmental credit has difficulty supporting the financing requirements of large-scale land transactions. Meanwhile, scattered households cannot directly cooperate with large external enterprises due to a serious information asymmetry between them and the lack of mutual trust, and they can only expect the government to act as an intermediary. This is why the government-controlled investment organization can hold a monopoly.

It can be seen from all above that in rural areas of China under current institutional conditions, the scarcest things are entrepreneurship and funding. In such a case where entrepreneurs are scarce in rural areas and the financial market is not well-developed, governmental agencies and officials become the last refuge for promoting rural reform and development.

---

[7]See *21st Century Economic Report* on November 13, 2009.

Unfortunately, these parties have also restrained the formation and development of the other factors needed. Rural finance needs to be liberated and relevant institutional innovations must be carried out in the form of mortgages, rural finance, and credit financing that is suitable for modern agricultural development. This is a problem that should be solved in rural reform and development in the next step.

5. Policy Suggestions

Based on all analysis and discussions above, we draw the following policy conclusions and suggestions:

(1) It is suggested to ensure the permanent stability of the rural land contracting system and to provide an institutional basis for rural long-term peace and order. The rural land contracting system and property rights for farmers conferred by law are generated through farmers' efforts and continuous deepening of the Party's rural policies. One of the important reasons why farmers' land property rights are usually violated is the lack of a system to ensure rights. So in order to implement the permanent stability of the rural land contracting system, the following measures should be taken: Firstly, conduct land affirmation, registration and certification for contracted land, homesteads, forest land, wasteland, etc. Secondly, based on village communities, conduct democratic affirmation for membership and commence a collective community. Solidify the relationship between farmer and land or other properties. Thirdly, delineate the owner and boundaries of collective land, specify the inner ownership relationship among owners, and conduct collective ownership affirmation, registration and certification, with respect to both history and reality.

(2) It is suggested to improve farmers' land property rights functions and to ensure farmers' property rights on the land by ensuring land contracting rights, liberating land management rights and giving farmers land disposition rights. Since rural reform, the relationship between farmers' land contracting right and management rights has evolved. In the first few years of fixing farm quotas for each household, the land yielded good crops and there were few non-agricultural job opportunities; the

land contracting rights and management rights were basically combined. But after township enterprises developed, the non-agricultural income became the major income source for farmers, and agriculture became a bypass business, and therefore land contracting rights and management rights were partly separated from each other. After farmers move across regions, they are separated from each other for a long time. When collective land is used for non-agricultural industry, land contracting rights become stock rights, while land management rights are transferred. With the advance of urbanization, farmers' lands are expropriated and both of them are lost. Thus, besides land being expropriated due to government-led urbanization, land contracting rights are fixed, but land management rights are variable. The core of the stability of the rural basic management system is the stability of land contracting rights, while permanent stability focuses on the stability of the basic system regarding farmers' permanent ownership of land contracting rights. Consequently, in order to achieve farmers' land property rights, it is required to first ensure the stability of farmers' land contracting rights, liberate land management rights and give farmers the land disposition rights. This includes conducting mortgage pilot projects for rural land and homesteads, achieving property rights for land, contracting rights, and usufruct of homesteads, and providing a guarantee of capital investment for farmers.

(3) It is suggested to set an institutional base line for land transaction and to establish exclusive policy arrangements for preventing the violation of farmers' rights and interests. In the past few years, land transaction has been accelerated in some areas, which is caused by the promotion of local governments and the requirements of rural structural reform on new land management pattern. In central and western regions, rural labor forces move across regions, which results in the aging and feminization of agricultural operators. The age structure of the floating labor force will be changed in the future and mainly composed of youths born in the 1980s and 1990s who may not return to villages for farming after several years of working in the city as their fathers did. Consequently, in addition to the interference of local governments in land transactions, the village itself also has the demand for land transaction and moderate concentration after it loses most of its population.

Another question is about whether enterprises are allowed to participate in agriculture. Since the issuance of the No. 18 document, the trend of enterprise participation in rural construction has certainly been strengthened. If policies have some prohibitions but no means to implement these prohibitions, they will have limited effects. Thus, for the problems regarding land transaction, the behavior of local governments and the participation of legal professionals in agriculture, it is suggested to establish a base line for farmer rights and interests and some exclusive clauses as follows: (i) No matter how the land is transferred or whoever it is transferred to, the land user should sign a contract with the household holding the land contracting rights; (ii) Rent should be possessed by the owner of the land contracting right; (iii) Specify the growth rate of rent at certain intervals; (iv) Collective economic organization can only play a role of intermediary but cannot obtain land rent; (v) The lessee of land cannot take the land for non-agricultural use. Violators will be punished by related laws and will be supervised by farmer collective; and (vi) The lessee should not destroy the arable layer within the lease period.

(4) It is suggested to improve the position of rural households as a main participant with a leading role in the decision-making of scale transfer and to further improve the marketization level of land transaction and scale management. The target of land transaction and scale management is land contractual management rights but not land ownership. And the transferors are households, but not rural collective economic organizations, and certainly not rural governmental agencies. All above have been clearly specified by the documents of the central government and local governments, but the question is how to further implement and explore a set of operation instructions. On the surface, a democratic process is important, operational methods also need to be accumulated and improved, but the transfer pattern is more important. Currently, large-scale transfer mainly occurs in suburban areas of cities. The enterprise's participation has become the most important part, but from a long-term view, the establishment and development of cooperative organizations may become the major pattern, so more attention should be paid on the exploration and research in this aspect. Obviously, if an enterprise structure and industrial structure mainly

rely on local enterprises while integrating foreign enterprises, family farm and large planting household, land transaction and agricultural modernization will be smoothly promoted and improved.

(5) It is suggested to utilize the government's role in promoting land transaction and scale management and to standardize the government's behaviors. Under the current situation in China, many things cannot be conducted without the participation and promotion of the government. Especially due to the dual segmentation of the land system and governmental control, large-scale land transaction and modern management require more support from the government. However, the leading position and participation of the government usually replace and weaken the position of farmer households as main participants, and may even directly violate farmers' rights and interests and make land transaction distorted. Unfortunately, it is difficult to determine the participation scope and depth for the government, and the inertia of the governmental behaviors make it difficult to quit. Therefore, it is quite necessary and important to standardize the government's behaviors in land transaction, specify the government's role, establish a rent distribution mechanism for land transaction, and strengthen democratic and social supervision.

(6) It is suggested to create a loose social environment and promote and protect the existence and growing of rural entrepreneurs. Obviously, the emergence and growth of cooperative entrepreneurs is the key for promoting the development of rural cooperative organizations. In fact, there may be many able farmers among large rural populations who come to the city, broaden their horizons, increase their abilities and may become entrepreneurs in the future. But in such a society full of official standards, due to rampant jealousy and the lack of a loose and comfortable environment and social conditions for entrepreneurs, it is unfavorable for entrepreneurs to emerge. It is also difficult for those emerging entrepreneurs to survive the strains of the bureaucratic jungle while the government's intentional promotion and support usually spoil them. In fact, many experiences have shown that the growth of entrepreneurs is usually unexpected, and the key for their free development and innovation is to create a loose and comfortable social environment and tolerate or understand behaviors that may not

comply with traditional concepts or dominating ideologies. Their various defects and even great mistake that are not incurable should also be understood.

(7) It is suggested to liberate and develop rural finance based on non-governmental capital and to solve the financing problem in large-scale land transaction and rural development. The lagged financial industry has affected China's economic development and cannot meet the demand of economic development on financing, which is more obvious in rural areas. There, the formal finance can only meet about one-third of the funding demand, while the rest depends on informal non-governmental financing that is considered illegal. The transfer to external enterprises becomes the major transfer pattern largely because enterprises can solve the problem of financing. Since the land contractual management right is confirmed to be the property right, it can be used as the guarantee for mortgage loans, but it is not confirmed nor will it be done through existing financial institutions in rural areas. Thus, the financing problem has become one of the most important obstacles hindering land transaction and scale management. Now that the state finance focuses on important fields involving the national economy and the people's livelihood, rural financing should depend on non-governmental capital, and all financial institutions and activities should be basically liberated under the supervision of the government. Only when financing develops will the financial activities such as mortgages, guarantees, trusts and loans be activated, and large-scale land transaction and modern agriculture actually develop.

(8) It is suggested to support and develop farmer cooperative organizations and family farms and to explore the issue of large-scale land transaction mainly for grain planting. In our investigations and research, there were only a few cases of land transactions involving grain planting, most of which involved large households and state-owned grain planting enterprises, but there were few cases of grain planting by other enterprises in rural areas. Such a situation is not only related to the extremely low income of grain planting but also related to improper incentive policies. The planting base of Chongzhou Grain Storehouse just aims to replace old grain with new grain and serve for grain processing. The major route to solve the problem is to increase

the planting income by providing a farmland protection subsidy and planting subsidy and increasing grain price, and thus to make the rate of return from grain planting approximate to the average rate. Besides, it also can support and develop farmer cooperative economic organization, family farms and state-owned grain enterprises and promote land transaction and scale management in grain producing areas. For this reason, in addition to some preferences and conveniences in the government procurement, the government can take some special supportive measures for cooperative organizations and family farms engaged in grain planting. It should give all planting subsidies to the grain planter rather than those households who transfer their lands. Nevertheless, the land transaction subsidy should be given to those households that transfer their land, which can encourage land transaction.

Bibliography

"Cigarette Quota Market" and Marketization Reform in Licensed Industry-Analysis on Adjustment of Cigarette Production Plan with Compensation by Jiang Xiaojuan and Liu Shijin, published in *Case Study of China's Institutional Change* (Volume 2) edited by Zhang Shuguang, China Financial and Economic Press, 1999.

Decision on the Reduction of Agricultural Tax by the State Council, 2003.

Decision on Several Major Problems to Improve Rural Reform and Development, 2008.

Decision on Several Problems about the Establishment of Socialist Market Economy System, 1993.

"Deepen Rural Reform" by the Political Bureau of the CPC Central Committee, 1987.

Foreign Exchange Quota Transaction: A Case of Planned Right Transaction by Sheng Hong, published in *Case Study of China's Institutional Change* (Volume 1) edited by Zhang Shuguang, Shanghai People's Publishing House, 1996.

Institutional Economics by Commons, Commercial Press, 1983.

Land Contract Law of the People's Republic of China, 2002.

Measures on Management of Rural Land Contractual Management Right Transfer, January 2005.

Notice on 1982 Rural Work by the CPC Central Committee, January 1982.

Notice on 1984 Rural Work by the CPC Central Committee, January 1984.

Notice on 1986 Rural Work by the CPC Central Committee, January 1986.

Notice on Proposal to Stabilize and Perfect Land Contract Relation by the Ministry of Agriculture Endorsed by the State Council in March 1995.

Regulations on the Transfer of Land Contractual Management Right, 2001.

Several Policy Measures on Current Agricultural and Rural Economic Development by the CPC Central Committee and the State Council, November 1993.

Thesis Seminar: Land System Reform of China*

On July 27, 2009, the "Seminar on Land System Reform of China", hosted jointly by the National School of Development at Peking University, Beijing Unirule Institute of Economics and the Boyuan Foundation, was held in the National School of Development at Peking University. At the seminar, several experts and scholars gave speeches and had discussions on land system reform in China.

A.1 Part I: Empirical Research

A.1.1 *Liu Shouying*: *China's road of land capitalization and urbanization*

The essence of urbanization is the relocation of production resources between urban and rural areas and the transition of economic and social structures, which focuses on population urbanization. However, it can be seen from our investigation in Beijing that the urbanization with Chinese characteristics has some unique features. The first feature is the urbanization

---

*Volumes 77 to 83 in 2009 edition of *Policy Research Bulletin* published by National School of Development at Peking University.

of land, that is, farmers' collective land is expropriated by the government and becomes state-owned with the advance of urbanization and continuous extension of urban territory. The second feature is the formation of rural–urban continuum (i.e., the areas that connect urban and rural land), which is a typical phenomenon in China that is quite different from slum phenomenon in other developing countries. The third feature is that the urbanization has evolved as a game between the governments and farmers on grabbing differential earnings from land. Actually, the urbanization brings clear and increased differential earnings from land for the governments, but simultaneously, farmers who live in rural–urban continuum also share the differential earnings from land by providing living space for external migrant populations from using the remaining lands and homesteads. Obviously, the source of the differential earnings is from the growth of the mobile population.

There are two groups that actively respond to the trend in rental markets resulting from inflow of external population. One is those rural homeowners, who can take advantage of the fuzzy policy concerning their homesteads, the expiration of homestead welfare distribution and difficulty in management of illegal building on their inherited land, which thus forms a unique scene in the rural–urban continuum. Another force is the village collective organization, who can develop non-agricultural industries, such as land renting and real estate transaction, in the remaining narrow space after most of the collective lands are expropriated, which will become the major source of income. Here, we can see from three cases.

A.1.2 *Gaobeidian town of Chaoyang District: Government-led urbanization*

In the late 1990s, as the urban construction of Beijing moved eastward, Gaobeidian became a typical rural–urban continuum, which has the following basic characteristics: (1) Farmers' lands have been basically expropriated; (2) Farmers who have lost land have no job opportunity and the unemployment rate rises; (3) Local industries are limited and farmers lose the space for survival and development; (4) The expropriation of large areas of lands results in the decline of farmers' living standard; and (5) The blending up of farmers and urban residents, the separation of residence from household registration and the concentration of external population bring some difficulties for social management and become a time-bomb endangering social stability.

A.1.3 *Zhenggezhuang Village in Changping District of Beijing*: *Collective land capitalization and farmer's spontaneous urbanization*

In the early 1990s, the village was mainly engaged in collective enterprise and constructional engineering. After the late 1990s, the real estate development was very active in surrounding areas, for which the village has taken the following actions: (1) Avoid selling the lands left from their forefathers and develop them by themselves; (2) Fully consider the sustainable development in land development; and (3) The land development is carried out in accordance with the planning and based on the stability of collective ownership.

After being integrated into the urban planning of Changping District, the village conducted consolidation, reorganization and fee collection for reclamation of most of its lands, by which farmlands were adjusted as construction lands. Meanwhile, the village-operated enterprise should rent land from the village committee with compensation not less than RMB 5,000 Yuan per *mu* (667 m²) every year. The village committee will distribute the rental income to those households with contracting rights. Through the actions above, the village has achieved the following benefits: (1) The capitalization of homestead has been achieved through village transformation and homestead activation, and huge benefit from land capitalization has been obtained; (2) The processes of urbanization and industrialization of the village have been achieved through the marketization of collective construction land. Besides, the village has adjusted the industrial structure, developed the tertiary industry and introduced some schools to the village, thus achieving the industrialization and the shift to urbanization. Thus, the model of Zhenggezhuang has achieved the win–win urbanization for farmers, the collective and the government.

A.1.4 *Beiwu Village in Haidian District*: *Government-led and farmer-benefited urbanization*

According to the urban planning, the original site of Beiwu Village will be used for constructing a green belt, and all villagers should be relocated to another residential area. In order to solve the problem of farmer's move into multi-storey buildings in a new location, the government conducts corresponding adjustments on its urban and land utilization planning. The start-up capital for construction will be funded by the governments at district and city levels as well as the town government, and public facilities will be funded and constructed by the governments at district and city levels. As for the construction of hotel and rental house, farmers will fund them with the loans obtained with their land as collateral. Meanwhile, the village collective organizes developers to build commodity houses and farmers' own houses to reduce the capital costs.

Meanwhile, the relocation has also increased industrial land and resettlement housing that can ensure farmers' income. Each household will obtain a house for self-living and at least one house for renting. Besides, the government uniformly allocates some industrial lands and construction lands for constructing housing for the external population, which will provide farmers with permanent income. Moreover, low density hotels will be constructed on the original site of Beiwu Village after the greening and the tertiary industry are developed to ensure permanent income from property for farmers. Finally, the social security of local farmers is integrated into the urban–rural society security system.

A.1.5 *Implications of the cases*

The three cases above have shown three different types of urbanization models. The first is a completely government-led model, in which farmers are excluded from the process of urbanization. While the government obtains huge income from land leasing and the urban real estate becomes very active, original local farmers' collectives have narrow development space. There are few job opportunities with declining income and living standards, and they can only build illegal housing for renting. This results in an environmental problem, difficulty in governance, an increase of mass disturbance and the rise of governmental cost. Therefore, it is unsuitable urbanization. The second is the model of urbanization led by farmer collectives, which can fully ensure farmers' land rights and interests and make farmer collectives participate in the process of industrialization and urbanization with their land and share the benefit from differential earnings from land. But unfortunately, such a model should be based on the marketization of land that is restrained by both homestead laws and non-agricultural land protection laws. Meanwhile, the earnings from land capitalization to farmer collective means that the government will lose most of earnings from land leasing, which will result in a direct conflict with the governmental interests under the current financial system that mainly depends on the income from land leasing and mortgage. So, it can only be analyzed as an individual case for the time being. The third model is a variation of the first model, in which the government makes some compromises in its interests, gives farmers a small space to share the differential earnings from land, gives up the income from land leasing, integrates infrastructure construction and farmer social security into urban–rural integration, which can avoid substantive infrastructure investment and welfare burden for the village in the second model. These policies have ensured the implementation of the governmental projects, but if it is conducted in hundreds of rural–urban continuums simultaneously, the government may not be able to afford it.

On the whole, the attribution of differential earnings from land determines the road of urbanization. The traditional government-led urbanization theory focuses on the attribution of land appreciation to the government for the reason that the government invests huge amounts of money for infrastructure construction and should enjoy land appreciation. But actually, the differential earnings from land are not from the government's infrastructure investment but from industry development and population urbanization. Besides, the one who shares the differential earnings from land is able to conduct infrastructure investment. Moreover, in order to solve the problems regarding rural–urban continuum and the advance of urbanization, some efforts should be given to solve the settlement of *mobile population* and the problem of becoming rich for local farmers, so it is urgent to construct low-rent housing for the external population. Finally, it is also urgent to innovate and experiment with the land system.

(Organized by WANG Tianyi and reviewed by the speaker.)

A.1.6 *Hao Shouyi: Land Use System Reform in Binhai New Area of Tianjin*

Binhai New Area is now in a period of rapid development, especially after the construction of the area has risen to the height of national strategy, for which the government of Tianjin has established the *Overall Plan for*

Synthetic Supporting Reform Experiment of Binhai New Area of Tianjin.
Generally, Binhai New Area is not only an area formed by rapid industrialization, but also a typical region to discuss how to consider both economic
development and land problems in the stage of rapid industrialization and
urbanization. Generally, Binhai New Area faces two major challenges during its development and opening-up. The first is the huge demand on construction land caused by rapid industrialization, especially after the
construction of the area has risen to the height of national strategy. For the
requirements of accelerating development and opening-up, the difference
between land quota and actual demand becomes larger. The second is about
how to save land and fully ensure farmers' interests during the processes of
rapid industrialization and urbanization. Binhai New Area now still has
large quantities of inefficiently utilized land resources and mainly relies on
the expropriation and transfer of land for agricultural use to meet the
demand of urban construction land under the premise of protecting farmland. So, it is important to solve the problem about how to protect farmers'
benefits and allow them to share the achievements of development during
the process.

The government has determined the tasks and objectives of land use
system reform by following the principles of uniform planning, lawful
management, market allocation and governmental coordination and has
established the land market system and land management system focusing
on the practical protection of farmland resources and practical utilization
of land asset benefits, forming a new intensive land utilization pattern
adaptable to the socialist market economy system that can provide
resource and social guarantees for the development and opening-up of
Binhai New Area. Meanwhile, the government has innovated land utilization planning management and farmland protection pattern, has reformed
the review system for farmland diversion and land expropriation, has
established a new mechanism for compensation for land expropriation and
the resettlement of farmers whose land is expropriated, and has reformed
the collective construction land use system and land income distribution
and use and management system. These works of government mainly
focus on the following two aspects:

Firstly, adjust land use pattern within its stock in an effort to provide
sufficient resources for the development and opening-up of Binhai

New Area. To this end, the government mainly conducts the following works: (1) Innovate land use planning management and explore a way of combing all three plans. In this respect the resource and environmental carrying capacities of the region are assessed to establish resource and environment planning, based on which the land use planning is then established, and then the urban overall planning is added and recent construction plans are restrained to specific projects. Finally, the management pattern of three planning on one map is formed; (2) Promote the reform for linking the increase in the urban construction land and decrease of rural construction land, namely that, the temporary land use right for turnover will be uniformly granted to the municipal government after one time verification, while the municipal government will determine the project area for demolition and new house construction and will prepare planning for the project of linking the increase in urban construction land and the decrease in rural construction land and organize the implementation of planning. Meanwhile, the project of demolition and new house construction is usually represented by small-town demonstration project, which should be carried out based on the principles of invariant contract responsibility system, invariant arable land and respecting the will of farmers. Meanwhile, rural collective construction lands with low output are intensively utilized through the homestead exchange for housing; the incremental part is transferred as urban construction land, and all original homesteads are uniformly organized for reclamation to achieve the balance of farmland; (3) Promote the reform to optimize the land use structure, especially transfer those lands with low output through circular economy; (4) Develop beach resources and seek land from the sea based on farmland protection; and (5) Conduct an experiment for farmland transaction, reform land expropriation reviewing system, and improve the land reserve system.

Secondarily, it focuses on the reform of urban–rural integration. There are mainly two patterns for urban–rural integration reform in Binhai New Area. The first pattern is represented by the resettlement project of new residential quarter for rural urbanization in Hujiayuan Street of Tanggu District that is located in the core of Binhai New Area. In this project land expropriation is rationally conducted based on linked urban–rural construction land. In addition to the compensation from land expropriation and settling-in allowance, farmers are also provided social insurance and job opportunities as well as 45 m²-residence for each person. During the process, the result of land to house property to assets is achieved, so farmers are very satisfied with the transfer in this pattern. The second pattern is the pattern of "One Town, One Industry and One Park" in Hangu District at the edge of Binhai New Area, namely that, a new town is constructed through the homestead exchange for house, while the replaced land will be used to construct an industrial park to create jobs and develop a grape planting industry. Through such a trinitarian pattern, the rural socialization, agricultural industrialization and industrial ecologicalization are achieved based on the stability of rural land property and the ownership of farmland. Such trinitarian pattern is favorable for farmers' life guarantee and industry development.

(Organized by WANG Tianyi and reviewed by the speaker.)

A.1.7 Zhang Hong: *Situation of rural collective construction land in Yunnan Province and suggestions for land system reform*

The use of rural collective construction land in Yunnan Province is as follows: (1) The landform has an obvious impact on the society and economy, and flat areas have higher production capacity and have a per capita GDP that is 2.7 times as big as that in hilly areas and over 3 times as that in mountainous areas; (2) The utilization efficiency of rural collective construction land and the differential rent of construction land have a steady decline away from central urban areas. Centered in Kunming City, Yunnan Province can be divided into four parts, including central urban area, 1st ring, 2nd ring and 3rd ring areas, and the utilization efficiency of rural collective construction land gradually decreases from central urban area to 1st ring and 2nd ring, and slightly increases to the 3rd ring, which is usually comprehensively measured by per capita GDP, per capita net income of farmers, per capita local public fiscal revenue, the traffic distance to central city, per capita construction land index for residential area in rural areas, etc.; and (3) Rural collective construction land is mostly used for residence construction but rarely for the construction for township enterprise and public facilities. Thus, it can be seen that township enterprises and the village collective economy in rural areas of Yunnan Province are relatively lagging behind.

According to the investigation on the situation of rural collective construction land transaction in Yunnan in 2008 conducted by my research group, we can summarize the following characteristics of collective construction land transaction in Yunnan Province.

Firstly, because township enterprises are undeveloped in Yunnan Province and there are only a few operational collective construction lands that are qualified for transfer, which is mainly the homestead. According to statistics, the amount of farmers' own housing and attaching homestead accounts for about 70% to 80% of total transferred land, which means that if the transaction is restricted to the operational collective construction land alone, the policy of land transaction will mean nothing to rural development in Yunnan Province.

Secondly, rural collective construction land transaction mostly occurs in suburban areas of the city and along the highway, besides that the transfer scale gradually decreases from the central urban area. In suburban areas and the areas along the highway in developed cities, there is a large demand on construction land. Thus, farmers in these areas have stronger awareness on homestead utilization and protection, the collective construction land scale (mainly homestead) is larger, and the land use is more intensive. Conversely, in those undeveloped villages far from the central urban area, there is only a small demand on construction land, farmers have weak awareness on homestead utilization and protection, and there are many idle homesteads with low rate of registration and certification, even in some villages, there is hardly any collective construction land transaction. However, these farmers far from central urban areas are also eager for improving their production and living conditions through land transaction.

Thirdly, most farmers have a positive attitude toward collective construction land transaction. The research group interviewed over 500 farmers in Kunming City and Honghe Autonomous Prefecture. Among 300 respondents in Kunming, about 54% of them know the central government's new policies of rural land transaction, about 60% of them agree with the transfer of contracted land and homestead, but 27% of them disagree.

Among nearly 200 respondents in Honghe Autonomous Prefecture, about 50.3% know the central government's policies of rural land transaction, about 76.3% agree with the transfer, and only 7.9% disagree. Those opponents mostly worry that the compensation for land expropriation may be too low and their living standard may fall after the land transaction through land expropriation. It is understood that the problems of housing, employment and social security are the biggest problems that the farmers in Yunnan Province face. Due to an undeveloped economy and low compensation for land expropriation, farmers whose land is expropriated use most of the compensation for daily life spending, new house renovation and children's education, and only a small proportion is used for purchasing various insurance. Meanwhile, many farmers want the government to issue related policies to provide job opportunities and social security. But unfortunately, due to the low degree of industrialization in many counties or cities of Yunnan Province, local governments are unable to settle the farmers who lose land. For this reason, many farmers ask the government to reserve some land for them, by which they can build housing and make a living by themselves.

The surveys above indicate that the current land expropriation system of China not only cannot benefit farmers in suburban areas, but also cannot deliver the benefit from land appreciation from the development of urbanization to those villages in outer suburbs. Thus, I think that the land reform should be conducted from the point of view of overall planning of urban and rural development that is favorable for urban development and farmers' income increase. In this respect, the most important thing is to utilize the differential rent to activate the collective construction land assets of villages in outer suburbs, to strengthen the collective economy, and to promote both urban development and new countryside construction.

Based on the discussions above, I have the following three suggestions on the reform of the land management system of China.

Firstly, accelerate the reform of rural land property rights system, specify rural collective land property rights, let the rural construction land have the same right, function and price with the urban construction land, and thus lay a foundation for constructing uniform urban–rural construction land market.

Secondarily, it should have provisions in the *Constitution* and *Land Management Law* specifying that the rural collective construction land transaction is allowable, and it should reform the current land expropriation system and make collective construction land transaction another form of urban construction land expansion. Especially, related regulations about forbidding rural homestead transfer in current land management law should be revised to allow idle homesteads owned by the village collective to be transferred.

Thirdly, establish a mechanism for rural collective construction land transaction across the regions, promote the rational cross-region mobility of rural collective construction land during the overall planning of urban–rural development, and thus achieve higher earnings from differential rent. It is found in the survey that the transfer across the regions is more favorable for promoting the development and new countryside construction in villages in outer suburbs.

(Organized by Huang Yue and reviewed by the speaker.)

A.1.8 *Xing Yiqing: Land expropriation system reform in Chengdu*

I am honored to represent the research group of land system reform of the National School of Development at Peking University to make a report on the land system reform of Chengdu. Entrusted by the party committee and government of Chengdu and led by Professor Zhou Qiren, our research group has conducted continuous surveying in Chengdu since January and has completed a 250,000 word report. Here, I will give an overview of this report.

The reform in Chengdu occurred when the difference between urban and rural areas in China became larger in 2003 to 2008. However, the difference in Chengdu is not enlarged but reduced. Generally, the success stories of Chengdu can be generalized as "Return of rights and functions, Overall planning of urban and rural development," that is, the local income from land appreciation is used to achieve the overall planning of urban and rural development. In recent years, the rapid urbanization and industrialization have resulted in huge aggregation and concentration of population and the soaring of land prices. This is also the premise of the whole story. The most important question is who will lead the change and how to distribute the benefit from land appreciation. As we know, in the current land expropriation system, this process is mainly led by the government and only a small part of the benefits are returned to farmers. In the reform of Chengdu, the government first distributes part of the local public financial revenues from land expropriation to rural areas, but the direct transfer by the government is far inadequate. In addition to the change in secondary allocation, we pay more attention to some practices generated from reforms of land and economic systems. In these practices, the village, production group and farmer household participate in the transfer of land use rights in various forms and share more benefits from land appreciation.

Firstly, I will give introduction to territorial management and the policy of linking the increase in urban construction land and the decrease of rural construction land, which are also common practices we are familiar with and occur in many areas. Actually, they are simple in economic logic, namely that, the construction land transformed from the additional farmland obtained from rural land consolidation is used to exchange for land revenue in the areas with high land prices. Such practices are within the framework of the land expropriation system, the only difference in Chengdu is to increase its flexibility and responsiveness, and to actively return more benefits to farmers, which is the so-called change in the amount in response to the price. Meanwhile, rural areas can obtain an economic investment of RMB 15,000 to 25,000 Yuan/*mu* (667 m^2). The second practice is about the land consolidation, called the increase–decrease linking policy. Such practice can return RMB 150,000 Yuan/*mu* (667 m^2) to farmers, which is mainly caused by construction land consolidation and it does not need to take the quota of urban construction land at that time. Moreover, the practice is stronger and has larger scale in Chengdu. The city has applied for a total turnover land use right of over 6,000 *mu* (4,000,000 m^2) and has constructed 5,331 *mu* (3,554,000 m^2) of new residential areas. Besides, the uniform planning and construction, as well as uniform planning and self-construction, are economically and practically within the range of quota exchange for capital.

It is worth mentioning that in such practices, rural areas can share the benefits from land appreciation from other areas through the policy of farmland balance. Because many areas have no potential for land appreciation and are meaningless for reform, the distribution of land benefits among different areas becomes more important. Certainly, whether the government should lead and determine the pilot area is worth discussion.

A series of other practices are on the edge of or beyond the law, all of them are cases about sharing differential benefit within local areas. The first practice is about the aggregation of industry. For example, Jiaolong Industrial Port, a completely private industrial park on the collective land in the suburban area of Chengdu, has a total area of 5 sq. kms, has made brilliant achievements, has orderly layout and standard factory, has 800 small and medium-sized enterprises, can provide jobs for 100,000 workers, pays an annual tax of RMB 100 million Yuan, has a vacancy rate of nearly zero, and still has more than 200 enterprises on the waiting list. This makes the pattern continue. More importantly, all infrastructures such as roads, water and electricity in the park are invested by privately operated funds. The most important success of the park is the pattern of double leasing, the first of which is to construct standard factories to rent to small and medium-sized enterprises for solving their limitation in funds, and the other is to rent land from the collective for staged development to solve the capital flow of the industrial park itself. During the process, each household can obtain an annual rent equivalent to the value of 600 kg rice, which will increase by 5% every three years. But another advantage is that farmers still own the right to share the benefit from land appreciation permanently. Certainly, the park has undergone a meandering process to comply with the law, which should be summarized when we formulate related policies and support.

The next case is about the commercial building or residential house that is called sub-right house on the collective land. I will take the case of Sandaoyan Town as an example. Because the town is located near the water source of Chengdu, it cannot develop industry, so it only can develop real estate and has built 700 self-constructed houses and 4,500 sub-right houses. The case of Sandaoyan Town has obvious characteristics; the first is the relatively complete planning and orderly street, the second is about the transfer of the "development right in the air", namely that, the houses with three floors with the first floor as shops are built, farmers will obtain one floor for living and corresponding floor shops.

The remaining floors will be sold by the entrusted developer, and farmers can obtain a rental income of about RMB 300 Yuan/month. In the process, the government can change urban landscape, improve the popularity, and ensure public finance by collecting town infrastructure construction fees at a standard of RMB 20 to 60 Yuan/m^2. However, there are still some worries about behavior beyond the law, and external purchasers cannot obtain the property right certificate, which is also the dilemma puzzling the prosperity of Sandaoyan Town.

Another case is about the urban–rural integration in construction in Chaping Village of Dujiangyan City. A large earthquake occurred in Chengdu last year, which affected a total of 270,000 houses and brought large public financial pressure for the government to conduct reconstruction. The urban–rural integration in construction is an innovation of system generated under this pressure. Chaping Village, a beautiful mountain village located in the tourist area of back peak of Qingcheng Mountain, has a large potential differential rent from land. Similar to subright housing construction, the joint construction is actually a measure in which farmers transfer parts of homestead to exchange the funds for reconstruction. However, the difference between them is that the joint construction has a legal framework in both economy and rationality at the beginning. Firstly, the joint construction can obtain a land property certificate and a house property certificate, especially for the joint construction party that is not the member of the collective economic organization. They can firstly obtain the collective land use certificate, but there is still a small difference in use life. The joint party's certificate has a time limit of 40 years for non-residential land, while farmers obtain the transfer land with permanent use life, so farmers do not lose the permanent interests on parts of their homestead. More importantly, although it is cooperation between farmers and joint construction parties, the contract is a tripartite contract involving farmer households, collective and joint construction party, which can well ensure the whole process. Meanwhile, the land right certificate also has significance in the enlargement of transfer range and in the guarantee of specification implementation. For example, the joint construction can only be carried out and obtain the property certificate after the reclamation is completed and the farmer's house acceptance is completed, by which the quality of both housing and reclamation can be ensured through the certificate. For the first household participating in the joint construction, 100 m² of homestead can be exchanged with 238 m² of undecorated house, and the investment is RMB 1.6 million Yuan/*mu* (667 m²). Besides, there are other forms of joint construction, such as the joint construction by seven households and that by 35 households, etc. As of January 2009, a total of 101 households in the village agreed with joint construction and obtained a total investment of over RMB 100 million Yuan. Thus, we can see the positive role of joint construction policy and certificate guarantee.

The final case is about the transfer of two collective construction lands in Jinjiang District of Chengdu in the last year through the form of bidding, auction and listing. These two lands are also the first rural collective construction lands transferred through bidding, auction and listing after the policy started in 1987. Such practice is also based on land registration, and the purchaser also can obtain the use certificate of collective land, while the income will be first given to the joint-stock company composed of farmers and then be distributed to shareholding farmers in various forms. Under such a system and rights guarantee, although the transfer income did not reach the expected rate, it still reached RMB 800,000 Yuan/667 *mu* (m²). The key of the whole case is that farmers are not passive participants like before but active transfer parties on an equal footing.

A series of practices above indicate that the determination of rights is actually a determination of distribution pattern. Meanwhile, the change of function of property rights will directly result in the huge change of income, and especially the more ensured property rights will make the whole transfer more smoother and will bring larger transfer value.

All practices or policy directions above transit from the executive power-centered to the property right-based. In such a transition, there will be opportunities for the involved parties to violate each other's interests, and especially the unclear boundary of rights and liabilities will cause various contradictions. We can see from all above that the most important reform experiences in Chengdu are as follows: The land property right is certified to each household, which can give farmers the right of self-protection. Generally, the land certification is an authoritative, abstract and legal expression of ownership, which is the first time to conduct so large-scale asset verification on such means of production and livelihood in the past

60 years since the foundation of China. Besides, that it has given the main status to farmers in land transaction is favorable for fundamentally solving the huge systemic risk in the reform, and can give a safety valve for the reform. Furthermore, the so-called contract is firstly based on the deed and then on agreement and only the normative ownership expression can enlarge the range of transfer needs, increase the economic aggregate of rural areas and well promote the economical use of land. As described in the horizontal scroll in the department of housing management of Daguan Town of Dujiangyan, the reform is registration-based, transfer-centered and support-ensured, which is a wonderful summary on the experiences of the reform. Thus, the land registration is actually an infrastructure investment under socialist market economy system, which is the premise of all reforms.

Although the land registration has a significant role, it is difficult to be carried out. But we can still seek some illuminations from the land registration in Chengdu: The first is to carry out a pilot project to seek the registration procedure suitable for the local reality. For example, the cost for the final registration process for each household is only RMB 10 Yuan/ *mu* (667 m^2), which allows the registration to be carried out within a larger range; the village-based senate is actually a village-level governance mechanism representing the transition from "Rule for the people" to "Rule by the people"; the third is to seek a balance between the actual situation and law during the process of registration.

In accordance with the experiences of Chengdu, we propose some policy recommendations as follows: The first is to carry out land registration to lay a foundation for all reforms and to remove all systemic risks in the premise of the stability of farmland; the second is to gradually increase the flexibility of land expropriation system and the returns of farmers' investments; the third is to gradually reduce the range of land expropriation and gradually enlarge the use range of non-acquisition model. It can be seen from the practices of Chengdu that the collective land can be used to develop industry, build houses and even conduct large-scale transfer, the key of which is the supporting from both policy and law. Thus, we can carry out some closed and controlled experiments in those conditional areas, enlarge the scale for those successful ones, and prepare for those areas with no conditions.

(Organized by Xing Yiqing.)

A.1.9 *Leung Chun-ying: Property right, land expropriation system and land use management in Hong Kong*

Before the foundation of the People's Republic of China, due to the lack of a complete property right system and law, Chinese lost much in property rights disputes. When the disputes over land and real estate occurred, most would devolve into social conflicts due to the lack of complete systems and laws. Most social conflicts were solved by force, which thus resulted in political events. The various disputes in property rights in China between citizens, society and the country that we encounter today also occurred in many foreign countries. However, we should see that those advanced societies, such as European and American countries and Singapore, do not have as many social conflicts as the Chinese Mainland does. Therefore, we should understand and learn more from foreign experiences in land property rights systems.

Here, I will introduce the development history of the land system in Hong Kong. Generally, the property right system of Hong Kong is fairly complete. The British government obtained the leasing right of New Territories in 1898, conducted the comprehensive survey and census for the land of each household in 1903, and canceled the original permanent ownership of farmers. Accordingly, the ownership and use of all lands in New Territories were fixed in 1903, and all the vegetable fields, rice fields and homesteads kept their original use. Meanwhile, the British government set the expiration date of all lands in New Territories on June 27, 1997. The government has issued strict land and property management systems, according to which all lands are owned by the government and will be rented for business development or some public welfare establishments such as building schools or hospitals. Such measures caused many conflicts between common people and the government, but the British government insisted on these measures, which indicates that the government has a very strong determination in land management.

Besides, the government of Hong Kong has a strict land property right registration system. In the system, all rights and obligations related to land or housing are clearly specified in law and should be registered. In the first example, someone decorates his own house and needs to hang a droplight on the ceiling, so he needs to cut a hole in the ceiling, but the hole should stop when reaching a certain point, otherwise he will violate the rights of his neighbor upstairs. This is clearly specified in the law of Hong Kong. The second example is about the elevator maintenance cost of public buildings. Mr. Zhang lives on the second floor and does not need to take a lift, while Mr. Li lives in the third floor and needs to take a lift up and walks down. Under such a case, should they both pay part of the elevator maintenance fee? This is specified in the management contract of the building. The third example is about the water right and road right of farmland. If you buy a land and then block a brook to construct a reservoir which will result in drought on fields downstream, under such case do you violate the rights of farmers downstream? The land purchasing contract is only between you and the seller (original owner), but the construction of a reservoir violates the rights of farmers downstream. So do you and the seller have some obligations to farmers downstream? In another case, suppose you purchase land from Zhang San, do you have a right to walk on the field of *Li Si* to reach the main road afar? For these third-party rights above, the government has issued comprehensive regulations. Taking the house mortgage and leasing as example, Mr. Wang pledges his house for a loan and then his house is rented to the lessee. Under such a case Mr. Wang and the bank are two parties of the mortgage contract, while Mr. Wang and the lessee are both two parties of a house-leasing contract. However, if Mr. Wang does not pay the loan to the bank, the bank will sell the house, which will influence the residential right of the lessee.

The government of Hong Kong implements land use management through land contracts. All lands are rented under a batch lease system, and the purchasing of land by the masses from the government is actually a leasing behavior. The government specifies the use of each parcel of land through the clauses in the land title. As the planning authority, the government may approve you changing the land use from the view of planning, but as the land owner, the government may not agree to change the land use in accordance with the clauses of the land title unless you pay the government (owner) a price difference (due to change of land title clauses), which actually reserves a right for the government to collect added-value tax, similar to the land added-value tax the Chinese Mainland levies.

The procedure of land expropriation in Hong Kong is generally the same as the Chinese Mainland, according to which once there is a demand, the government will issue an announcement. As for the compensation, there are the following characteristics: (1) The compensation is equal to the market price of land; (2) All fees for the transferor including legal fees, real estate appraisal fee and accounting fee generated during the process of land expropriation will be paid by the government and be used as one part of the compensation. In Hong Kong, lawyers and accountants have strong public trust in the society, so lawyers can deal with legal problems, accountants can deal with financial problems, and all of them can bargain with the government; (3) The citizens who lose their land can obtain certain compensation for further land appreciation. During the land expropriation, the expropriated party will obtain an official letter from the government, in which both land type and the date of expropriation will be specified, and the expropriated party can use the letter to obtain other land, which thus can make up the expected value of farmland appreciation. Basically, 5 ft of farmland can exchange for 2 ft of construction land.

Finally, I think that no matter how complicated the problem is on the surface, either the relation between farmers, or between farmers and society, or between the state and farmers, all relations should be considered as property rights relations. There are a lot of experiences we can take as reference to solve problems in the reform. For example, the land appreciation formed by changing land use can refer to the measures in Hong Kong, namely that the government or the state can serve as the contractor and deploy some executive capacities to solve operational problems, and the credibility of lawyers, appraisers and accountants should be ensured. Meanwhile, the property right registration system should be implemented to prevent various social conflicts caused by the violation of the interests of a third party.

(Organized by Huang Yue and reviewed by the speaker.)

A.1.10 Part I Comment

Zhou Tianyong: (1) The Third Plenary Session specifies that farmers beyond the planning area can directly participate in the use of construction land by way of becoming a shareholder. After referring to the practices in some areas like Chengdu, I suggest the government further extends the regulations issued by the Third Plenary Session and allows farmers within the planning area to directly participate in land use. I found from the investigation in Guangdong in the last year that after issuing the lowest price for land transaction, the government basically does not participate in the commercial land expropriation but lets the land user directly negotiate with farmers. Farmers in some areas can become a shareholder, while some farmers in other areas can obtain 10% to 15% reserve land as compensation. Whether these measures can be used in the planning area? (2) The key of the reform in some areas is to obtain the annual construction land quota, either the conservation of land quota by homestead consolidation in Chengdu or land bill transaction in Chongqing is to solve such problem. But, as a unified policy for the whole country, how to design the annual construction land?

Chen Jiaze: Actually, the land policies in Hong Kong have the consanguineous relationship with that in the 11th century in Britain. At that time, all lands are owned by the royal family and all farmers only have the possession right of land, so that the land system in Hong Kong does not have the farmland collective ownership of the mainland. When we carry out the reform of the rural land property right system in Chengdu, we hope to draw upon the rationality of the land system in the UK. Although the continental law system and anglo-American law system are quite different, we think that the right of possession can greatly weaken all disputes.

Leung Chun-Ying: In the UK, parts of lands are not owned by the state. The nationalization of all lands in the UK started from 1066, but after that, the permanent property rights of parts of lands were sold. Compared with the rural collective land ownership in China, most farmlands in the UK are owned by farmers. Thus, the UK is now facing the same problems as us, including farmland expropriation, and the land appreciation when the land use is changed. However, they have some legal systems to solve or prevent these problems, so that I think that the legal system regarding land in the UK has a certain reference value.

Zhou Qiren: When we carried out investigation on system reform in Chengdu, we found the multi-level elasticity in the current system. The system difference between planning and non-planning areas mentioned by Jianguang before is actually a hard-and-fast rule. We found from the investigation in Chengdu that the land registration is only carried out for farmers beyond the planning area but not for farmers within the planning area. Because cadres at basic level think that if the land certification is conducted for farmers within the planning area, they will have some troubles when conducting land expropriation. For this reason, we report the situation to the government of Chengdu, and the land registration is also conducted within the planning area. Only when the land expropriation is conducted based on clear property rights can the concept of the compensation at market prices emerge. As mentioned by Mr. Leung Chun-ying before, there are two different concepts for the compensation for land expropriation, including the compensation at market price and in accordance with original use, which are actually the determination of the right. For this reason, the land registration is also carried out within the planning area in Chengdu. We think that such a measure is meaningful and its final effects should be observed. After the land registration, there will more leeway in the negotiation of land expropriation, and the price will be different too. All local governments face the problem about whether farmers within the planning area can share the benefits in a certain way, e.g., the problem of urban village. There are no villages in Shenzhen, but there are still some farmers who have lived there for generations and take a tough stance, and they often build buildings with even 13 floors for renting. Thus, there is something there worth studying, e.g., how to expand the elasticity within current system framework and the degree to be reached.

Gong Qiang: I just heard some thoughts about the participation of farmers in sharing the achievements of urban development through land transaction, but I think that farmers should obtain both rights and responsibilities simultaneously. I think that only those areas that conduct farmland protection well have the right for land transaction. For example, in many remote mountainous areas in Yunnan, farmers can build a house in a mountainous area to exchange with a house in the town provided by the government, so that these farmers can build other houses to obtain the interests continuously. Consequently, I think that only those areas with enlarged farmland area have the right for land transaction.

(Organized by Hong Hao without the reviewing of the speaker.)

A.2 Part II: Problems and Proposals

A.2.1 *Qin Hui*: *Urbanization and land system*

Many disputes about land and the issues of agriculture, countryside and farmers have now reached a dead end. For example, we often discuss whether land transaction should be promoted, whether land should be collectively owned or privately owned, how to strengthen the ability of collective bargaining, whether the farmland should be protected, etc. Meanwhile, we also discuss about whether to promote urbanization or revive rural areas, someone says that the movement of the new countryside is certainly a movement to promote non-agricultural industry, but someone says that the urbanization has reached a dead end and the countryside should be revived. However, all measures about these disputes may increase the strength of one party but worsen the weakness of the other party ("Single-direction Move").

For example, for the dispute about the red line of 1.8 billion *mu* (1,200,000,000,000 m^2), some reports think that the red line may be broken this year. But, the red line is normally broken in the way of land enclosure by the government in China rather than the way with which to strengthen the rights of farmers. Thus, the problem is this: If the farmland needs to be protected, farmers cannot sell it, but there is no effect on the governments' activities in this regard. In other words, enclosure continues. If, on the other hand, the farmland does not need to be protected, the government will carry out the activity at an even larger scale, and yet, farmers still cannot sell it. Thus, whether the red line is observed or not by farmers is rather irrelevant; the system is one that only serves the government but not farmers, under which it is hard to tell whether the system is state ownership, collective ownership or private ownership.

Someone said that the clarification of property rights is impossible, because the right of land ownership all over the world is not a completely absolute right, but the clarification of rights and absolute rights were originally two different concepts. Actually, the rights like land ownership include various rights as early as in Roman law and is the so-called right cluster. However, each right in this cluster should be clear and should not make those people with power possess excessive rights of discretion. It would be a quite different thing if the rights could be determined by someone powerful just because they are not absolute.

Similarly, for other problems we now face, some say that the urbanization should be accelerated so the so-called enclosure investment attraction
and building of large cities emerges. Some say that the urbanization road in
western countries is not suitable for us and we should revive the village, so
the phenomena of land collection, demolition and building new villages
occur. Some say that the scale operation should be promoted, so the enclosure is carried out to develop large farms. Some say that the stability of small
households should be ensured, so small households are not allowed to sell
their land to large households, otherwise these households will rebel because
of the lack of land. If these things are not solved properly, some problems
will occur in all cases. Thus, I think the problem about current property rights
in China does not lie in state ownership, collective ownership or private ownership, but in the situation where the system of allowing the government to
carry out enclosure but not allowing farmers to sell. If the system still exists,
the interests of farmers will be violated no matter which policy is adopted.

The so-called capacity of collective bargaining is a political concept,
but not an economic concept or ownership concept. Moreover, the
Collective is the opposite side of Individual, but not the opposite of Private.
The single-owned is Private, but the ownership of 10,000 people is also
Private in the premise that these 10,000 persons are combined with each
other freely. Someone asked me whether I propose Private or Collective.
I actually propose the concept of Private Collective, called Civilian
Collective. Here, Private does not mean Individual but Civilian. The Private
is not opposite of Collective but of State, or is opposite of those things
regulated or compelled by the official. Thus, farmers certainly have the
right for collective bargaining that should be a right of Private Collective.

Now, many village collectives can represent farmers for collective bargaining, which certainly has maintained the rights and interests of farmers.
However, the role of the so-called collective of land property rights is the
same with that of the productive collective. After the contracted responsibility system, most farmers quit the collective, but there are still some farmers
who do not leave and carry on well. Even the micro-economic system of the
collective has no difference with that in the times of Mao Zedong. The participation of farmers in the collective after obtaining the right to quit is
fundamentally different from the case that they are forced to stay in the collective owing to the lack of a quitting right. Generally, some productive

collectives have become star villages, because farmers will leave if these collectives have not developed as star villages. Although productive collectives are now not compulsory, those collectives with land ownership are still compulsory with varying degrees of ease. If farmers have the right to quit the collective with land ownership, the remaining collectives with land ownership will become the really autonomous collectives that can ensure the interests of farmers. Thus, as previous productive collectives, the collectives with land ownership also can exist and can play a positive role, but also should have both exit and entrance mechanisms as productive collectives do.

Now many people say that the collective ownership is a membership right or identity right. The identity right is actually a right that can make you own certain identity as well as some unshakable obligations. However, there is a large risk now, that is, the identity can be canceled by the government. In many cases, the government can deprive farmers' land by canceling their identity. Thus, the real problem is not about collective or private ownership, but about whether we have a real civic right but not a so-called special identity. Put it another way, if governments can intervene at will, the collective ownership will become meaningless. Hence, the system that integrates both government and community, resulting in the situation where the government means the community, should be changed. That is to say that we should cancel the right of people beyond the collective to change the identity of members at their will.

For this, I have two suggestions: (1) the collectives with land ownership should have both exit and entrance mechanisms, namely, the separation between government and community, but farmers can have an identity to quit or participate in a collective; (2) someone says that the land ownership cannot be given to farmers, which usually means that once farmers have land ownership some of them will lose their land. There are two meanings of farmers' land ownership. One is that farmers can sell their land at their own will, and the other is they can keep their land when they do not want to sell it. Since we worry that farmers without land will affect social stability, we can specify rules that govern the sale of land by farmers. Similarly, we should let farmers keep the land if they do not want to sell it, for the prevention of emerging of numerous farmers without land.

(Organized by Lu Qian without the reviewing of the speaker.)

A.2.2 Cai Jiming: *Exploration of staged reform of the urban–rural land system*

The current land expropriation system has an antinomy. On one hand, over the past 30 years of reform and opening up, most of the government's land expropriation behaviors during urbanization have been unconstitutional, as the vast majority of them are not for the need of public interest. On the other hand, all land expropriation behaviors have abided by the Constitution, because either the lands for public interest or non-public interest are obtained through the government's expropriation, which thus can ensure the state ownership of all incremental lands during the urbanization and complies with related regulations on urban land ownership in the Constitution. Thus, such land expropriation is both legal and illegal. To eliminate such an antinomy, there are three approaches:

The first is to expand the land expropriation range of the state under the current structure of the land ownership system, i.e., specify in the Constitution that for the need of public interest and economic development, the state can collect or expropriate farmer's lands that are used for economic development, regardless of public interest or non-public interest. But I think it is inadvisable for the state to expropriate lands for non-public interest or collect private or collective properties through its administrative power. Meanwhile, considering pervasive corruption under the current political system, 8 of 10 corruption cases are related to land, so if the range of land expropriation is enlarged, corruption behavior will be more pervasive.

The second approach is to change the structure of urban land owner-ship system. For public lands, the state can appropriate them as state land, while for non-public land, the user can directly purchase or rent them from land owner. This way, the state would not involve in the expropria-tion process for the land that will not be used for the public interest. Considering that over the past 30 years of reform and opening up, China has formed a situation of the coexistence of public ownership and various ownerships, the change of the ownership of urban land from single state ownership to the coexistence of various ownerships complies with the basic spirit of the constitution.

The third approach is to collect or purchase the land before the Constitution is revised, besides that the government can collect public lands, while the government can act as a market player and equally negotiate with farmers to purchase non-public lands, which can not only meet the demand of public land but also can maintain the state ownership of urban land. Meanwhile, if the government and farmers have equal rights in land transactions, the land price can really indicate the value of land, so that the government does not need to play an intermediate role between farmers and land users. Nonetheless, under current system imbued with rent-seeking activities, government officials may buy the land at a low price but sell it at high price to obtain benefits. For this reason, this approach is unadvisable.

If the second approach is adopted, the land ownership of urban and rural areas should be unified, that is, public lands in either urban or rural areas can be state-owned or collective-owned, while non-public land can be non-state-owned or non-public. Non-public land should be obtained through market transaction but not by compulsory land expropriation. For state land, I think that the situation of unclear property rights and responsibility rights should be broken and the classified ownership can be adopted. Meanwhile, the lands owned by the central government, provincial government or the governments at prefecture level or county level should be classified clearly, which can prevent the current government to consume all construction land quotas reserved for the next 5 to 10 future governments in pursuing political achievements and can prevent the continuous expansion of urban land boundaries in the future.

The research group on land reform of the National School of Development at Peking University summarizes the experiences of Chengdu as "Return of right and function." The real question is that which right or function should be returned. As for the ownership of collective land, which cannot be transferred freely yet and cannot be completely achieved in the economy. From an external perspective, the government's forceful collection of non-public land is the negation of the ownership of rural collective land. However, from an internal perspective, farmers' contracting on rural collective land without compensation is another negation of the collective ownership. Thus, the so-called "Return of right and function" is to return all property rights to the collective land. As for the homestead of villagers, although its ownership belongs to the collective and cannot be transferred, its use right should be allowed for leasing and transferring. Current laws and regulations not only forbid the leasing and transfer of the use right of farmers' homestead, but also forbid urban citizens to purchase housing or rent land for building houses in rural areas, which obviously results in a non-identity in the property right of homestead between urban and rural areas. For this reason, I think that the so-called "Return of right and function" should not only return the so-called collective ownership and contracting right regulated in current laws to the people, but should return all property rights for farmers in the 1954 edition of the Constitution, by which the rights and interests of farmers could really be indicated and respected. Moreover, the homestead of rural residents should become private-owned, and the building land should be distributed to each household except the part that is already used by farmers for self-construction, by which the authentic "Return of right and function" can be achieved.

Finally, whether the privatization of farmland violates the constitution and cannot be promoted. It is certainly not, because the 1954 edition of Constitution has endowed the farmer with land ownership, and the 1975 and 1978 editions of the Constitution did not neglect the land ownership of farmers. Thus, if we want to promote land property rights reform, it is completely feasible to propose some suggestions to revise the Constitution if necessary or the central government agrees. From the Thirteenth to Sixteenth National Congresses of the CPC, the Constitution has been revised many times. Thus, it is groundless to restrain the land property right reform in the name of violating the Constitution.

(Organized by Hong Hao and reviewed by the speaker.)

A.2.3 *Zhang Shuguang*: *General thought and action framework for solving land problems in China*

The speech I will make today aims at pointing out the problems with current land policies, proposing a general thought and action framework to solve the land problem in China, making land policies clearer in direction and more flexible, and promoting and guiding the innovations and experiments at a basic level, thus accelerating the process of urbanization in China.

Urbanization is the key to China's development, reform and adjustment. Generally, urbanization is a process of decreasing the rural population and increasing the urban population, which is a process of the re-allocation of resources from rural areas to urban industries and service sectors owing to the urban expansion and industrial advance. There are three major problems in the process of urbanization in China: (1) The urbanization of China is an uncompleted urbanization, in which 140 million rural migrant workers do not give up everything in rural areas to become a complete urban citizen, who are usually called urban farmers, which undoubtedly results in many characteristic social economic phenomena of China, such as left behind children, schools for children of migrant workers, the separation of new husband and wife, group renting and heavy traffic during Spring Festival; (2) Large quantities of sub-right houses have emerged during the urban development. According to the statistics of the Ministry of Land and Resources, the total area of sub-right houses in the whole country reaches 6.6 billion m^2, while the total area of complete property rights houses is only 12 billion m^2, even in Shenzhen, the percentage of sub-right housing in all houses reaches 49%, but the government strictly prohibits the development of sub-rights house, which has resulted in an enormous contradiction and conflict and may endanger social stability; (3) The government intends to maintain grain security through farmland protection, but current measures cannot protect farmland but encourage farmland occupation.

The three problems above are interrelated and restrained by one another, which also corresponds to three types of farmers who have different preferences and relations on land. The first type refers to rural migrant workers in the city, among them 20-year-old to 30-year-old youths do not want to return to their hometown and want to become urban citizens. The second type refers to those who live in suburban areas, and they work in the city due to urban development and expansion but still live in their original place, so that they will not abandon land and the benefits from the land. The third type refers to those engaged in farming, especially those farmers engaged in grain planting. They do not become rural migrant workers for various reasons, but they still undertake all costs for farmland protection.

From history, the complete change from countryman to urban citizen is the only way to achieve urbanization in all countries, the key of which is to carry out population mobility and land mobility simultaneously. But unfortunately, population mobility and land mobility in China are now separated from each other, e.g., rural migrant workers still have contracted land in rural areas and have not changed their rural idea, living and consumption styles. Some of them still will build houses in rural areas after they earn money in the city, which has resulted in a high housing vacancy rate in rural areas and a serious wasting of resources. For this, I propose three measures here: (1) Those rural migrant workers who live in the city, have permanent jobs and a fixed address and have worked for a certain number of years (e.g., three years) can become urban citizens with their family members and enjoy the rights and treatment of urban citizens; (2) After obtaining the identity and treatment of urban citizen, rural migrant workers should give up their membership right and land property right in rural areas, but still have the right to sell or rent their houses on the homestead; (3) The urban construction land quota should be increased in accordance with the amount of rural migrant workers who become urban citizens to expand the space for urban construction and development.

As for the problem of sub-rights housing, the fundamental method is to use lands in suburban areas for urban construction, but the primary income should be returned to farmers to give them urban real estate and long-term income. All sub-rights houses should first be classified in accordance with their construction ages, the older ones can become legal after paying related taxes and the existing problems can be solved gradually. The newly-constructed houses should be released when they comply with urban planning and integrated into urban commodity housing, but those newly-constructed houses that do not comply with urban planning and the standard of building should be absolutely demolished, which is different from the previous manner of all talk but no action. Meanwhile, under urban planning, several construction patterns should be developed, e.g., the construction by farmers themselves, the cooperative development between farmers and the enterprise, the overall planning of urban and rural development, and the construction by the developer.

Finally, in order to solve the problem of farmland protection, the income from grain planting should be gradually made close to the average income in accordance with the principle of compatible interests. Besides that farmers should be encouraged to actively protect farmland. One of the most important reasons for the government's tardiness is the concern about that the release of sub-rights housing may make farmland protection policies difficult to be implemented. But actually, current management and control policies have stimulated the development of sub-rights housing, the key of which focuses on incompatible interests, namely the incompatibility in interests between the central government and local governments, as well as between local governments and farmers, which have resulted in a dilemma. Farmers who have the most effective measures do not want to protect farmland, but the central government that is far from the land and has no way for farmland protection pays much effort for farmland protection. For this reason, I think that the problem should be solved in accordance with the principle of compatible interests. Firstly, scientific verification should be conducted to determine the amount of farmland required in China; secondarily, the farmland protection fund should be established to make developed areas and cities undertake the costs for farmland protection as well; finally, in the key protected areas of farmland, the income from grain planting can be increased to the level of local average income through transfer payment, planting subsidy and the increase of grain price, and thus to encourage farmers to protect farmland by themselves.

(Organized by Tan Li and reviewed by the speaker.)

A.2.4 *Huang Xiaohu*: *Re-thinking about the real estate industry of China*

The relationship between housing price and land price has long been a very sensitive topic. All parties think that the housing price is too high, but the dispute is about whether the housing price pulls up the land price or the other way round. Theoretically, the relationship between housing price and land price has been discussed in the writings of Karl Marx and Friedrich Engels, in which the housing price is considered as a sum of land price, building capital, profit, interest and maintenance fee. Thus, current urban housing prices of China theoretically consist of land price, building and installation investment and profit, as well as management and service fee of the developer if the developer organizes the construction.

Construction investment and profit, commonly called the cost of construction and installation, are relatively fixed costs. Generally, there is a small difference in the cost of construction for the houses with the same standard, and besides, the price of building materials and the wages of workers are stable within a certain period. Even from long-term trend, as other commodities, the price of building products may decrease with the advance of technology and the increase of labor productivity. But the land price is quite different, which is a capitalized land rent that will form excess profit with the change of land conditions, so both land rent and price will have a long-term tendency of increase, especially for urban lands. Meanwhile, the short-term change in the relation between supply and demand will also cause some fluctuations in both land rent and price around the excess profit of land.

The demand includes self-living demand and speculative demand, besides which the supply is also divided into the supply for actual demand and speculative supply, such as indemnificatory housing, cooperative construction, self-constructed farmer house, etc. Marx noticed the change in building industry and described it as follows: Houses were all custom built at the early stage, but houses of this type became few around the 1850s, while builders began to purchase large tracts of land to construct many houses for customers to select, so the land properties operated by builders themselves could be tens of times more than their own property and they have the risk of bankruptcy due to market fluctuations. Generally, such a construction pattern is actually a speculative behavior, because the construction has small profit, while the speculative object is land rent. The so-called builder for speculative construction concerned by Marx is the earliest real estate developer in the world, who served as builder, developer and maintenance provider in a whole. However, current developers in China are responsible for neither construction nor maintenance, but are engaged in speculative construction. The combination of speculative supply and speculative demand will have great effect on housing prices and can attract public funds to participate. It can create many rich men, but the fall of housing prices will also form create debtors, which is something happening in China now.

The establishment of an indemnificatory housing system allows the housing supply for the poor not depend on developers anymore. If the supply system of cooperative housing construction can be developed, the housing of low and medium income citizens will also no longer depend on the developer. At that time, the speculative behavior in real estate will become a game among rich men and will have nothing to do with common people. Certainly, there is a contraction in supply and demand between indemnificatory housing and cooperative housing construction, the prices among them will also fluctuate, but the house with sky-high price will not occur if there are no speculative behaviors, and at that time, the effect of the government's policy of bidding, auction and listing will be clear. Because of the speculator gamble on land rent, the state that is the land owner should not always maximize the land revenue in any case. The price-capped housing actually restrains land prices, and when carrying out the cooperative housing construction pattern, the government can supply land at a low price by way of assignment, which indicates the superiority of public ownership of land.

There are still some problems in land use system and management in China. In the case when the developers still monopolize most housing supply, the land policy of bidding, auction and listing, it becomes an important driver of speculative behavior on land. The high land price will harm common people, and therefore when there is a serious bubble caused by speculative behavior, the government should be scrupulous to supply land, and should not supply the land to those who can give a higher price but should increase the land supply for indemnificatory housing and price-capped housing. However, if the monopolization situation of the developer is not changed, all measures are merely temporary solutions and are unlikely to curb the injury on consumers caused by speculative behavior.

Unfortunately, current urban development excessively depends on the real estate industry, some local governments issue rescue policies when the housing price falls, with which common people are very dissatisfied. Meanwhile, because of urban construction investment, public land finance, taxes related to land and land banking account for a large proportion in the economy, the current development pattern of China is actually borrowing from the future and will be unsustainable. For this, there are many reasons, including guiding thought, development strategy, governmental function, cadre system, public finance and financial system, land system and land management. In the aspect of land, the government forbids collective land to enter the market, and it collects land at low price but sells it at a high price. The former actually strengthens the monopolizing position of the developer, while the latter provides the space for investment speculation. Besides, the non-standardized use of land revenue also encourages the shortsightedness behaviors of local governments. The Third Plenary Session of the Seventeenth CPC Central Committee has specified the direction for reform, and we should accelerate the implementation and promote steadily.

The relation between housing price and land price can be summarized as follows: Land rent and price are the important parts of the housing price and have a tendency for long-term increase, so that the housing price will increase too. But the short-term fluctuation in housing prices is caused by the relation between supply and demand, and the speculative supply and demand will result in sharp fluctuation in housing prices because land rent and price are speculative objects. Meanwhile, the harm of speculative activities on common consumers is mainly caused by the monopoly situation in the housing supply market, so the key to solve the problem is for the construction department to break the monopoly, which needs to reform the housing system further and deepen the reform in the land management system.

(Organized by Tan Li and reviewed by the speaker.)

A.2.5 *Zhou Tianyong*: *Selection of living pattern and land management system for urbanization*

Urbanization is an inexorable trend of the mobility and concentration of rural surplus laborers and populations toward the city, which will not change its course with people's will. The living pattern during urbanization refers to that of land distribution in urban areas, existence of slums, residential areas, courtyards, buildings with several floors, etc., due to the mobility and concentration of rural populations into the city. However, different residential patterns will have different effects on land use ratio, urban–rural structure of population and age, social safety, etc.

When studying the problems of urbanization, land and dwelling, we found that the typical living patterns in the world can be summarized into three types, including East Asian pattern, Latin American and Indian pattern and Chinese pattern. In the pattern of East Asia, urban citizens have increased income and most new migrant citizens have the capacity to purchase the normative house during the process of urbanization. Meanwhile, some citizens should temporarily live in the slum during the stage of transition, but the slum will gradually be transformed and disappear with the increase of citizens' income and the enhancing of governmental financial resources, and the housing conditions of urban citizens will gradually become the same. Such pattern is adopted by Japan, Korea and Taiwan.

The second living pattern is the pattern for Latin America and South Asian countries. Compared with East Asian countries, the resident income increases slowly and there is a large difference in resident income. In India, public land will become privately-owned if actually occupied by individuals for more than 10 years, while in Latin American public lands will become privately-owned if they are actually occupied by individuals for over half a year. The private occupation on public land in these countries is due to the fact that in these countries, the president is elected through the direct general election, the candidate needs to court people in the slums to win votes. In such a living pattern, rich men can live in a good house after they come to the city, while numerous surplus rural laborers still live in the slum. As a result, the slum becomes the major living pattern for the urbanized rural population.

The third pattern is the current living pattern of China. We have conducted some research in the purchasing capacity of urban citizens and found that the income-house price ratio for the resident with the highest income reaches 2.4:1, namely 2.4 years of income can afford one house, while for the residents with the lowest income, it will take more than 20 years to be able to afford a house. Besides, we have conducted an estimation on the whole rural population and found that the house price–income ratio averages at 18:1, which is three times the recognized highest house price–income ratio of 6:1. Under such a case, most of farmers certainly cannot afford the house, so an amphibious living pattern is formed, namely that, rural migrant workers can only live in urban work sheds, dormitories or small rooms rented in urban villages, but they still own houses in rural areas that remain empty. Obviously, the higher the amphibious occupancy rate is, the more the per capita residential land is. Furthermore, if these rural migrant workers purchase a house in the city but still do not abandon the right of habitation in rural areas, it will occupy more land. Besides, the living pattern, such as high-rise housing, courtyard, cottage, the rate of one household occupying several houses, will have an effect on the degree of land occupation. For example, according to statistics by the Ministry of Land and Resources, cottages constructed from 2003 to 2007 only hold 27,000 people, but if the pilot ratio reaches 1:3, it can serve over 300,000 people.

Different living patterns have not only different land occupations, but also have different effects and hidden dangers etc. on social structure and social stability. Compared with other counties in Latin America and East Asia, China has too powerful of a government, no privatization and basically no slums. The lack of slums will directly result in the higher degree of aging in rural areas, because rural migrant workers will return to their hometown after they become middle-aged and elderly. It is estimated by us that if such an amphibious living pattern continues, the degree of aging, i.e., the percentage of above 60-years-old population, will reach as high as 69% in 2030. The lack of slums will result in serious population mobility that will have an effect on social stability. In other countries, the population mobility is mainly business or leisure mobility, but the population mobility in China is mainly for livelihood. If rural migrant workers can live in the slum, such serious population mobility will not happen between urban and rural areas, because if a family lives in the same place, the social risk caused by bachelordom or population mobility will be smaller. For this reason, we need to think about whether the society with slum is more stable than the society with serious population mobility.

In order to prevent the doubled increase of residential land, the phenomenon of amphibious living between urban and rural areas should be prevented. If numerous urban citizens come to rural areas and purchase a house with courtyard, the cost to reclaim these lands as farmland will be high. Besides, the prevention of amphibious living can not only prevent serious and durable population mobility between urban and rural areas, but also prevent the speeding and worsening of aging in rural areas. Moreover, we should prevent the phenomenon that 10% of populations with several houses in urban areas lease their houses to 90% of the population without a house. We also do not agree with some scholars who said that those who cannot afford house can rent house, but we think that if 80% to 90% of populations in a society cannot afford house, the society will have serious problems. If each rich man can afford 5 to 6 houses, their children can depend on the rent throughout their life, and such society is very terrible.

So, how we can prevent the phenomenon of amphibious living between urban and rural areas? I think that the key is to reduce the housing cost of rural migrant workers. The largest obstacle for farmers to come to the city is not the household registration policy, but the high housing costs. The key for reducing the housing cost is to adjust the strategic thought of land utilization and management. When we started to draft the outline of our report, we thought it would be necessary to control construction land and urban land, but the results of research indicate that the real problem is not that. Actually, villages use large quantities of land. Since the reform and opening up, the absolute rural population has decreased by over 60 million and land used by villages has expanded by 200 million *mu* (133,333,333,333 m^2), while the urban population has increased by over 420 million simultaneously, but the area of urban construction land has only increased by 50 million *mu* (33,333,333,333 m^2). At the beginning of the reform and opening-up, the per capita housing area for farmers was about 8 m^2, but it has increased to about 30 m^2 or nearly 40 m^2 as the housing construction on the contracted land is not strictly controlled, and large quantities of farmlands are occupied. Thus, the key to land control is not in cities but in rural areas. We have also found from the research that the government of the city uses large quantities of lands to construct development area or industries, such as constructing refinery and steel works, and only provides a smaller part of residential land, which results in the boom of housing prices. But, we should think deeply about why the tertiary industry does not develop well.

We have been following suggestions to adjust the land use and management systems. Firstly, it should encourage the transfer of homestead and contracted land. For example, if I want to work in the city and my homestead and contracted land can be transferred, the income from land transaction will greatly improve my house purchasing power in the city. But unfortunately, large quantities of land assets are "dead" and cannot be transferred at all, and as a result the rural migrant workers cannot afford housing in the city. Thus, it should accelerate the rectification in the household registration for those villages with small scale and scattered living pattern. Many villages with small scale, scattered living pattern, low land utilization rate and no scale effect are doomed to decay, as in Russia, Brazil and India. The key is to conduct land consolidation after villages decay. For instance, Germany has issued a series of measures for land consolidation, similarly, China should conduct land consolidation to obtain farmland and construction land for transfer.

Secondarily, we should think about the existence and development of slums. The key for the problem focuses on whether the government has the capacity to provide low-price housing or price-capped housing for numerous migrant populations. Especially, the rate of urbanization in 2040 will reach 80% and the urban population will increase by 560 million. I think that no country can afford the construction of price-capped housing and low-rent housing. Under such case, we can try to modify our tolerance on urban villages and rental houses in suburban areas, to moderately relax the limitation on slums, and to gradually transform the slums with the development of the economy, which can not only reduce the housing costs during the process of urbanization, but also can reduce the possible effect on social stability caused by serious mobility for livelihood and the lack of slums.

Thirdly, we should think again about the tolerance on sub-right housing. We think that it is completely necessary to develop sub-right houses in small towns and suburban areas, which can prevent the government's land transaction fee and various taxes and can reduce the housing price to allow farmers to afford it. We have conducted some investigations in some areas and found that many farmers can only afford sub-right houses but cannot afford complete property right houses. Thus, the sub-right house should not only be developed but also should be treated differently. Meanwhile, the government can support the construction of land-conserved or multi-story sub-right houses in suburban areas or small towns, but it should control the behavior of urban citizens to purchase courtyard-style buildings in rural areas, while the reason should be discussed in detail.

Finally, it should increase income and decrease housing prices. In order to reduce housing prices, the supply of residential land should increase. It can be seen from our analysis that the supply of residential land is inadequate, so that besides local governments increasing the supply of residential land, the rural collective construction land should be allowed to enter the market and form a competitive land supply market to effectively increase the supply of residential land. Meanwhile, if the commodity house is allowed to be constructed on collective construction land, the supply of housing will effectively increase. Besides, the high rate of urban citizens with several houses also increases the contradiction between supply and demand, which is difficult to be reduced unless the house property tax is levied. In addition to house property tax, the government can also levy land use tax and levy graduated tax for the household with over two houses, which can reduce the rate, improve the structure of housing supply and demand, reduce housing prices and improve the rate of satisfaction of self-living house purchase. Besides that, these taxes can reform current public land finance of local governments. In order to increase income, we think that the fundamental way is to vigorously develop micro, small and medium-sized private enterprises with the best employment-absorbing ability by relaxing the threshold for market access, reducing taxes and decreasing oppression on them and fee charge during executive law enforcement.

(Organized by Yi Shengyu and reviewed by the speaker.)

A.2.6 *Hu Cunzhi*: *Build a free flow mechanism for factors of production by certifying exchange entitlement*

The current land transaction has many obstacles that have bad effects on transfer, of which the major three are as follows. Firstly, multiple burdens on land transaction cause obstacles and difficulty. Land trade should not only need to meet the requirement of productivity development but also ensure the stability of contracting rights for the need of China's actual conditions. The obstacle and difficulty are mainly indicated by five contradictions: (1) The contradiction between land scale management and the maintenance of family land basis required by the household responsibility system; (2) The contradiction between the promotion of intensive management or the encouragement of capital to the countryside and land annexation caused by aggressive capital; (3) The contradiction between the long-term stable environment for the transfer of farmers' contracted land and the land stability for farmers such that they have a place to return as the last resort; (4) The contradiction between socialized and specialized farmland transaction and the forceful power of powerful groups (including village committee, agricultural company and the governments at basic level); (5) The contradiction between land transfer and reclamation after its transfer for production and living. All contradictions above have resulted in the first obstacle or difficulty in land transaction.

Secondarily, land lacks the channel and guarantee of two-way flow. Because current flow direction is by and large one-way, the change of farmland from scattered to scale management becomes the main stream, but the inverse process becomes scarce and non-mainstream; the concentration of construction land to urban areas with the process of urbanization becomes the mainstream, but the inverse process is secondary and rare; farmers considering land as leeway is also rare and has small probability of occurrence. Under such a case, the explorations in all areas carry out the reform from the direction of mainstream but do not provide a guarantee from inverse flow direction, which will result in a problem that the factor flow only has forward direction but no inverse direction, so that it not only does not belong to the market economy, but also does not belong to the actual factor flow.

Thirdly, the space and location of land restraint management pattern and influence land transaction. Unlike capital, which can be used for scale management if only it is concentrated, without the limitation in source and location, land faces a problem of special location in its scale management, that is, lands should be continuous but not scattered, as the scattered land is difficult to utilize. After achieving the utilization of continuous land, the lands in the central area should be protected from being segmented, otherwise the scale management of land cannot be sustained. Therefore, the core for land scale management is the management of continuous land. However, in order to achieve such management, the phenomenon of forcing farmers to transfer their land may occur in most cases.

For the reasons above, current land transaction does not have such good effects. We conducted statistic research before the Third Plenary

Session of the Seventeenth CPC Central Committee, which indicated that
the percentage of land transactions on total farmland only reached 4.75%,
even in the areas with a higher percentage only reaching 20% to 30%,
which is lower than the percentage of rural laborers that come to the city.
The bad situation of land transaction is not only related to an incomplete
system but also to imperfect channels for factor flow.

In response to the three problems above, I propose providing a guarantee for reverse flow of land by the way of exchange entitlement. The
reverse here means that there should be an arrangement for the route of
opposite direction, whether positive or negative, mainstream or non-
mainstream, which thus can form a free and two-way factor mobility that
can ensure a market economy and overall planning of urban and rural
development. It can be seen from the analysis that two characteristics are
important here. The first is the major flow direction of land from scattered
to concentrated and from rural areas to urban areas, but the inverse process
will be scarce and sporadic; the second is about the higher requirement of
scale management on land location, but in order to provide a leeway for
farmers, the social security function of land is mainly related to land area
but not to land location. Thus, we can solve the problem by land substitu-
tion and setting up the reverse mobility route, so that we can meet the
requirements of scale management and social security. The innovative tool
we introduce here is called certificate of "exchange entitlement", which
not only centers on land area, but also is based on land location. We hope
this can solve the problem of land transaction, provide a policy tool for
reverse mobility, and thus form a complete market for land trade.

Exchange entitlement is a legal certificate that symbolizes the right on
land. It can be exchanged with land under certain cases. The certificate
can be exchanged with certain land area or certain land value due to its
location or both of them. As a policy tool, it can break the obstacle in land
mobility and reduce the effect of land location. As a legal certificate,
exchange entitlement can be issued by the government or statutory body
during land resumption, recording original area, class, price and other
information, and can be exchanged with land when necessary. Exchange
entitlement is mainly used for land consolidation and land exchange in
Europe, for land development in America, and for land expropriation
in Hong Kong. Especially, exchange entitlement can be combined in

Hong Kong and can also pay some premiums. The Chinese Mainland has begun to issue exchange entitlement in Hainan since 1999, which is still in use now after 10 years of practices.

Exchange entitlement has various forms, one of which records land area and can be exchanged with the land with equal area, the other of which records its value and can be exchanged with the land of the same value. In order to ensure farmers obtain original land, a land with larger area according to the distance from the original one can be exchanged with if the original land cannot be obtained. Only when we conduct complete regulations will farmers know expected results during scale management, and disputes can be avoided in the future. For the exchange entitlement of construction land, it not only can be exchanged with the construction land in local villages but also with the construction land in other areas, which is favorable for the development from rural areas to urban areas.

Exchange entitlement will result in a series of management challenges because it is a legal certificate requiring not only public trust but also legal seriousness. For this reason, I suggest that it should be uniformly managed by the government at county level. If exchange entitlement involves a large range of land, it can be adjusted and exchanged within the whole range. Besides, it should assign a special organization to manage, reclaim and rescind exchange entitlement when the household redeems the land; same for homesteads. Thus, farmers' interests can be practically ensured under scale management or the concentration from rural areas to urban areas.

Finally, as a new institutional arrangement, exchange entitlement can achieve a win–win situation if it is treated properly. Firstly, farmers do not worry about losing of land and will be assured of a transfer of land. Secondarily, the company can conduct scale management and the collective economic organization can obtain benefits from scale management. Furthermore, the state can break the dual urban–rural structure and can promote overall planning of urban and rural development. Certainly, if it is treated improperly, it will cause many problems. Thus, we should be scrupulous about this new institutional arrangement and should be cautious to promote it after full demonstration and pilot implementation.

(Organized by Yi Shengyu and reviewed by the speaker.)

A.2.7 Part II Comment

Sheng Hong: I personally think that exchange entitlement is a good design, but there is a more common transaction method between land and currency. Exchange entitlement certainly has more attached conditions as it requires no full-payout during land expropriation, and so it is a quite intermediate way of reform. Meanwhile, the one-to-one replacement will actually hinder the transaction and is not necessary for the mobility between urban and rural areas. For example, someone is tired of urban life and wants to come to rural areas, who can obtain land through a common transaction by currency. The benefits of exchange entitlement are only limited to the current situation, but if it is promoted, it should demonstrate that it can reach more policy objectives that the more common transactions cannot reach.

Hu Cunzhi: I agree with Mr. Sheng's opinions, the key is that land has some social functions, and leeway should remain for farmers. Exchange entitlement can solve the problem about whether the leeway should be left for farmers, namely that, farmers have the right to choose whether or not to exchange it for land.

Chen Jiaze: I think that the benefit of exchange entitlement is to promote transaction. The design of land bank in Chengdu is close to the thought of Mr. Hu. The land exchange has an important limitation in land location. Exchange entitlement is actually a concept of stock and is favorable for progressive reform, so I agree with this system.

Sun Youhai: We now should consider the actual situation, namely that, there is a difference in land utilization between urban and rural areas, urban land increases with the increase of population, but rural construction land increases with the decrease of population. In 2005, rural construction land had a total area of 165,600 sq. kms, accounting for above 51% of total land area of the whole country, which was two times larger than all urban construction and industrial lands, but the rural population is 1.4 times larger than urban population. In 1991, the per capita land area in rural areas was 123,600 sq. kms. Obviously, rural land has increased by 42,000 sq. kms, which occurs in the case that the rural population has decreased by 110 million. Besides, we should be aware that the urbanization of population lags behind land urbanization and rural construction land is now increasing.

Hu Cunzhi: Does the concept of Private Collective proposed by Mr. Qin Hui has a Chinese translation? Are there any similar practices in foreign countries? What are the differences and relations between this concept and the subsidy cooperative system for rural community that centers on land and has been developed for over 10 years in China?

Qin Hui: In foreign countries, the concept of Collective does not exist in either the continental law system or common law system. The reason why I propose the concept of Private Collective is to consider Chinese characteristics. In the early stage of Roman law, the collective greatly interfered with rights, and there was still no concept of Collective. If there was to some extent, it is only attached to the execution of rights, e.g., the limitation in family for rights of succession. For another example, Boeing Co. is a company with hundreds of thousands of shareholders, and the number of these shareholders may exceed the population of some small countries. But no one would consider it as the collective ownership. If only a property is civilian and can be combined with free will, it is deemed to be Private, no matter whether it is owned by hundreds of thousands of people or by a single person. Similarly, we do not consider many large stock companies as non-Private. However, China's laws regulate that the land should be Collective-owned, but any system can be elastic, the individual should be endowed with the exit and entrance rights. We adopted the measure for the destruction of productive collective, as repeatedly discussed by Mr. Lin Yifu, why the measure cannot be adopted for the collective with land ownership? There are some obvious differences between the land ownership system of Private Collective and the current system. The first difference is whether there is an exit mechanism, for the current collective system or stockholding system the share is combined with the rights of members and has no right of entrance or exit. Given that such a system can give farmers certain benefits, e.g., giving parts of benefits from land appreciation to farmers who do not need to labor or invest (actually they cannot) and can do nothing except indulge in eating, drinking, gambling, and visiting prostitutes, is it a normal phenomenon? If the so-called identity system is canceled, it will cause two changes, including the canceling of so-called identity rights and so-called integration of government administration with commune management. I agree with one statement Mr. Chen Xiwen proposed in the last year, namely that, although we need to maintain the collective ownership, the economic functions of administrative village should be gradually stripped. If we can specify the identity property and build an entrance or exit mechanism of collective ownership, the so-called collective will become the stockholding system or Private system. Meanwhile, the property rights reform will also be carried out smoothly. However, on the surface, all clauses of the Constitution are completely satisfied.

As described by Tianyong on the difference in living patterns between East Asia and South Asia or Latin America, I think that it is actually not a difference, because all of them allow the existence of slums. The only difference is that the East Asian type has rapid economic growth rates and a relatively average distribution, and the slum can be dispelled by itself. But considering respecting the existence of slums, there is no any difference between them, so the two patterns can be combined into one. Meanwhile, China is not the only special case in the world, and I think that China is similar to South Africa before the democratic reform. There were some common words in South Africa at that time, one of which is "Migrant workers", referring to those black people who worked but could not settle in the city. Another was "Ordered urbanization", referring to the case that the city of white people became neat and luxurious and had good public order due to black people not living in the city. When discussing ordered urbanization, scholars in South Africa take America as a counter example. According to my classification, East Asia, South Asia, Latin America as well as the early stage of developed countries are classified into one class, while the second class refers to the living pattern based on identity characteristics, such as China and South Africa.

Zhou Tianyong: The results of urbanization in South Asia, Latin America and East Asia are different. We have conducted comparison research on the system of small and medium-sized enterprises all over the world and found that the systems of South Asia, Latin America and East Asia are different, which result in the difference of income, employment, living, and business starting up, etc. Thus, I think that the roads of urbanization and population mobility in South Asia and Latin America are absolutely different from those in East Asia. Certainly, both Latin America and East Asia allow the existence of slums, but Latin America has the same rigorous limitation on small and medium-sized enterprises as China does.

Leung Chun-ying: I heard for the first time about the concept of Private Collective proposed by Mr. Qin Hui. Hong Kong has some similar real estate collectives. For example, in a certain period, the British government of Hong Kong provided the land to civil servants at a certain level to establish the housing cooperative for these servants owing to high housing prices. The government approved land use and issued land title at a premium lower than the market price. These lands could be used for construction but not sold. The constructed houses by the cooperative will be distributed to qualified civil servants who can only sell the house to other qualified civil servants. Because the plot ratio for housing construction is low, and the land title obtained from the government does not have the limitation on plot ratio, many developers want to use these lands. However, only when all members of the cooperative agree can the land property right of the collective be sold, and the selling has to obtain the consent of the government, which will collect a land payment. The Private Collective at least in Hong Kong has the experiences to deal with land transaction in this way. Thus, there are many experiences for reference.

Hu Cunzhi: What is Private Collective? The system of Private Collective is first to quantify land property right to individuals, based on which the community-based land cooperation system is established in addition to land exchange certificates.

(Organized by Hong Hao without the reviewing of the speaker)

A.3 Part III: Land Law Revision

A.3.1 *Jiang ping*: *Interest conflict and balance in Land Management Law*

After the approval of *Property Law* in 2007, the department of land management has now completed the amendment draft of *Land Management Law*. There are many different views on the draft, but I will only give my thought on four problems in the draft.

A.3.2 *Conflict between public right and private right*

The *Property Law* focuses on private rights or civil rights, while the *Land Management Law* focuses on public rights. Generally, the land problem is one problem with the closest relation between public and private rights, and many land management problems are also the problems about public rights. The public rights obviously cannot excessively be provided for in the *Property Law*, so it should depend on the revision of the *Land Management Law*.

The *Land Management Law* has greatly enriched the regulations on land right, but also has greatly expanded the range of public management. Generally, the executive range of private rights will decrease if public rights increase. Conversely, if the governance scope of public rights shrinks, the private right will expand. Thus, it is hard to imagine that the power of governmental management is strengthened while the guarantee strength of private rights is improved simultaneously. From this view, the existing *Land Management Law* has problems.

The *Land Management Law* mainly strengthens the execution of public power in two ways, the first of which is to strengthen the management on land use planning, namely that, the governments at all levels should formulate the general planning of land use, and the planning formulated by the lower level should not be beyond the planning range regulated by higher levels. Thus, as it did in the past, it still conducts multi-level control in the way of land management. But can such control solve the problem? From the current situation, the land problem is one of the problems with the largest gap between law and practice, and the actual illegal phenomena of land use has moved far beyond the provisions of law. It is still uncertain whether these problems can be solved by using old laws. The second is to strengthen the protection on farmland, which is greatly concerned in the revision draft of the *Land Management Law*. The law specifies that the people's government at all levels should ensure the stability of total amount of basic farmland, the unchanging of use and the improvement of quality within its administrative area. It provides that the total amount should not be reduced, rather than stating that it can be reduced properly. Another rule is about "Supplement before occupation", specifying that the people who occupy farmlands should supplement them by themselves and can apply for land use procedure after it is accepted by the department of land management of the county-level government. But the real problem is that such a requirement on land utilization poses great obstacles to land development. Besides, the farmland supplement in different areas has different degrees of difficulty. To solve this problem, is it possible to allow some large cities to pay certain fees instead?

From this view, the *Land Management Law* lacks the foundation for implementation. The administrators may think that farmland will still decrease after being strictly controlled, but it may decrease more seriously without strict regulation on it. Obviously, in both fields of public and private rights, our policies now are still to strengthen the management on public power to solve the problem of land loss and other problems.

A.3.3 *Conflict of interests between state-owned land and collective land*

During the drafting process of the *Property Law*, someone has discussed the use right of collective construction land, and finally Article 151 of the *Property Law* specifies that the collective construction land can be managed in accordance with the *Land Management Law*. The *Land Management Law* specifies that the use right of collective construction land within the range of urban land delineated by the general planning of land use only can be transferred in the case of bankruptcy, clearance and merging of the enterprise. The land within the regulated range by land planning can be transferred, but if it involves urban construction land, the transfer cannot be conducted. But we now face a question about whether the collective land beyond the land construction planning can be used as the reserve of construction land. This possibility is completely denied in the revision draft of the *Land Management Law*. Thus, the revision draft does not comply with the reform policy that the group can deal with construction land within certain range, or does not comply with the reform policy well.

Particularly, the problem of sub-right houses, which are actually the commodity houses built on the collective land, becomes serious. Meanwhile, all people in the country are concerned about the route for the existing sub-right house becoming legal. However, the current *Land Management Law* clearly regulates that commodity houses should be built on the state land, namely, the construction of commodity house on the collective land is illegal. I think that it does not solve the problem at all, and it seems that there is no way for the house built on the collective land to become legal.

A.3.4 *Conflict between public interest and commercial interest*

The *Property Law* has two views about the problem. Firstly, it is not realistic to assume that all developments in urban areas over 30 years of reform and opening up are public interest. Secondarily, it is difficult to distinguish clearly public interest from commercial interest through one law. However, it cannot be distinguished in law but may be distinguished in reality, which should be realized.

In fact, worldwide, all countries have land expropriation for public interest. But in many countries, the state does not intervene with the land obtainment for commercial interest, which is completely left to the market. Unfortunately, no provision can be found in the *Land Management Law* to specify that the land for commercial interest can be addressed through the methods of market economy such as equal negotiation. In the current draft, only an article specifies that some business lands such as industry, business, tourism, entertainment and commodity houses or the land with two potential users, should adopt the competitive modes such as bidding and auction. But now, whether the collective land is for bidding and auction or it is for bidding and auction only after being appropriated by the state is still uncertain. Now, there is only a way for bidding and auction, namely, land should be first appropriated by the state and then be used for bidding and auction, which does not comply with the requirement that the land for commercial target does not need to be appropriated but can be completely negotiated by two parties. Thus, the *Land Management Law* should consider more market factors.

A.3.5 *Conflict between national and local interests*

The draft of *Property Law* had many regulations on how to use homesteads, but the final law uses Article 153 to specify that the obtaining, execution and transfer of the use right of homestead should comply with related laws such as *Land Management Law* and other national regulations. However, the related regulations of the state certainly include local laws, and some provinces such as Guangdong Province issued some regulations on homestead use, specifying that the house on homestead can be sold without any payment to the state. But if the owner sells the house, he may not apply for a new homestead. Such regulation can shut off all leaks and can ensure the circulation of house on the homestead in the market. As the original *Draft of Property Law* does, the draft of *Land Management Law* issues some national regulations on the use right of homestead. In such a vast country as China, it is difficult for the practice of Guangdong to become the regulation of the state, so the national regulation is not always suitable in certain areas. Therefore, I quite agree to allow all local governments to issue some local regulations or laws on the *Land Management Law*. The current draft only specifies that the local government can determine the area of homestead of each province or region, but does not allow local governments to make their own decisions on the circulation of homestead. This lays too much limitation on the rights of local governments.

(Organized by Zhao Qiong and reviewed by the speaker.)

A.3.6 *Sun Xianzhong: revision of Land Management Law and land right of farmer*

In the process of the revision of *Land Management Law*, the Ministry of Land and Resources entrusted the Research Office of Civil Law of the Academy of Social Sciences to compile the scholar suggested draft. There is a large difference between the suggested draft and the final draft for comment issued by the legislative body, so the suggested draft can only be considered as the early-stage results.

The revision of *Land Management Law* has its reasons and objectives. Before 1986, China did not have the *Land Management Law* but only the *Regulations on the Land Expropriation for State Construction*. The regulations specified that all construction projects belong to the scope of state construction, any land for construction should be arranged by the state uniformly, and individuals should obey the state. Focusing on the service for construction, the Regulations did not consider the land other than that for construction use. The Regulations reduced the cost for China's industrial development and construction and effectively promoted the industrialization under the system of a planned economy. But after the liberating of the land market, the hidden problems of the regulations were exposed.

For this reason, the state issued the *Land Management Law* in 1986, but it was still restrained and affected by the historical background at that time. One of the most important problems is that if all construction projects are called State Construction, farmers cannot properly ask for their rights when their lands are appropriated by the state. Meanwhile, because the individual interest cannot be equal to the state interest, individuals will not maintain their rights when the demolition occurs. However, if all construction should be conducted by the state, the development of land market will be out of the question. Thus, during the revision of *Land Management Law*, all participants agree to modify State Construction Land into Urban Construction Land, which thus can lay the foundation for farmers or individuals to ask for parts of rights. After nearly 20 years of development, the market economic construction of China has achieved great advance, the understandings of common people on their property right have been greatly improved, and some problems of *Land Management Law* have shown after the impact of urban-rural dual structure in recent years. Thus, the state has continuously issued and formulated the *Property Law* and *Rural Land Contract Law* and proposed some thoughts on land system reform in the Third Plenary Session of the Seventeenth CPC Central Committee in 2008. However, there are still some conflicts between *Land Management Law* and important thoughts of the state, so the law should be revised.

The original design of *Land Management Law* focuses on the administrative management of the state on the land as an important natural resource. The administrative management only focuses on construction land management and lacks the concept of general land (including forest, mud flat, steppe and water surface). It excessively stresses the administrative management of the state on land as an important natural resource, but neglects the regulation on market transactions and especially on land rights, so it should be adjusted. However, land management is also indispensable. History shows that the impact of public rights on private rights always exists, but it can be seen from our surveys and research that there are no random or independent land utilizations in the world, and the application of administrative right should have a proper reason. For example, the building on the land should comply with the planning of the state and the use of farmland should be controlled too. The basic role of the law should exist and cannot be weakened or canceled because of the market economy. Currently, the management of land right of China is seriously segmented and has low efficiency. We expect that through law revision, the development of land management law to land law can be promoted. All above are proposed from the lawmaking background of the suggested draft of scholars.

Next let us discuss some considerations on the lawmaking framework. Firstly, the law mainly consists of the content of administrative law, but also includes many contents of juridical law and civil rights law, and there is a conflict between these contents. Secondarily, we should pay enough respect on the regulations of current law and the constitution on land ownership. Laws related to land also include land contract law and property law, as well as steppe law and forest law. We can only coordinate all laws and lay a foundation for the unification of law in the future from the view of a law on general land law. Thirdly, we widely study foreign experiences. Besides, we adopt the structure of general rule and detailed rule for legislation, in which the general rule is about the general system, while the detailed rule specifies some detailed systems.

Finally, I will introduce the legislation structure of the scholar suggested draft. There is a large difference in structure between the scholar suggested draft and the current revised draft. The *Land Management Law* originally had 7 chapters with 86 articles, while the scholar suggested draft has 10 chapters, of which the first chapter is the general rule that is basically not modified and generally introduces legislation aims and the basic system, while the second chapter introduces land rights. We have extended the concept of land rights in accordance with the *Property Law*, have established the entire system from the views of ownership, usufruct, guarantee right, real right for security and quasi-property. Meanwhile, we also clearly list the rights limitation in public law and civil law and specify some unclear land rights in the original law. For example, the definition of the use right of collective construction land is unclear in the *Property Law* and is even deliberately blurred to some extent. This is especially proposed in the legislation. We also propose that the right of state land includes the right for urban construction land and other use rights of farmland, e.g., the right of state-operated farmland to use state land.

The third chapter is about the establishment of land registration system, which is basically not mentioned in the original *Land Management Law* but is very important. From the view of real estate law, the land registration is the core content. A land may generate several rights. Which rights are the basic rights? Which rights should be protected or be achieved first when a legal conflict occurs? Such kinds of questions should be clearly answered. For this reason, an order of legal rights should be established by means of the register book of real estate. Essentially, the registration of real estate does not aim for administrative management, and since the Han Dynasty, when the land title system was established, it has been considered as the system of civil rights but not the means of administrative management. Thus, we propose to establish five unifications, including uniform legal force, legal basis, registration procedure, registration organization and registration right certificate. Article 10 of *Property Law* has some provisions on real estate registration, which are controversial in the initial stage but finally are formulated. The reason why the land registration system should still be formulated after the issuance of the *Property Law* is that after the issuance of the *Property Law*, the registration by multiple departments or even at multiple levels occurs. These behaviors that do not seriously carry out the *Property Law* make us a little passive, so we want to promote the implementation of registration principle through the *Land Management Law*.

The fourth chapter "Overall Plan for Land Utilization" and the fifth chapter "Farmland Protection" are not revised significantly. In the sixth chapter the contents of land development and reclamation and land consolidation are added. The final part is about land supervision and legal liability.

Finally, the largest difference between the scholar suggested draft and the current law is that the former distinguishes urban land property rights from rural land property rights and establishes the land law based on land ownership. In my opinion, the marketization of urban land has no problem, but the marketization of rural land has not been achieved, and the most important thing now is to solve the problem of marketized rural land. Thus, in the scholar suggested draft, we set more careful mechanisms for different types of land rights to enter the market based on two different land ownerships including collective and state ownership. Particularly, we greatly strengthen the use right of collective construction land, which is different from the use right of homestead, so we propose to recover its position.

(Organized by Huang Yue and revised by Hong Hao according to the opinions of the speaker.)

A.3.7 *Sun Youhai*: *Historical review and revision suggestions for Land Management Law*

Today, my speech will have two parts, the first of which is the simple historical review on the revision of *Land Management Law* in 1998, and the other is several suggestions about how to conduct land legislation under new tendency.

A.3.7.1 *Experiences and lessons in the revision process of Land Management Law*

Firstly, it should affirm that the revision in 1998 has obtained historic advances in the following aspects: (1) Establish land use control system; (2) Establish farmland occupation and supplement balance system; (3) Increase the compensation standard for the economic losses of farmers during land expropriation; (4) Establish the approval system for farmland transaction, adjust the approval right of land expropriation, etc.

There are mainly three successful experiences for the revision in 1998: (1) Boldly conduct the reform on the basis of reality, e.g., establish the land use control system for excessive utilization of farmland, it plays an important role in farmland protection; (2) Scientifically refer to international experiences, e.g., the land use control system refers to the experiences of countries such as Korea and performs localization of them; (3) Formulate, issue and implement supporting laws and regulations for the *Land Management Law*.

There are mainly six lessons worth paying attention to: (1) The ecological and environmental destruction caused by the pursuit of gross balance of farmland amount does not receive enough attention. In this revision, some experts proposed to manage the large-scale newly developed farmland as construction project and conduct the environmental impact assessment.

But this important suggestion was not accepted and the environmental impact assessment system for newly developed farmland is not established; (2) The position of overall planning for land utilization, which should be higher than that of the urban overall plan, remains too low. The urban overall plan is always approved by the People's Congress, but the overall plan for land utilization has nothing to do with the People's Congress, which indicates that the relation between local planning and overall planning is not properly treated; (3) The same compensation for the same land in land expropriation has not been achieved; (4) No legal norm for the transfer of rural collective construction land is formulated in a timely fashion; (5) The law has weak operability, especially in judicial processes. When the parties of some land disputes resort to the court, the court has no law to depend on to settle the disputes. For example, when Tianjin Binhai New Area began to attract investment, the land price was very low, but when some enterprises were closed or went bankrupt for various reasons after several years of operation, the land ownership may be controversial. The government and enterprises are entitled to the land in their own minds. Unfortunately, the current law neither mandates that such land disputes shall be solved by the court, nor specifies the specific norm for the court to depend on, which thus results in social contradictions that have not been solved for a long time; (6) Lack of a guiding thought. So far, the practical rule for solving the relation between national industrialization, modernization and the protection of farmers' land interests has not been issued.

A.3.7.2 *Specific suggestions for land law construction*

Firstly, the problems regarding guiding thought and principle of interest adjustment should be solved. We should insist on the guidance thought of serving rural reform proposed in the Third Plenary Session of the 17th CPC Central Committee, such as the stability of rural land contract relation and accelerating the process of urban–rural integration.

Secondly, the interest balance principle should be taken as the basic principle for land system construction. The reason why social contradictions caused by land expropriation become more and more serious is actually that the problem of interest balance is not solved well. The so-called interest balance is a process in which the authority of law is used to coordinate the conflicts between all parties and make the interests of all parties rationally optimized based on the principle of coexistence. The method to satisfy the desire of parties to the utmost within the range of social general objective is to understand all involved interests, evaluate the position of these interests, balance them using the justice balance, determine the preference of the most important interest in accordance with certain social standards, and finally to reach the most desired balance. The interest balance has a natural appetency with basic legal values such as fairness and justice. Only when the interest relation between all parties is dealt with properly can the society be stable. In other words, the interest balance is the fundamental way to achieve fairness and justice in the land system.

Thirdly, I propose several specific suggestions for the revision of *Land Management Law*: (1) Clearly specify the permanent stability of land contract relation according to the law; (2) Insist on the process of urban–rural integration in rural land reform and conduct effective legal protection on the economic interest of land transaction for farmers; (3) The uniform land registration should be promoted on the basis of *Property Law*, and the specific organization in charge of land registration should be specified according to the law to terminate the chaotic situation of land registration; (4) Improve the legal position of the overall plan for land utilization, and the overall plan for land utilization and urban–rural construction planning should be submitted to the People's Congress for discussion, review, approval and revision; (5) Strengthen the protection of the ecological environment, introduce a system of environmental impact assessment for large-scale development of new farmland, and give special regulation on the quality of farmland; (6) Create favorable conditions for introducing judicial intervention to solve social contradictions caused by land development and utilization and issues related to operational regulations to solve the disputes such as land ownership.

Finally, in order to solve the problem about the *Land Management Law* focusing on administrative management and public right but neglecting private right, which has been mentioned by Professor Jiang Ping and Professor Sun Xianzhong, I think that land legislation should be on the different way. Owing to the limitation of legal capacity, position and property, the *Land Management Law* will not solve many problems. Thus, I propose to formulate the *Land Law* when necessary and to entirely adjust the land relation from the perspective of both public and private rights. Besides, many foreign countries have formulated the *Land Law*, but none of them has formulated the special *Land Management Law*.

(Organized by Hu Yun and reviewed by the speaker.)

A.3.8 Sheng Hong: Critique on Land Management Law and its Revision Draft

As an economist, I am different from all the jurists who made speeches just now. But I think that laws should have underpinning economic rationality, so my speech is arranged here to give a favorable supplement to the previous speeches. My topic is *Critique on Land Management Law* and its Revision Draft. Firstly, I stress that I have two objects for criticism. One is the *Land Management Law* revised by the Standing Committee of the National People's Congress in 1998 and the other is the *Exposure Draft of Revision Draft of Land Management Law* issued by the Ministry of Land and Resources in March 2009.

To criticize the current *Land Management Law* in a word, it is "weakening and grabbing the rights of rural collective land and improperly expanding and strengthening the rights of the government sectors in charge of land expropriation and land management." For example, Article 47 of the Law specifies that the compensation for farmland expropriation shall be 6 to 10 times the average of the production values in three years before the land expropriation. Suppose the rent rate is 50% and the interest rate is 2.52%; it means that only a compensation of RMB 30.2 to 50.4 Yuan is made for RMB 100 Yuan. Moreover it is not a currency of RMB 100 Yuan but a stock of RMB 100 Yuan that is likely to appreciate. This is very irrational.

The revision draft of *Land Management Law* does not amend the existing problems of the law, but further weakens and deprives the rights of rural collective land, increases the power of the government sectors in charge of land expropriation and land management, and continues to promote the law in a wrong direction. The draft does not face up to seven major land problems occurring recently in China. The first problem is the large-scale and serious social conflict caused by land expropriation. The second is that numerous farmers lose their lands due to land expropriation but do not obtain a rational compensation and stable working post. The third is that the government's forceful land expropriation at low cost results in excessive land urbanization and the improper allocation, abuse and waste of land. The fourth is that most state lands are freely occupied by enterprises, public institutions and government agencies, but they share land rent and other land incomes. The fifth is that due to the lack of systemic supervision on the government sectors in charge of land management and expropriation, the related departments of land management abuse their power for rent setting and seeking, leading to rampant corruption. The sixth is that in addition to the harm suffered by the rural collective during the process of land expropriation, due to the unclear concept and the problems in the public decision mechanism and supervision mechanism of rural collectives, such low compensation for land expropriation cannot be distributed fairly. The seventh is that owing to the limitation in the determination of land use of rural collective and farmers in current law and policy, the efficiency of land use in rural areas of China is very low.

There are five constitutional errors in the current *Land Management Law* and its revision draft. The first is that in the expression "in order to strengthen land management" in Article 1, the means is considered as the end. The second is that the expression of "Maintaining the socialist public land ownership" neglects serious problems in current public ownership of land. The third is that the so-called "farmland protection" is placed in an improperly high position. The fourth is that the law implies the principle of the sacrifice of local collective or individuals for public interest. The fifth is that it implies the principle that the people who live in different regions and are engaged in different industries can be differentiated.

Meanwhile, there are another four major errors in the revision draft. The first is that the concept of public interest is defined too generally. As all construction lands of urban planning are included in public interest, both the concept of public interest and the range of governmental land expropriation are expanded. This does not comply with the reform orientation of the Third Plenary Session of the Seventeenth CPC Central Committee to gradually reduce the range of land expropriation. The second is that the important exception article (Article 43) about reserving the right of rural collective to construct on their reserved land is deleted. The third is that the article without economic rationality and legal basis is added, namely "Commodity house should be constructed on state-owned land." The fourth is that both pricing power and dispute adjudication rights concerning land expropriation are endowed to one party (the county-level and municipal governments).

However, there are still some positive clauses in the draft. The first is to add the clause of market-based land allocation. The second is that several land property rights are determined in detail and the interests of land owners are specified to be protected. The third is that the clause of land market is added. Unfortunately, the principle for formulating these clauses is weakened, disintegrated and off-contact in all specified clauses. For example, the third clause can be indicated by following three analogies, including that television can be freely transacted; the television above 21 inches and below 19 inches cannot be transacted; and the transaction of the television of 20 inches should be approved by the government.

Besides, there are four omissions in the revision draft, including the lack of institutional arrangement to ensure the effective execution of state land property rights, the lack of institutional arrangement for the position, limitation and supervision on the department of land management, the lack of judicial settlement mechanisms for land conflict, and the lack of clear definition of rural collective subject.

Finally, I think that the revision draft is unfavorable for all parties and will only aggravate the tense situation, intensify conflict and inflict heavy losses on society. Thus, I oppose the legislation by single department and suggest establishing a healthy legislation procedure. I advise the National People's Congress and its standing committee to entrust organizations other than the Ministry of Land and Resources to make the revision draft; even several organizations can propose different competitive drafts that will finally be reviewed by the standing committee.

(Organized by Hu Yun and reviewed by the speaker.)

A.3.9 Chen Jiaze: The route for farmers to express their subject desire during the revision of Land Management Law

I proposed an important idea in the meeting in Chengdu held by the Ministry of Land and Resources in the last month, that is, the core of revision of *Land Management Law* is the sharing of interest and cost. I am glad that the thought is responded to by Mr. Sun. As time is limited, here I will just discuss how to reflect the desire of farmers, who are the main users of rural land.

If the land law wants to set a specification for land resources allocation, the opinions of the subject of land resources should be considered. Confucius said that "the gentleman focuses on basis," and the basis refers to common people. The farmers are concern over their respective land interests and the legislation process of this interest. We have understood the thoughts of farmers through numerous field investigations. We think that the subject of law revision, whether the competitive subject or the department of land and resources even representative institution should consider the interests of farmers.

I personally think that the creation and revision of any public law to adjust or standardize private rights should be conducted by the representative institution of legislation. Under the management structure of China characterized by superincumbent entrusting or agency relation, the government sector is a foremost subject for the revision of economic law. Therefore, a module required for the representative system should be considered during the process of law formulation, namely that, the public selection should be used to reach the balance of social preference. The balance is the basis of sustainable legal order, while such basis is based on public selection of the subject of land interests.

Specifically, there are several ways for farmers to express their desires. The first is to conduct hearings, discussions and integration on the revision draft of *Land Management Law* through a hierarchic representative system; the second is to depend on the department of land and resources; and the third is to form the revision of *Land Management Law* by matching the preference of common people through a straw poll in the villagers council. Here, the only problem that needs to be considered is the cost of collective action. The cost may be very high, but if the sample space is representative enough, the cost will be sustainable. More importantly, the process of this voting makes farmer's thought clearer, which will provide a direction for law revision. The lawmaker should consider the interests of common people other than himself when revising the law, so the maximized support of public choice should be pursued. Only when this maximization is combined with maximizing farmer's interests can the law be successfully revised.

(Organized by Hu Yun and reviewed by the speaker.)

A.3.10 Part III Comment

Wang Weiguo (Dean of the School of Civil, Commercial, and Economic Laws, China University of Political Science and Law): My view on the *Land Management Law* can be summarized into one core and five basic points. The core question is about whether the reform of *Land Management Law* should focus on the pattern of urbanization or the pattern of urban–rural integration. China has undergone a transition from farming, to industrialization and to urbanization, but the latter two develop at the expense of rural areas and farmers. Thus, the Third Plenary Session of the Seventeenth CPC Central Committee proposes the urban–rural integration, which is the basic point. Unfortunately, current *Land Management Law* is based on the pattern of industrialization, but its revision draft is based on the pattern of urbanization, which is also the origin for errors. Mr. Sheng Hong just now pointed out the forms of errors in the revision draft, but he did not note the origin of the errors.

Now I will talk about five basic points, which are also five indexes for the assessment of *Land Management Law* I will use in the future. The first is about respecting civil rights. The revision of the law should comply with an important clause added during the revision in 2004, namely about the protection of citizens' legal private property. The *Property Law* issued in 2007 also proposes to respect farmers' land right. The land right is not a public right but a private right, and the intervention of public rights on private rights should be limited and have reason and procedure. The revision of *Land Management Law* should first respect farmers' land right, including land ownership and usufruct, and should provide a uniform market space and regulation for urban and rural areas in accordance with the requirements of the Third Plenary Session of the Seventeenth CPC Central Committee. The government has no right to suppress the freedom of farmers' property or, in particular, to deprive farmers of their land at will. If the revision of *Land Management Law* is considered as an opportunity to expand the space for the government to deprive farmers of their rights, it not only violates the *Constitution* and *Property Law*, but also violates the ruling objective of the Chinese Communist Party. The second is about the comprehensive development. In the stage of industrialization, farmers are considered to only be engaged in agriculture, but the revision of *Land Management Law* is to break the pattern, besides that farmers should be allowed to capitalize their lands and to be engaged in various forms of operations, including real estate business that complies with urban–rural construction planning. The third is about benefiting farmers. The revision should be favorable for improving farmers' welfare, respecting farmers' land rights and property freedom, and should make farmers' land rights become wealth, while the route includes land transaction and capitalization. As for the question about how to maximize farmers' interests in land transaction, I suggest that all experts, scholars and officials believe that farmers have adequate wisdom to deal with it, and our legislation need not do it for them. The fourth is about the orderly management. The orderly and effective land management includes property right registration, land use management, and transfer market management, all of which comply with the demand of rural construction and development and the requirements of farmers' interests. The management order is both the boundary and guarantee of the freedom, while the persuasion of management rule, the credibility of management department and the normalization and transparency of management behaviors should be carefully considered during the revision of *Land Management Law*. The *Land Management Law* should do something to curb illegal land behavior, especially land speculation and market manipulation behavior of real estate developers. The fifth is about governmental reform. Actually, land reform is fundamentally a governmental reform, and the crucial reason for Chinese land dilemma is that the land is operated by the government. Thus, we should formulate practical systems and measures to implement the publicity and non-productiveness of land management by the government, should terminate the land dilemma characterized by land GDP, public land finance, land monopoly and land corruption, prevent the continuous development of the political pattern of alienation between officials and citizens, by which the long peace and order of China can be reached.

Huang Xiaohu: All experts just now proposed many opinions on the *Land Management Law*. I think all are reasonable, but most of them cannot be achieved now. Based on my working experiences in the department of land and resources, I think that many problems are not the problems for the department of land and resources only but for the entire system, including public finance, finance, investment system, and cadre system. I think that the staff members of the department of land and resources have tried their best to reflect the spirits of the Third Plenary Session of the Seventeenth CPC Central Committee as far as possible during the revision of *Land Management Law* and to make larger breakthroughs in some problems. For example, the homestead mortgage system is specified in one of the drafts, but it may be canceled in the future. Those clauses that should be revised from an abstract view will become complicated if they involve the entire interest pattern and cannot be changed at one time.

Thus, I agree to conduct some practical promotions in special aspects and to create more favorable conditions and experiences to fully promote the law when conditions are available. For example, a special rule can be formulated individually for land expropriation, because land expropriation involves private right and does not belong to the scope of administrative management of land. Besides, current laws have a mechanical damage, namely the pricing right of the government in land expropriation, which causes many manipulations. But because it will have too big influence on interest pattern, it is impossible to revise such mechanical damage at one time.

Sheng Hong: I think it doesn't need to issue such a revision that may cause more terrible results, and I personally think that at least the land expropriation regulation in this draft is backward.

Zhang Shuguang: This section causes vigorous discussions, and there may be other opinions. Five speakers just now proposed many opinions on the revision of the current *Land Management Law* and have inspired our thought. The basic attitude for such a complex problem of land reform should be correcting the direction first and specifically promoting it later. Besides, some cases proposed in the morning are quite important, which includes some innovations that can break the current system and have strong vitality.

(Organized by Hu Yun without the reviewing of the speaker.)

A.4 Part IV: Government and Decision

A.4.1 *Hu Cunzhi*: *Relative separation between land use right and ownership*

I am glad that the meeting can give me another chance to give a speech from the view of an insider without representing any department, as hoped by Mr. Zhou. Because I just went out to learn in the last half year and did not participate in the whole process of revision of *Land Management Law*, so I can only make a report on something I know. Here, I first thank you for your criticism of myself and my colleagues, but I hope that you criticize our competence but not our motivation. Under such case, I will have little nerve to tell all of you about something I know.

As for land system reform of China, I will talk from the following aspects. The first is about how to improve the reform on rural land property system. The current land property system has many flaws that need to be reformed, which also suffers from many criticisms, even someone criticizes that the current land property system is a system of urban areas bullying rural areas and the state bullying the collective, but actually the statement is not correct. Actually, when the land system is designed, all protection and management measures for the property right of two public land ownerships of both state and collective are the same. At that time, in order to protect farmers or rural collective property rights and avoid uncontrolled land occupation in rural areas, only the state was allowed to use rural lands through land expropriation. As for what happens now, like the state power being abused and some local governments using protection measures as the means to bully farmers, it is a later story. Certainly, the principle and objective of the legislation are to equally protect property right, and otherwise, both the *Constitution* and *Land Management Law* will be thought as evil laws or laws to harm common people, which come back to the question of motivation. Both of the two property right systems have equal legal basis and the same management measures. But, the difference or the reason why the situation today is formed is that the functions of rural collective land property rights are restricted due to lagged reform. We can see that the land use with compensation is first adopted for state-owned lands in urban areas but not for rural lands. Besides, urban land is already in trade and close to the market, so it can meet the demand of the market economy, but the reform in rural areas is lagged behind and still stays the same as in the time of the planned economy. There are three real problems, the first of which is that the ownership is clear, but the holder of ownership is quite different; the second is that the equity of ownership is unclear; the third is that the way to obtain the use right is not the marketing way. All of them are the same with the situation when state land is not reformed.

As for the way of reform, previously, we tried to clarify those unclear ones in both areas of property rights and ownership. Yet, after 20 years' effort, it has not worked out. Thus, I propose to seek a different way to adapt to the demand of market economy, stop tangling with the complexity of ownership, and to stress use rights. I propose to relatively separate land use right from ownership and particularly to make a breakthrough on the use right of construction land, to promote the successful reform on state land, to copy the reform for the use right system of state-owned construction land, to achieve the system of land use with compensation based on the separation between collective construction land ownership and use right, and to spare no effort to solve the problems such as the equity, subject, obtaining method and transfer method of use rights. The use right of collective construction land will especially be reclassified in accordance with the characteristics of function and equity, and different measures will be taken for the land with different characteristics, i.e., homestead is allocated to farmers without compensation, hence, it cannot be transferred but whose land use right can. The collective construction land for public facilities is also the same; while the use right of collective operational land can be classified into the transferring or renting land use rights in accordance with current rights and functions. Under such status of property right, the time limit, transfer method and other factors can be set accordingly, and the system shift can be conducted the same way as the property right reform of state construction land does. In this way, the route of reform will be clear. Meanwhile, because the current situation of public ownership is not changed and some existing rights and interests are not touched, a progressive reform can be achieved. Besides, the problem of sub-right housing can also be solved in this way. As we know, the sub-right house is a house without land property rights, but the public house we lived in before was also the house without land property rights. I think that all of you are clear about how these houses enter the market, how to balance the interest relation between all parties and how to reform; here I will not extrapolate.

The second question is about how to promote the reform of the collective land use system. Currently, the Ministry of Land and Resources mainly implements the spirit of the Third Plenary Session from the following aspects: (1) The transfer of collective construction land should be promoted according to the law, certainly, some experiments that are thorough, operated in local areas and have controllable results can be conducted in some special regions, such as supporting region or pilot region for comprehensive reform. The region with trial demand and the region approved by the state council, e.g., Tianjin Binhai New Area has the special reform scheme approved by the state council. The real problem is that there are still some defects in the law, some ways for the transfer of construction land are not allowed (vividly described as no door is open), and some ways are allowed but lack the route, which is vividly described as "the door is open but there are no stairs." If you dare to walk down, you will fall to your death. Thus, some joint procedures are needed; (2) The conditions for collective construction land transaction should be strict. The transfer of collective construction land should meet the requirements of land use control, should have a planning, cannot be used for commodity house development, and should be registered. Besides, homestead cannot be transferred now. Since 2000, the Ministry of Land and Resources has explored some measures to promote the management on homestead, but all of them have had some problems in both law and management. Although there are some good reform ideas for collective construction land, they are not operational in reality, especially if there are no management measures, it may get into trouble; (3) Specify the transfer procedure of collective construction land. The Ministry of Land and Resources has issued a process that is now seeking opinions and being revised, including the procedures of applying, reviewing, public transaction, signing transfer contract, registration and use control; (4) Strictly conserve land and intensively use land; (5) Straighten out the income distribution system for collective construction land transaction, which is very important and cannot be solved only by our department but through the cooperation between several departments such as agriculture and finance. Because if no income distribution system exists under the condition of market-based transaction, some problems will occur when the collectives manage these incomes; and (6) Strengthen the management on the transfer of collective construction land, including land registration and certification, the establishment of uniform land market, uniform publishing of intermediary service information, and the building of a transfer system.

The establishment of uniform urban–rural land market mainly involves the following aspects. Firstly, one land market can have two ownerships. Because the system of land property has the same basic structure and transfer method, the land with two different ownerships can be seamlessly joined in land transaction. For example, the age limit of rural land use right can be set at 70 years as that of the state land is, and it can be the same case for the transfer rule. Meanwhile, if the land use right of the allocated rural collective land wants to enter the market, transfer fee should be paid, like that for state land. In such a way, both types of land can be freely transacted or transferred in the market under a uniform land property system and the objective of the same land with the same price and rights can be achieved. As for the system of state land, some commercial land for industry, business, tourism and entertainment should adopt the system of bidding, auction and listing. The bid winners should be transparent, and the contracted stockholding pattern can be adopted, but the transaction price should not be smaller than the minimum price. All of these market regulations are the same. Secondly, set the scale and operational space of collective construction land. There are no limitations on the amount of collective construction land in current laws and common practices, the laws only provide that the collective construction land can only be used through joint operation, shareholding, cooperation, etc., but the amount of collective construction land is not specified. I also see such a special case that a village changes all its collective land into construction land. In this case what will the government or society do when they want to use or expropriate these lands? Thus, the amount of collective construction land should be determined by the whole society in the initial stage of the reform.

(Organized by Huang Kai and reviewed by the speaker.)

A.4.2 *Wu Xiaoling: Properly manage four kinds of relations in the legal system*

I am very glad to attend the meeting today, and I benefit a lot from the meeting. Owing to the limitation of time, here I will only discuss several problems. Firstly, I think that the revision of the law aims to improve the allocation efficiency of land resources and to protect farmland. Secondly, we should fully use the experiences of legislation and revision last time around for reference. Therefore, the report of the Chief Mr. Sun Youhai is very important, covering the disputes in the revision in the last time, which opinions are accepted and which opinions are not accepted. Based on previous experiences we should learn lessons from the revision in the last time, which is very important. Firstly, I will give my personal opinions on four problems mentioned by Mr. Jiang Ping. I am a deputy of the People's Congress, as well as a member of the standing committee. I can participate in legal discussions and have the final voting right. Thus, by listening to your opinions I hope to make my opinions at the NPC meeting represent better the public will.

The first question is about how to deal with the relation between public power and private rights well in law. I think that the core is how to deal with the issue of status of law in the planning process. At present, for a governmental institution, the unauthorized acts cannot be done, even if it is lawful, while for a citizen, any action that is not forbidden by the authorities can be conducted, even if it is illegal. Thus, to define the boundary between public power and private right and protect the private right from being violated by public power, the law on planning must be a law approved by the People's Congress at all levels and approved by the representative of popular will, and it should be the institutions representing public opinion instead of government or a party secretary that authorize the national authority to implement the law. In many cities, when a secretary leaves the position, the planning will be revised once. In this case the city cannot be constructed.

The second question is about the relation between state land and collective land. Our laws and constitution equally protect all property rights, especially for property rights of public ownership, so that we should fully protect the collective land. The protection involves the following aspects: (1) The property right of collective land should be clearly determined, which has no problem in law under the background of land registration by the Ministry of Land and Resources. But the definition is difficult to reach the level of farmer household, which belongs to the jurisdiction of collective ownership, namely, about how to deal with the land after the collective owns the land. Under the background of China, it is still impossible for members of a collective to have freedom in forming their own organizations. Then the question is how to enable the collective to have a good governance structure. Therefore, I appeal to pay attention to the *Villager Organization Law* which will be revised by the People's Congress, make villagers' self-governance more sufficient, and restrain the committee of villagers to make it actually represent the interests of all farmers. (2) We should give the usufruct to the rural collective land that is capitalized, and land usage and its percentage in each use should be determined during rural planning. Meanwhile, the usufruct should be given to other lands based on farmland protection. (3) The collective land should be endowed with the management right within the planning. In order to ensure the management right, farmers should be provided with the choice of judicial protection and administrative arbitration. China now suggests conducting administrative arbitration, and only to conduct judicial arbitration when the administrative arbitration is not accepted. The original intention of system design may aim to save cost, but management right of the party can be ensured only when the choice is given. Finally, in order to protect the property rights of collective land, the same land should have the same price, and the uniform land market should be established.

The third problem is about the relation between public interest and commercial interests. From the law, the Third Plenary Session of the Seventeenth CPC Central Committee has proposed that the construction land of farmers can have the right of free transfer, and if construction lands beyond the city are not for public facilities, they should be negotiated, which is a good legal origin. But what is the contradiction now? I think it is the unlimited expansion of the city. Generally, urban land belongs to the state. If the boundary of the city is limitless, all lands in China will become state-owned. This is the reason why the state fails to keep the farmland area above the line of 1.8 billion *mu* (1,200,000,000,000 m^2). The only way is to determine the boundaries of cities using the satellite location map. If the satellite surveying map on December 31, 2008 is used to determine the boundaries of cities, and to specify that all lands beyond the boundaries are rural areas, and that lands for public facilities in rural areas should be expropriated by the state and lands for non-public facilities should be subject to negotiations between local governments and farmers, it can not only ensure the capital income from the commercialization of rural construction land but also save land. But the difficulty is that local governments will not agree with the resolution. Therefore, the reform on public land finance should be conducted. Now, local finance is unmatched with administrative power and has few financial rights, so it can only depend on public land finance. If the budgeting way is changed to the pattern that local governments will obtain financial resources related to the affairs they undertake, and local governments will not depend on land finance, by which the opposition of local governments on the determination of urban boundary can be reduced.

The fourth problem is about how to deal with the relation between state interest and local interest, which focuses on farmland. After farmland is protected, the problem of homestead and construction land can be negotiated by local governments after major laws are available. We should respect the pioneering spirits of local governments, for the principle of the uniformity on general matters and freedom in details has been the experience of the Communist Party in its ruling for many years. Besides, both the central government and local governments should be provided with incentives. As Professor Jiang Ping mentioned, local governments should be endowed with certain decision-making power to regulate the method of transfer and management within the total amount of construction land and homestead stipulated by the state.

All above are my understandings on the Four Relations proposed by Professor Jiang Ping. Finally, I will talk about the technology for legislation. I think that we should promote our process of democracy and legislation based on previous works. According to current legislation procedures, it is difficult to make the legislation department accept the suggestions of scholars or accept several drafts. I quite agree with Mr. SUN that not the *Land Management Law* but the land law should be formulated. As the revision of *Land Management Law* is put on the agenda of leadership, we should take the opportunity to reflect the common view we reach today in the law. Thus, we should set limited objectives but not limitless objectives. Under the correct direction, every advance will be precious. Through the meeting today, we can comb those key problems that cannot be negotiated and form a common view, based on which the best results of law revision can be reached.

(Organized by Huang Kai without the reviewing of the speaker.)

A.4.3 *Chen Xiwen*: *Correct wrong and stick to right*

I am glad to be invited to attend the meeting today and have been very much inspired by the meeting. All of you have proposed many opinions with great reference value on the current problems and the direction of reform from multiple levels and perspectives. Here, I will share my personal thought.

The current land management system has two basic characteristics, including classified management on land use (called land use control) and collective ownership of rural land. Now, there are enormous powers to liberate both of them, which aim to liberate land use control and to change rural collective land into social construction land. Both of them are two major problems for us to discuss regarding the land system.

Land use control is conducted all over the world and urban citizens are accustomed to it. Similarly, the management of lands such as collective construction land, farmland, forest land, steppe and water surface in rural areas are also land use control. No matter how the land system is changed, the control of land use will not be changed. If rural areas want to pursue the interests, all farmland will be changed into construction land. Thus, the control of land use is formulated in accordance with the planning and cannot be simply described as the control of governmental administration. The real issue is whether the formation process of the planning is scientific, democratic, public or transparent, and indicates the most long-term basic interest of society and common people.

Some think that the collective land ownership of rural land has caused great harm to farmers, but it is not always the case and depends on the following: (1) whether the amount of the compensation for land expropriation is enough; and (2) whether farmland can be changed into homestead at will and whether homestead can be changed into sub-right house or other factories at will, which is a question of land use control. But at the same time, we should see that the collective ownership still gives certain guarantee for farmers to a large extent, according to which farmers obtain the most basic living materials. Now, all regions want to break the circle of the collective to make all lands that originally could only be used by the members of the collective available for the whole society, and some capital or powers that cannot enter the circle originally now are eager to enter it.

As for these two questions, I think that some concepts cannot be applied simply. For example, the differential rent from land is only applicable to the land of the same use. The key factor of differential rent from land is soil fertility, but once farmland is converted into construction land, soil fertility will become meaningless. If all price differences between different lands are generalized as the differential rent of land, farmland can obtain the highest differential rent of land only by being converted into construction land, and this is very unfavorable for farmland protection. Actually, I think that the differential rent of land is the result of land transaction and the planning, but not the result of continuous investment on soil or location. For another example, the land capitalization indicates the non-agricultural tendency of farmland, and the land appreciation can only be reached when farmland is changed into construction land. Besides, land marketization is also highly concerned. This concept should also comply with the control of land use, and the marketization can only be achieved between lands in the same category.

Considering that farmers are relatively the weaker group, rural lands are not nationalized when urban lands are nationalized, which is also because certain compensation should be paid when farmland is converted into state-owned land. In the nationalization of urban land in 1982 when the Constitution was revised, farmers obtained no compensation. But now, farmers obtain more and more compensation from 6 times, to 10 times, to 16 times and to above 30 times. They can even obtain compensation from the income from land transaction ring fees.

The decision of the Third Plenary Session of the 17th Central Committee has proposed three important measures for land system reform: (1) It clearly specifies that if the non-public construction project beyond the urban planning area complies with the planning and related departments have land quota and approve the land use, the land where the project is may be utilized in other ways other than land expropriation, namely that the land owner can participate in the development and operation in several ways, which is a large breakthrough in the reform of land expropriation system; (2) For the existing collective construction lands, including homestead, the land for township enterprise and the land for the enterprise engaged in rural public facilities, the documents of the Third Plenary Session clearly propose that for the operational construction land operated by the village collective, i.e., the construction land for township enterprise that is legally obtained, if the enterprise is closed, such approved land quota can enter the uniform urban–rural construction land market and can change from community-operated land to society-operated land; (3) It stresses land renovation and consolidation and clearly proposes that new lands from land consolidation should be first reclaimed as farmland, if they are intended to be changed into construction land, they should comply with the planning and be included into the land use quota in that year, and should preferentially meet the demand of the collective construction land. All above is great progress compared with in the past, but the real problem now is that many fundamental works in construction land are not conducted well in rural areas. Particularly, those lands for township enterprises are very chaotic. Because the concept of township enterprise is unclear, the user of the land for township enterprise cannot be specified.

Besides, the reason why the homestead is not liberated in the decision of the Third Plenary Session is that the homestead has a nature of welfare and is equivalent to public housing, for which the owner should pay fees if selling it. The homestead should be equally distributed within the collective economic organization, but without the requirement above, it will fall in the hands of cadres at village level or the powerful ones. Conversely, it can be transferred as public housing is, which only needs certain use fees or transfer fees.

How should the land expropriation be reformed? Today, several experts here mentioned the *Constitution*, but how should we understand the *Constitution*? In my opinion, the problems are: Whether urban lands are for public interest or not, they are all state-owned. Besides, if those lands beyond the range of urban land are for the public interest, they should also be expropriated. Actually, there is no need for urban land to be state-owned, so the article should be revised. But what is the limitation of land expropriation? It is difficult to know the boundary of state land owing to so fast a velocity of urbanization.

We have reached a common view that the land system should be reformed, but we also have realized that the reform is very complicated and difficult and needs overall consideration. Only when some problems such as the basic requirement and objective of the reform are clear, or when we can know that all we do now violate the objective or create conditions for it, the contradiction can be reduced. The land system reform is not invertible, as the land that is cemented and used for building construction cannot be recovered and the interest losses of farmers are difficult to be compensated. So an in-depth study and experiment should be conducted. I always agree to conduct experiment based on some basic principles: (1) It should comply with the procedure; (2) It should be controlled; (3) It should have a pre-arranged planning; (4) It should be conducted seriously. Meanwhile, the experiment conditions should be closed, which will be changed when failure occurs and will be insisted on when no failure occurs.

(Organized by Lu Qian without the reviewing of speaker.)

A.5 Meeting Summary

Zhou Qiren: In the morning, I welcomed all of you, but now I am surprised that all of you are still here. It seems that it is quite wise for three organizations to hold the meeting in Peking University, because one of the spirits of Peking University is absorbing anything and everything, which complies with the complex land problem. I think that all different academic viewpoints need a platform for mutual communication and discussion. Generally, finance is considered as an allocation of time resources. The recent financial crisis indicates that such an allocation alone is very complex. But the land problem we discuss now requires the allocation of both time and spatial resources, so it may be more difficult. I think that there is no acknowledgement that is in-depth enough to answer the question about how to allocate the resources well, distribute the income well and arrange the system well. China, in particular, is a very large country with a level of urbanization 5% lower than the average world level and mountainous lands account for 70% of its total area of territory. It is experiencing very rapid economic growth recently and is seriously expanding economic freedom. All these push the historical debts of urbanization and the current contradictions on land use to the land problem. All three aspects, namely resource allocation, income distribution and institutional arrangement, are now encountering big problems.

In view of resource allocation, the population mobility to the city may conserve land from the global experiences. But actually, both our urban and rural areas are expanding. As both of them expand the use of construction land, the farmland will be squeezed. Undoubtedly, the urbanization should promote the optimization of resource allocation, but actually construction land increases in both urban and rural areas in China, which is the problem we should face.

In view of income allocation, the inadequacy of domestic demand is caused by the fact that the income of farmers who have the largest proportion of the total population does not increase rapidly enough. After 30 years of reform and opening up, farmers have obtained the rights of farming, selling grain and working, but the shares of rural areas and farmers on the total income are still small. Thus, even though urban areas or industries develop, the problem of farmers' low income will still exist.

In view of institutional arrangement, no institutional arrangement is completed overnight. My old friend Mr. Wen Guanzhong is not here today. He has insisted on his view about land privatization since land investigation in 1988. I admire him a lot but do not agree with him. I have drawn a conclusion from my research on land reform that any property system formed by a political campaign can be removed by another political campaign. Land reform is first to distribute land to farmers, but when the movement of collectivization came, all lands allocated to farmers before were reclaimed, because all lands were distributed by Chairman Mao and can be integrated at his will. Consequently, the land has become the Collective concerned by Mr. Qin Hui, a collective emerges after the extinction of farmers' private property right. For this reason, I think that any property system depending on legal power will not exist. The real permanent stability of the property system only can be reached after it becomes a custom of the society, which should be gradually changed and should be waited for patiently. Actually, the obtaining of farming rights of farmers in the rural reform is a process. Today, although rural collective ownership is not changed, the farming has become household-based. Recently, the Third Plenary Session stressed the permanent stability of land contract relation. For this reason, during the land certification in Wayao Village, Shuangliu County, Chengdu Province, the contract period in the land certificate is not 30 years but a permanent period. In the first News Conference of Premier Mr. Wen Jiabao, some western journalists asked him "Why does China not implement a land privatization system." He answered, "Our land contract relation is stable permanently." I think that the property right is supported by multiple factors and cannot be changed by a word. Generally, our state authority has great effect on many fields of the social economy, which only can be utilized properly in a slow and progressive way. Moreover, the transaction, transfer and pricing of property rights are more complicated.

Since the problem is complicated, the results obtained from different prospectives can be entirely different. We need a platform for the government, civil organizations, scholars and front-line practitioners to discuss its restraints from different aspects. I have worked in all these circles, so I know there is an information limitation in each of them. For example, scholars and decision-makers respectively have their own logic. I originally thought that the land use control could only be carried out in developed countries after urbanization is completed, but the urbanization of our country has a long way to go. How to carry out the urbanization if the land use control is implemented? However, after conducting an investigation in Chengdu, I found that the land use control should be carried out and is necessary. Obviously, farmers in Chengdu will not obtain compensation as high as RMB 25,000 Yuan/*mu* (667 m²) without land use control and the system of balance between land occupation and supplement, so that I think that something should be considered from different perspectives.

I am not blurring the line between right and wrong but have my own thoughts on many problems. Most of my viewpoints will be criticized by Mr. Chen Xiwen, but I also disagree with many viewpoints of his, and it does not matter. Because we all live in China, and we all hope the country can develop well. This is a common ground of our thoughts. With this common ground, we will not be afraid of the non-conformity between our viewpoints. Another important aspect is that you can criticize the quality of research but cannot doubt the motivation, as Mr. Hu said. The meeting today is generally very successful, and we should insist on such an atmosphere of discussion. I think that the opinions from scholars, field investigations, front-line practices or the decision-making departments, may still be different after the meeting, but the difference may become smaller. Thank you!

(Organized by Hong Hao without the reviewing of the speaker)

List of speakers (in speaking order)

Liu Shouying: Researcher of the Rural Economy Research Department of the Development Research Center of the the State Council

Hao Shouyi: Deputy Director of Tianjin Binhai New Area Management Committee

Zhang Hong: Dean of the School of Urban Management and Resources Environment of Yunnan University of Finance and Economics

Xing Yiqing: Member of the Land System Reform Research Group of National School of Development at Peking University

Leung Chun-Ying: Chairman of DTZ and Convener of Executive Council of Hong Kong SAR

Zhou Tianyong: Professor of the Research Laboratory of the Party School of the CPC Central Committee

Chen Jiaze: Director of the Institute of Economics of Chengdu Academy of Social Sciences

Zhou Qiren: Dean of the National School of Development at Peking University

Gong Qiang: Assistant Associate Professor of the National School of Development at Peking University

Qin Hui: Professor of the School of Humanities and Social Sciences at Tsinghua University

Cai Jiming: Professor of the School of Humanities and Social Sciences and Director of the Center of Political Economy at Tsinghua University

Zhang Shuguang: President of Beijing Unirule Institute of Economics

Huang Xiaohu: Vice President of China Land Science Society/China Land Surveying & Planning Institute

Hu Cunzhi: Chief Planner of the Ministry of Land and Resources

Sheng Hong: Director of Beijing Unirule Institute of Economics

Sun Youhai: Research Director of the Supreme People's Court

Jiang Ping: Lifetime Professor of China University of Political Science and Law

Sun Xianzhong: Researcher of the Institute of Law of Academy of Social Sciences

Wang Weiguo: Dean of the School of Civil, Commercial, and Economic Laws at China University of Political Science and Law

Wu Xiaoling: Member of the Standing Committee of the National People's Congress and Vice Chairman of the Financial and Economic Committee of NPC

Chen Xiwen: Deputy Director of the Office of Leading Group for Finance and Economics of the Central Committee and Vice Director of the Office of the Leading Group for Rural Work of the Central Committee

Afterword

The transition of the land system in China is closely linked with the transition of Chinese Society. During the Communist Revolution, the Party gained the most fundamental and widest revolutionary power through land revolution.[1] During the stage of socialism, the land reform and cooperative movement have provided important support for industrialization of the country. In the stage of reform and opening-up, the system of contracting land by farmers has not only provided an initial impetus for marketization reform, but also created a relatively stable social environment for the transition of the economic system over 30 years. Meanwhile, in the process of current urbanization, the transition of the Chinese land system will still become the most fundamental and important field for all system transitions. Certainly, the origin intention for Boyuan Foundation to fund the research project is to focus on the transition process of the Chinese land system, particularly its profound effect on the transition of Chinese society.

As the leader of the project, Mr. Zhang Shuguang is one of the most famous leaders engaged in the research of Chinese systems and system transition. In recent years, he has focused on the research of Chinese land system changes, has conducted large quantities of case studies and empirical

---

[1]Land revolution (1927–1937) was carried out by the Communist Party of China in the revolutionary base areas during the Second Chinese Revolutionary Civil War. During the revolution, landlords were cracked down and their land was confiscated and redistributed to farmers, with an aim to abolish the feudalist exploitation and debts and meet the farmers' demands for land.

analysis, and has provided original insight in the reform of land system and the adjustment of land policy. Here, we offer an aggregation of his research results in the field to the reader.

Mr. Zhang takes the transition of the land system during the process of urbanization as the research object, observes the interaction and game between the central government, local governments and farmers through 16 cases, and has revealed the specific process of the transition direction of the Chinese land system to property rights subdivisions and limited property rights. He thinks that "from the reality of institutional change, whether the property is public or private, state-owned or collective-owned, is not the essence of the problem. The most important aspects are the ability to exercise property rights and the disposition and usufruct rights." With the advance of the research, he further points out that "the subdivision of property rights has not changed the collective-owned property of land, but has greatly expanded and improved the implementation ability of property rights of farmer households, by which different rights owners can have their own limited property rights, can implement their functions in their own ways and can jointly promote the production development. It is not a typical privatization in the classical sense, but in the sense of the implementation of property rights, it is rational to consider it as privatization." Therefore, he thinks that if the differentiation of property right is assumed to be meaningful and the exercising of property right is assumed to be important, our policy conclusions will be clear: "The existing legal system of land is established based on the protection of ownership, which is suitable for the classical property right form with non-differential property rights, but not for the modern property rights form with subdivided property rights. After the usufruct property of land contracting rights is affirmed by the *Property Law*, all land laws should be adjusted and modified toward this direction. That is, all current land laws should focus on the protection of usufruct."

Here, it should be mentioned that for a traditional research project for public interest, a research framework is firstly designed according to the requirements of the project, and then researchers are organized to carry out an investigation based on the framework. Finally, the investigation report is completed and the research results are submitted. However, the Boyuan Foundation is not complacent with this pattern but tries to explore a new way, in which the whole process of the project is closely tracked, the communication and interaction between funding party and recipient party are formed, and symposiums are held based on the project for communication and interaction between the members of the project group and the experts, scholars and officials in the field. For this reason and in order to promote the research on the Chinese land system, the Boyuan Foundation, the National School of Development of Peking University and the Beijing Unirule Institute of Economics have held three symposiums presided over Mr. Zhou Qiren. The most wonderful of them was the one held on July 27, 2009. In that symposium, the experts, scholars and government officials establishing land policies have carried out a heated discussion and drastic thought confrontation on land privatization, the red line of 1.8 billion *mu* (1,200,000,000,000) for farmland protection, and the profound effect of the property rights subdivision in land scale transfer on institutional change. Thus, the research project funded by the Boyuan Foundation has not only improved the research competence of the members of the project group, but also has become an academic exchange platform to promote research in this field.

We sincerely hope that the book can further expand the academic discussion in this field and readers can give academic criticism and participate in the discussion. Meanwhile, we think that Chinese intellectuals have a historic responsibility to focus on and research subtle institutional changes in the reality and their profound effects on the transition of Chinese society.

Edition Group of Series of
Economic Observation of China
Boyuan Foundation
November 12, 2010

Index

Printed in the United States
By Bookmasters